Scenic Driving

A L A S K A

and the

Y U K O N

Erik Molvar

FALCON

HELENA, MONTA

For my Mother,
who has never ventured far from the car.

FALCON GUIDES

Falcon Press is continually expanding its list of recreational guidebooks. All books include detailed descriptions, accurate maps, and all the information necessary for enjoyable trips. You can order extra copies of this book and get information and prices for other Falcon guidebooks by writing Falcon Press, P.O. Box 1718, Helena, MT 59624 or calling toll-free 1-800-582-2665. Also, please ask for a free copy of our current catalog.

Cover photo: Alaska Highway ALISSA CRANDELL
Back cover photo: Aurora Borealis (Northern Lights) STEVEN NOURSE
All black and white photos by the author.

Library of Congress Cataloging-in-Publication Data
Molvar, Erik.
    Scenic driving Alaska and the Yukon / by Erik Molvar.
        p.   cm.
    Includes index.
    ISBN 1-56044-489-4 (pbk.)
    1. Alaska--Tours.   2. Yukon Territory--Tours.   3. Automobile
travel--Alaska--Guidebooks.   4. Automobile travel--Yukon Territory-
-Guidebooks.   I. Title.
F902.3.M65   1996
917.9804'5--dc20   96-8579
                                                           CIP

CONTENTS

Acknowledgments

Long before this book was conceived, researchers at the Institute of Arctic Biology were filling my head with the natural history of the Far North. I am particularly indebted to Dave Klein, Terry Bowyer, Dale Guthrie, Doug Schamel, and Gary Laursen for sharing with me their fascinating tales of the ecology of the subarctic and arctic regions.

This book is really a compilation of the interpretive efforts of scholars of all stripes, including historians, biologists, geologists, and Native American scholars. Deserving special mention are Alaska's great Quaternary geologist, Péwé; Christopher Burn of Carleton University; and the often nameless researchers who have compiled historical resource studies for the Bureau of Land Management in Alaska. Agency personnel in both Alaska and Canada brought forth a wealth of information on wildlife viewing, fire history, and place names.

It seems as if every town in the Far North has an active historical society, and this book has profited immensely from the help of archivists at the many local museums. Particularly outstanding and helpful were staff members at the museums in Keno City and Mayo, Yukon Territory; Atlin, British Columbia; and the University of Alaska Fairbanks. Various Native American groups also provided a great deal of information on the history of their homelands, particularly the Kenaitze, Tahltan, Gwitch'in, Tlingit, Kaska, Gitksan, Nisga'a, and Inuit peoples.

Everywhere in the North Country, I met locals who were only too happy to share their wealth of knowledge. Dan Renshaw, who runs the Gold Cord Mine high in the Talkeetna Mountains, astounded me with his encyclopedic knowledge of the local geology. Chuck Dart brought forth a collection of colorful tales (some too colorful for this book) concerning the history of Manley Hot Springs. Other locals who made notable contributions to this book include Carol Gracious of Gracious House on the Denali Highway, Mike Mancini of Keno Snack Bar in the heart of the Yukon's silver country, and the staff of the Stikine Riversong Lodge in Telegraph Creek, B.C. Thanks to Eric Rock and Shawn Osborne for sharing their respective corners of Alaska with me.

Locator Maps

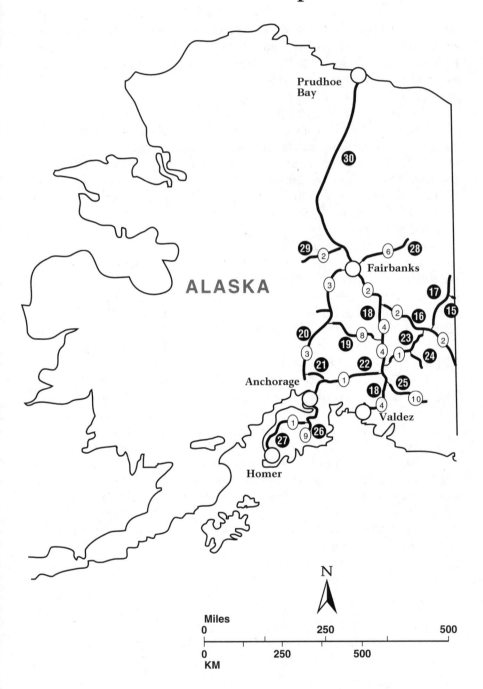

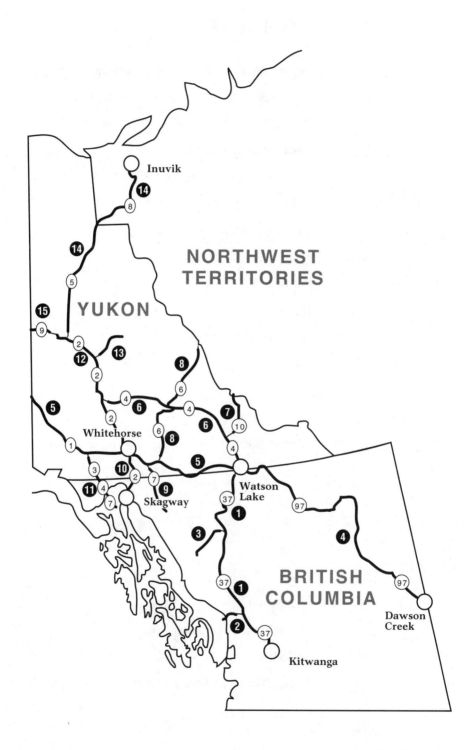

Map Legend

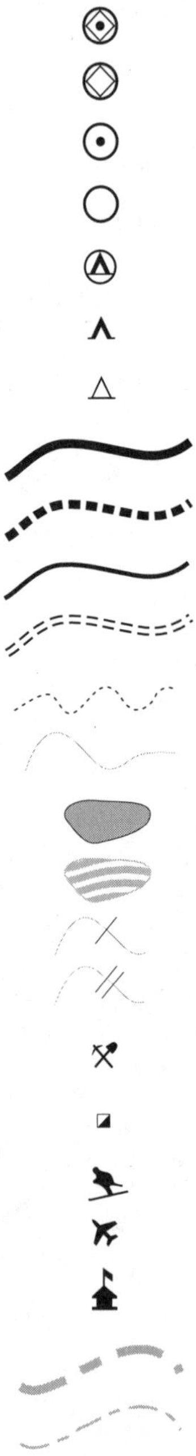

◉ Settlement with gas and other services

◇ Settlement with some services but no gas

⊙ Settlement with gas but no other services

○ Settlement with no services

Ⓐ Privately-run campground

Λ Public campground, fee charged

△ Public campground, no fee

〰 Featured road, paved

▪▪▪▪▪▪▪▪ Featured road, gravel

〰 Non-featured road, paved

=========== Non-featured road, gravel

〰 Trail

〰 River

▬ Lake or sea

▬ Glaciated area

✕ Falls

✕ Rapids

⚒ Mine

◪ Ruins

🎿 Ski area

✈ Military airbase

🏴 Ranger station or visitor center

～～ State boundary

～～ National or State Forest boundary

Introduction

Alaska and the Yukon are part of a vast and untamed Arctic landscape that stretches across the Northern Hemisphere in a broad band. They are magnets for solitude seekers, wildlife buffs, anglers, and folks who simply want to return to the slower pace of times gone by. A network of paved and gravel highways crosses this remote and primeval landscape, and a vacation on the roadways of the Far North provides outstanding opportunities for adventure. This is a land of stunning natural beauty, intact and functioning natural ecosystems, and a rich pioneer heritage.

Scenic Driving Alaska and the Yukon is an interpretive guide that covers the natural and cultural history of this great land, along with all of the major roadways in the Far North. This is the story of the land and its people, as told through the highways that wind through a magnificent landscape.

The Land and Its People

There is nothing ordinary about the northwestern corner of North America. Much of the land in Alaska and the Yukon was not originally part of the continent but drifted in as small "suspect terranes," or land masses that floated freely on the molten magma of the Earth's mantle before collid-

Liberty Falls is one of the hidden attractions of the Edgerton Highway.

ing with the continent and becoming stationary. The edges of these wandering plates are defined by spectacular mountain ranges that were pushed skyward by the collision. The origin of these suspect terranes has been a puzzle to geologists for decades, but finally, with advances in technology, some light is being shed on the issue. Some terranes came from as far away as the Tropics, sliding up the western coast of North America before grinding to a halt at the northwestern corner of the continent.

Much later, during the ice ages, a land bridge linked Alaska with Siberia. Ice covered the polar seas, and cold, dry winds swept over the arid steppes of the interior. Pleistocene mammals such as the saber-toothed cat, cave lion, woolly mammoth, and giant ground sloth crossed the land bridge into the new continent. Great ice fields surrounded this arid landscape, posing a temporary barrier to dispersal.

Close on the heels of the Ice Age mammals came small bipeds that hunted them. These Paleolithic hunters and gatherers became the first Alaskans, and they gave rise to the rich and diverse native cultures that inhabit the Far North today. Their descendants are fiercely proud of their 27,000-year history of habitation in Alaska and the Yukon. The Canadian bands now call themselves the First Nations, so that all people might recognize their sovereign claim to the land. Many of the land claims of these natives have never been addressed, leading to a painful and divisive battle over ancient homelands and hunting grounds.

Western culture has been a recent import to the Far North, and most of the towns there have existed for less than a century. The frontier days of the Northland have scarcely passed, and reminders of a wild and free-spirited past are visible everywhere. The dry, cold climate has preserved many original log cabins and other structures in excellent condition. If you take a walk through the old ruins, you can almost hear the voices of the miners and the trappers, the hustlers and the dance-hall girls.

Today, Alaskans and Yukoners draw heavily from the cultures of the past, both native and white. Old traditions die hard up here, and there are a few nooks and crannies where life goes on in much the same manner as it did a century ago.

Getting There

Most travelers bound for the Far North have to drive a long way to reach the point where civilization falls away and the subarctic region begins. From the United States, the most common route to the Alaska Highway is from Great Falls, Montana, through Calgary and Edmonton, Alberta— a distance of 867 miles. This route crosses prairies and wheat fields and passes small farming communities on the Great Plains. A scenic route from Edmonton to Dawson Creek via Lesser Slave Lake is 37 miles longer.

Black Rapids Glacier descends from the forbidding crags of the Alaska Range.

An alternate route crosses British Columbia via Prince George, a distance of 817 miles from Seattle. This route follows low valleys between ranges of impressive peaks. If you are approaching from the east, you can intersect this route by driving westward from Calgary through Banff and Jasper National Parks and following the Yellowhead Highway to Prince George. This inland city is also the jumping-off point for the Cassiar Highway, which leaves Highway 16 some 307 miles to the west.

Canadians approaching from the east can reach the beginning of the Alaska Highway from Calgary (866 kilometers) or Edmonton (591 kilometers). A slightly longer but more scenic route runs northward on Highway 2 via the Lesser Slave Lake, adding 60 kilometers to the overall distance. From Vancouver, it is 752 kilometers to Prince George. From there, the Cassiar Highway begins 493 kilometers to the northwest, while the Alaska Highway begins 402 kilometers to the northeast.

If you want to skip the long approach, the Alaska Marine Highway System operates ferries that serve the towns of the Inside Passage. Travelers approaching from the south can embark at Bellingham, Washington, or Prince Rupert, British Columbia. The ferry connects with the highway system at Haines and Skagway, two ports in the northern part of the Alaskan panhandle. The voyage from Bellingham to Haines takes two days. Ferry rates for vehicles are fairly expensive and vary according to the length of the vehicle. Staterooms for sleeping are available for an extra charge.

If your time is limited, you can fly into one of Alaska's international airports at Anchorage or Fairbanks or into the Yukon capital of Whitehorse. Rental cars are available in all of these cities, and several companies also rent recreational vehicles. However, some rental companies may restrict RV use to well-maintained roads. Some cruise lines offer package tours that combine a cruise along the Inside Passage with independent forays into the interior in rental RVs.

Driving in the Far North

Highway travel in Alaska and the Yukon can be a bit more challenging than in more southerly regions. Service stations are few and far between, and the surrounding country is sparsely populated. Many highways have gravel surfaces, a new experience for most drivers. Those that are paved may be marred by "frost heaves," or dips and rises caused by the freezing and melting of the soil beneath the roadway.

If you plan to venture into the Far North, you would be wise to carry this "Far North survival kit:"

- Two spare tires
- Jack and lug wrench
- Tire patch kit
- Bicycle pump
- 5-gallon jerry can of fuel

- Flares
- Spare fan belt
- 2 quarts of motor oil
- 5 gallons of drinking water
- Food for three days.

Gravel highways are commonplace in northern latitudes. They can be graded more easily than paved roads and thus are much less expensive to maintain. However, they do have drawbacks. Precipitation can result in pot-

Along Kluane Lake. (Alaksa Highway, Drive 5)

holes, a frequent cause of flat tires, and decelerating trucks can create "washboards," or long series of ridges in the roadway that can cause cars to skid. Sharp edges on the gravel may puncture tires. In the words of one travel-wise Yukoner, "Slow down and your tires will stay round."

Passing cars also may spray gravel, which can crack or chip your windshield. If you meet oncoming traffic on a gravel road, you should slow down and pull as far to the right as possible to save wear and tear on the windshields of both cars. This also reduces the amount of dust thrown up by the tires, improving visibility for the other driver. It is considered good manners to slow down when passing through settlements, in order to reduce dust pollution.

Frost heaves may create a bumpy driving surface on paved roads that cross permafrost areas. When driving across frost heaves, slow down and swerve slightly at each rise and fall to slow the rise and fall of the vehicle.

Polite driving is a hallmark of the North Country, and you should be aware of a few unwritten rules of the road. Roadways in the Far North are often clogged with tourists, but it is important to bear in mind that not every driver here is on vacation. Many are local residents who may have tight schedules and want to travel as quickly as possible. If a driver overtakes you in an area where passing is unsafe, pull to the side and allow him to continue on his way. When stopping to take pictures or watch wildlife, pull completely off the road. It is illegal to stop in the middle of a roadway throughout the Far North. Finally, it is a northern tradition to stop and help motorists who are stranded because of car trouble.

You should drive with your lights on at all times, on both paved and gravel roads. During the summer, long days produce lots of low-angle light, and low-beam headlights increase your visibility and reduce the chance of accidents. This practice is recommended by the Alaska Department of Transportation and is required by law in the Yukon. Remember to turn off your lights each time you stop; it's mighty inconvenient to have a dead battery in the middle of nowhere.

Crossing the International Border

You will have to clear customs before crossing the U.S.-Canadian border. Customs houses are located on all major roadways that cross the border and are typically open during the day (8 a.m. to midnight). If a customs station is closed, you must wait until the following day to cross or you will incur a heavy fine.

For the most part, citizens of the United States and Canada have little trouble clearing customs. Bring a valid driver's license or passport as proof of citizenship, and be sure that your vehicle registration and insurance papers are up-to-date. Customs officials in both countries are concerned about the kidnapping of small children, so all children traveling with you should have identification papers. Customs officials have the right to search vehicles for contraband materials, and visitors who decline this search will be denied access into the country. Most travelers are allowed to cross the border after answering a few simple questions.

A few restrictions apply to motorists crossing the U.S.-Canadian border. First of all, you must carry enough money—either in the form of cash or traveler's checks—to afford your trip. Personal checks and credit cards are not acceptable. Customs agents expect you to carry a minimum of several hundred dollars for a brief stay in the country and more for a longer stay. You must declare all firearms at the border. Automatic weapons and handguns are not allowed into Canada without a special permit (which is rarely granted). Items that are made from parts of game animals or endangered species are typically difficult to get through customs, and they often require special permits. It is unwise to try to bring fresh fruits and vegetables through customs, as these may be quarantined to prevent the spread of crop diseases. You must pay a duty fee for all goods you purchase in a foreign country and bring home.

Fishing, Hunting, and Panning for Gold

You will need special permits or licenses for some recreational activities in the Far North. Fishing licenses are required in all parts of Canada and the United States, even for catch-and-release angling. These licenses are issued by the individual states, territories, and provinces, and are good only within the region in which they are issued (for example, a Yukon fishing license is not valid in the Northwest Territories). Fishing licenses are more expensive for non-residents but are still quite affordable. When purchasing one, be sure to pick up a copy of the fishing regulations. Seasons and catch limits often vary widely within a state, province, or territory, and you will be expected to know and obey the rules. In Alaska, a fishing license is also required for clamming.

Hunting in the Far North is an expensive proposition for non-residents. Licenses and tags typically cost hundreds of dollars, and regulations often require visitors to be accompanied by a resident or a licensed guide. Special tags are issued for each game species, so the cost of a hunting trip depends in part on how many tags you purchase. Check with local wildlife management agencies for current regulations, seasons, and limits. Successful hunters may have to obtain special permits to transport their game through customs.

Panning for gold is a unique and popular pastime in the Far North. Because gold is heavier than water and other kinds of rock, it settles to the bottom of a gold pan when you swirl gravel with water. Gold-panning is free in all streams of the Far North, with a few restrictions. Recreational gold-panning is not allowed on the right-of-way of the Trans-Alaska Pipeline, nor is it permitted on claims staked by prospectors. Claim markers may not always be obvious, so it is wise to check with local authorities to find out where panning is allowed. Do not trespass on private land.

When panning for gold, take precautions to protect the stream from degradation. Dig gravel from bars in the streambed rather than from the banks. Dump waste water and gravel on the shore, never directly into the stream. By heeding these guidelines, you can be sure that you will not destroy the aquatic habitat of spawning fish.

How to Be a Welcome Visitor

The North Country is famous for its hospitality, and you can return the favor by learning the unwritten rules of northern culture. Bear in mind that Alaska and the Yukon are swamped with tourists every summer. Many Alaskans who came to the state to seek solitude have had a difficult time finding it. Privacy is particularly hard to come by in resort areas, where

Woodland caribou.

Cow moose and yearling on Kelly Flats on the Richardson Highway.

historical structures may also serve as homes for local residents.

Respect the sanctity of homes, mineral claims, and private land. If you wish to explore historical ruins and are unsure of the land ownership, ask first at the local visitor center. Private landowners are often happy to grant permission to visitors who want to explore old ruins on their property. The same courtesy applies to crossing private lands to go fishing or gold-panning.

The Northland is full of colorful characters, but not all of them look upon themselves as tourist attractions. Always ask permission before snapping pictures of local residents. It helps to bear in mind that these are real people with hopes, problems, and frustrations of their own. A friendly and polite approach is the best way to form lasting friendships in the Far North.

Some tourists give visitors a bad name by barraging local residents with questions and demands. It is much more rewarding to be patient. The pace of life is substantially slower in the Far North, and folks like to take their time spinning their yarns. To get a real feeling for this engaging culture, slow down and let the locals tell their tales at their own pace. They will appreciate the consideration and generally will try to be as helpful as possible.

Finally, drive courteously and have a safe and rewarding trip!

THE SOUTHERN APPROACHES

The roads to the Far North lead through northern British Columbia, a wilderness of endless forests and towering mountains. While Alaska and the Yukon boomed during the gold-rush era, the northern half of British Columbia remained untamed and uncharted. Modern industry has just begun to discover this remote region, and most of the population lives in widely scattered outposts at the edge of the unknown.

For many travelers, this area is a destination in itself, while for visitors bound for Alaska and the Yukon, northern British Columbia offers a fitting introduction to the wonders to come. The pioneer days are a recent memory here, and the land is home to entire ecosystems that have never been disturbed by man. Wildlife waits around every bend, and the waterways teem with fish of all kinds.

The coast of British Columbia is defined by the Inside Passage, a protected waterway that winds among countless forested archipelagos and gives access to hundreds of glacier-carved fjords. The sea merges with the land here, and rain and fog create a misty landscape of rain forests and shrouded peaks. The rugged Coast Mountains guard the coastline, and valley glaciers pour from the ice fields that crown the tallest peaks. Mountain goats clamber on the cliffs, and brown bears and bald eagles feast on salmon along the rivers.

This is the homeland of such Salishan tribes as the Bella Coola, Haida, Tsimshian, Gitksan, and Nisga'a. These coastal peoples have traditionally enjoyed a rich culture, traveling the inland seas in war canoes, holding elaborate potlatch ceremonies, and building great villages of plank houses. The rich salmon runs of the coast have provided a plentiful food supply, giving the tribes ample free time to develop a rich artistic tradition, which focused on the carving of elaborate ceremonial masks and impressive totem poles.

The climate of the inland mountains is typified by dry summers and cold winters. The northern marches of the Rockies offer a landscape of barren peaks and glacier-carved valleys. This is a land of endless spruce forests,

I

populated by pine martens, lynx, wolves, grizzly bears, and moose. The alpine tundra of the higher elevations supports populations of woodland caribou and Stone sheep, and golden eagles nest among the tallest crags. The streams are home to whitefish, arctic grayling, and rainbow trout, while lake trout and northern pike inhabit the lakes. This area was originally inhabited by nomadic tribes of Athapaskan descent: the Tahltans, Sikannis, and Kaskas. Calling themselves Déné, or "the people," these wandering hunters were attuned to their natural surroundings and survived in perfect balance with a harsh and unforgiving land.

From the mountains, a forested lowland stretches eastward all the way to Hudson Bay. The cold winters and brief summers here result in vast tracts of permafrost, where the soil never thaws. These have become muskeg bogs populated by spindly black spruce and mats of sphagnum moss. This is the land of the black bear and the moose, and the wolf reigns supreme during the silent winter. Athapaskan tribes such as the Beaver, Sikanni, Slavey, and Digrib peoples formed the basis for a rich fur trade that supported the economic growth of Canada during its infancy. This vast and featureless land has always been thinly populated, although in modern times the quests for oil and timber have attracted heavy industry.

The two primary routes to the North Country are paved along most of their length, and services are available at frequent intervals. The Alaska Highway has earned enduring fame and popularity as the pioneer route to the Far North. It follows the Front Range of the Canadian Rockies northward to the Yukon. The Cassiar Highway is gaining in popularity. Once a gravel haul road for asbestos carriers, it is now a paved or coated thoroughfare used primarily by tourists. Spectacular mountains make it the more scenic of the two routes, and it is also a faster and more direct route to Alaska.

1

The Cassiar Highway

Official Designation: British Columbia Highway 37
Description: A paved or coated highway with a few gravel sections; 733 kilometers (456 miles) from Kitwanga, British Columbia, to junction with Alaska Highway
Recommended Maximum: 80 kph/50 mph on gravel sections
Distance Markers: Kilometer posts count northward from Kitwanga, reset at zero at Meziadin Junction and again at Dease Lake
Further Reading: *Nisga'a: People of the Nass River*
Information Sources: Kalum Forest District, Cassiar Forest District, North by Northwest Tourism Association

 The Drive

This remote roadway follows the Coast Mountains through British Columbia to join the Alaska Highway in the Yukon Territory. It was conceived as a gravel haul road for the heavy trucks bringing asbestos south from the mines at Cassiar. The mines are closed now, and most of the roadway has been paved or coated (which is almost as effective as paving). It provides the most direct access to the Far North, crossing a wild and mountainous landscape that has changed little in thousands of years. Services are available at regular intervals but are still far enough apart to give you an appreciation for the immensity of this beautiful corner of the continent.

The highway makes an auspicious beginning by crossing the Skeena River, one of the great inland waterways of northern British Columbia. Called "River of Mists" in the local native dialect, this deep and powerful river flows between steep slopes covered with a lush coastal forest of hemlock and Sitka spruce. Stern-wheelers plied its green waters between 1886 and 1913, bringing supplies to the fur-trading posts and mining centers of the interior.

On the north bank of the river sits the Gitksan Indian village of Gitwangak. Its white companion settlement, Kitwanga, occupies the bluffs farther inland. *Gitwangak* means "People of the Place of the Rabbits," and the village was built at a strategic position on the pre-Columbian trading routes between the coast and the interior. These trade routes were known as "grease trails." Coastal Indians rendered an oil from a smelt known as the

The Cassiar Highway (Part 1)

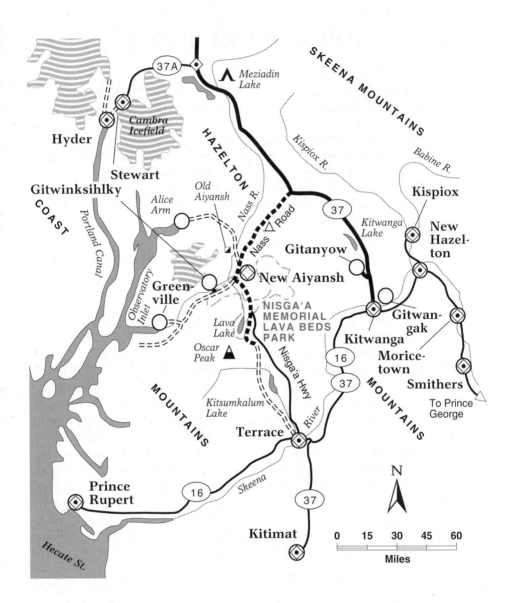

eulachon, or candlefish, and used it to barter with inland Athapaskan tribes for furs, meat, and hides. Eulachon oil was considered a delicacy and was used to enhance the taste of a variety of foods in much the same way as butter.

In 1893, Anglican missionaries established St. Paul's Church in Gitwangak, and it still stands on Bridge Street as one of the finest examples of early Victorian architecture in the province. A scenic riverside park is the site of a dozen authentic totem poles bearing heraldic crests and relating the stories and legends of the Gitksan.

Just north of Kitwanga, on a short loop road to the west, a historic Indian stronghold has been preserved at Kitwanga Fort National Historic Site. Here, atop a conical mound on the flood plain, the native people built plank houses and surrounded them with a palisade of sharpened logs. A short interpretive trail tells of the frequent battles fought here between feuding bands of Indians. From the heights, the defenders could roll spiked logs down upon their foes. One of the last defenders to fight here was the fabled warrior Nekt, who was believed to have the powers of a grizzly bear and who wielded a club named "Strike Only Once." He wore a suit of armor cunningly constructed of slate that protected him from the blows of his enemies.

As you leave Kitwanga and the highway begins to climb, watch for

Mountain scenery near Kitwancool.

views of the Seven Sisters, a magnificent chain of sawtooth spires that rises in the Roche Deboule Range. The road follows one of the "grease trails" along the Kitwanga River. The spectacular Coast Mountains rise to the west, and as you move northward the coastal forest is replaced by stands of balsam poplar and white spruce. To the north and east, broad forested basins are flanked by isolated peaks.

About 15 kilometers north of Kitwanga is the Gitksan village of Gitanyow, marked on maps as Kitwancool. *Gitanyow* means "People of a Small Place." The village once stretched for 9 miles along the river, but intertribal warfare and diseases spread by white traders wiped out most of the population. This village has one of the oldest and most outstanding collections of totem poles in the world, including the famous "Hole in the Ice" totem pole. These poles are the cultural record of the native people, and on ceremonial occasions, the owners of the poles gather together and recite the stories depicted in the wood. If you are lucky, you may get a chance to see native craftsmen carving these monumental works of art.

Beyond Gitanyow, the bottomland is choked with tall cottonwoods. The seeds of this tree must fall upon bare soil to take root, and so it is typically found along major watercourses where floods periodically scour the riverbanks. At Kilometer 31, the road reaches Kitwancool Lake. Snow-dappled peaks rise beyond its deep blue waters. The old highway leaves the main route here and heads westward, providing access to boat-launching spots and primitive campsites along the lakeshore. To the north of Kitwancool Lake, the highway descends gently through marshy country along the Cranberry River. Tall peaks give way to low, wooded ridges. The Nass River Forest Road takes off to the west at Kilometer 76, following the Cranberry into the mountains and to the native village of New Aiyansh and the Nisga'a Lava Beds Memorial Park (see Nass River Forest Road Sidetrip at the end of this chapter).

The Cassiar Highway continues northward through heavily logged forests. Small placards along the road record the dates that stands were logged and when they were replanted with seedlings. It is interesting to compare the regenerating plant growth on stands of different ages. Several small lakes lie below the highway to the west, and you can reach them via short spur roads. Before long, you will be able to glimpse the Nass River and the wooded ridges and glacier-clad summits that stand above it. *Nass* is an Indian word that translates roughly as "satisfier of the belly." The river abounds in sockeye salmon and eulachon, or candlefish.

The Cassiar Highway passes a cluster of service stations at Kilometer 139 and then crosses a bridge over the Nass River. The dramatic summits of the Coast Mountains loom to the west as the road climbs to the top of a bluff. Among the peaks is a huge cap of glacial ice known as the Cambria Ice Field.

The Cassiar Highway (Part 2)

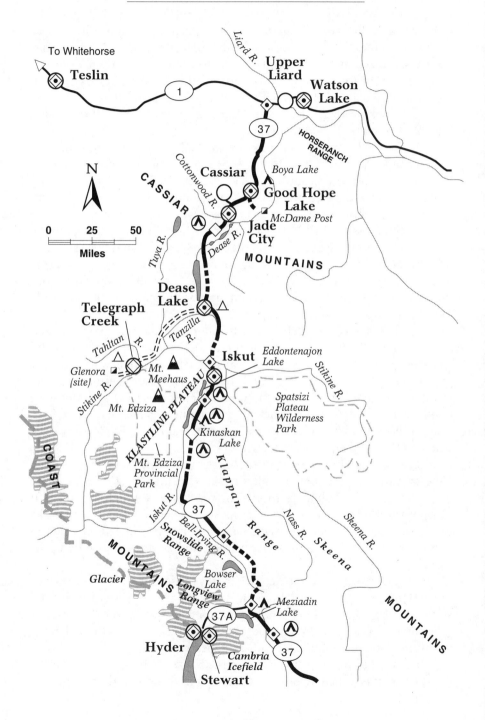

A glittering expanse of water soon appears to the west, nestled in the trees on the valley floor. This is Meziadin Lake, and a spur road runs westward to reach a provincial park near its south end. The highway follows the lakeshore at a distance and soon reaches Meziadin Junction. The Glacier Highway (Route 37A) runs west from this point (see Drive 2). Kilometer posts reset to zero here and count northward from Meziadin Junction.

Turn right to continue northward on the Cassiar Highway, which traverses hilly country dotted with small lakes and isolated clearcuts. The mixture of spruce forest and small clearings is excellent wildlife habitat. Watch for black bears and moose.

As the road approaches the Bell-Irving Valley, it enters a zone of massive clearcuts. Vast areas have been denuded, creating a stump-filled moonscape that was once a beautiful valley. Well-planned timber harvests can actually enhance the value of the forest as wildlife habitat, but few species can survive in enormous clearcuts such as these.

As you cross the Bell-Irving River for the first time, you can see to the east the Klappan Range, a western arm of the Skeena Mountains. The road follows the turbid river, and soon the snowy Longview Range rises in the west, forming the edge of the Coast Mountains. After 30 kilometers of continuous clearcuts, the forest returns and the graceful spires of the Snowslide Range rise ahead.

Before you cross the Bell-Irving River for a second time, you will pass a rest area at Hodder Lake. This gemlike pool is surrounded by graceful spires of spruce, and snow-mantled peaks are reflected in its water. Beyond the bridge, the road begins to climb toward Nigunsaw Summit, passing through marshy country along the way. Watch for beavers and moose in ponds surrounded by willow thickets. The mountains rise sharply on both sides of the road as it approaches the summit, and beyond the pass are the wild and brawling rapids of the Nigunsaw River.

At Kilometer 136, the highway climbs to the top of a rise above Echo Lake, and an interpretive sign commemorates the first effort to build a telegraph line into the Yukon Territory. The road traverses high ground as it runs northward from this point, offering superb views of the rugged peaks to the west. A Forest Service road soon drops away to the left, en route to Bob Quinn Lake. Just beyond it, a heliport and airstrip appear along the road.

Thomas Creek, at Kilometer 162, marks the southern edge of the Iskut Burn. Here, silvery snags rise from the midst of a new growth of alders and young conifers. In 1958, a lightning strike burned about 65,000 hectares (250 square miles) here. In the wake of the fire, huckleberries thrived in the sunny clearing, providing a feast for local bears.

The road ultimately dips down to the banks of the Iskut River at the point where it is joined by Burrage Creek. From this point, there are excellent views of Hankin Peak to the southwest. As the road climbs back onto the elevated benches, watch the northwestern horizon for views of Mount Edziza, an extinct volcano that rises from the Klastline Plateau. Lodgepole pines form dense thickets in this high country. In areas that burn frequently, the lodgepole has a competitive advantage over other trees because fire stimulates its cones to open and release their seeds onto the newly burned ground. The Iskut Burn ends at Eastman Creek, where there is a rest area in a pleasant woodland. The creek was named for George Eastman, one of the founders of the Eastman-Kodak Company. He traveled to this remote corner of British Columbia on a big-game safari early in the 1900s.

The road leaves the glacier-clad peaks behind as it climbs into the basin containing the Iskut Lakes. The surrounding mountains are barren and brooding. Forested slopes sweep upward to blunt summits crowned with windswept tundra. The flat-topped peaks to the east are outriders of the vast Spatsizi Plateau. This rolling upland of bare tundra has been protected within the Spatsizi Wilderness Park. It offers outstanding backpacking and horse-packing possibilities. Spatsizi translates as "red goat" in the local native dialect. The mountain goats here often wallow in the iron-rich dust found on the plateau, and it turns their fur a dull shade of red. The plateau is also home to grizzly bears, moose, and the endemic Osborn caribou.

Natadesleen Lake is the southernmost of the Iskut Lakes, and a short hiking trail leaves the highway at Kilometer 207 to reach it. The highway soon reaches the southern end of Kinaskan Lake, where a provincial park offers camping on the water's edge. The Mowdade Lake Trail into Mount Edziza Provincial Park is accessible by boat from this campground.

The highway follows the long shoreline of Kinaskan, then makes a brief swing to the east to cross the Todagin River. On the way, openings in the hills reveal the stark peaks that guard the western edge of the Spatsizi Plateau. The road passes Tatogga Lake, and just beyond it a 12-kilometer gravel road leads eastward to a primitive campground on the shores of Ealue Lake. This road also provides access to the Spatsizi Wilderness Park.

The highway continues northward and soon strikes the shoreline of Eddontenajon Lake. The austere peaks of the Klastline Plateau rise beyond its waters. A dry climate prevails here, and the copses of wind-blasted aspens along the shoreline are reminiscent of the Front Range of the Rocky Mountains.

The village of Iskut is scattered along the eastern shore of the lake, and it offers a variety of services. Here, the Sikanni tribe has made a home among the Tahltan Indians of the interior mountains. The Sikanni, a small band of Athapaskan Indians, were driven from their ancestral homeland on the prairies in the 1800s by the much larger Beaver tribe, which had acquired guns from fur traders. Although they sought refuge in the rift valleys, the Sikanni suffered repeated raids at the hands of wealthy and powerful coastal tribes from the west. After decades of wandering, the Sikanni band settled among the Iskut Lakes, where its members have finally found peace.

There is another cluster of businesses at Fortymile Flats, just beyond the head of Eddontenajon Lake. About 5 kilometers beyond Fortymile Flats, there is a pullout on the west side of the road that offers a view of Mount Edziza. This peak is a dormant volcano that first erupted 4 million years ago and continued to spew lava until only 10,000 years ago. The successive eruptions covered 162,500 hectares (630 square miles) with lava and cinders. Native people used obsidian from Mount Edziza to make blades and points, and the volcanic glass became an important trade item. Obsidian implements found as far away as Idaho and the Arctic Ocean have been traced to this source.

The highway soon begins its tortuous descent to cross the mighty Stikine River, which established its present course 7 million years ago as it cut downward through the uplifting Stikine Plateau and Coast Mountains. Downstream from the bridge and out of sight is the Grand Canyon of the Stikine, where fast currents and sheer walls form an impassable barrier. The current through this canyon is so strong that migrating salmon are unable to swim through it. As a result, they are absent from the upper reaches of the river.

As the road climbs into the highlands beyond the river, notice the railroad grade to the east. It was built at enormous expense by BC Rail, which envisioned it as part of a rail link to the Yukon. Like many construction projects attempted in the North Country, this scheme folded in 1977 in the face of mounting costs. The landscape now takes on the appearance of the Alaskan interior. The lush forests of the coast are gone, to be replaced by open forests of spindly white spruce that rise from an undergrowth of tundra shrubs. Valley bottoms are covered by brushy tundra, dominated by dwarf birch and low-growing willows.

The highway tops out in the open basin that holds Upper Gnat Lake. Woodland caribou inhabit the arid mountains to the east in the winter and early spring. The road then descends to the Tanzilla River, which bears the Tahltan name for the warm springs that feed it. There are primitive campsites along the river, and the tall willows found here make excellent moose habitat.

The highway follows the clear Tanzilla to the town of Dease Lake, on the drainage divide between the Pacific and Arctic oceans at Kilometer 338. To the south, all of the waterways in interior British Columbia drain into the Pacific; to the north, the Dease River and its tributaries flow into the Mackenzie River system and eventually into the Arctic Ocean.

At the center of town, the Telegraph Creek Road runs westward to the

The Dease River flows through the heart of the Cassiar Mountains.

head of navigation on the Stikine River. (This route is discussed in detail in Drive 3.) From Dease Lake, kilometer posts on the Cassiar begin counting northward from zero.

Dease Lake has long been a focal point of human settlement. The first permanent structures were built by the Hudson's Bay Company, which came to trade for furs with the Tahltan Indians who lived here. The gold rushes in the Cassiar Mountains and later in the Klondike caused the town to boom briefly. It has never been much more than a wilderness outpost, and it remains so to this day. Dease Lake is the hub of Tahltan Indian government. The Tahltans were traditionally a nomadic tribe, roaming the interior of British Columbia to take advantage of seasonal abundances of salmon, berries, and wild game. Today, government programs have encouraged the Tahltans to adopt a more settled existence and to move away from the traditional subsistence lifestyle.

As the highway moves northward, it follows the eastern shore of Dease Lake for 25 kilometers. Forested ridges rise on both sides of the lake, and bald eagles are often spotted in the skies above it. An access road drops to the lakeshore from Kilometer 42.

Gold-seekers first came to this area around 1870, moving north as the California and Cariboo gold fields petered out. The boom towns of Laketon and Porters Landing were built on the distant shore of the lake, but they were soon abandoned as mining activity shifted to the mountains north of the lake. The Dease River flows from the foot of the lake into the heart of these mountains, and the highway follows its wandering course. Tall spruce trees lean from undercut banks, and oxbow lakes mark the locations of old channels that were abandoned by the river after spring floods.

As the hills turn to rocky peaks, the highway crosses the river at the spot where it flows into Joe Irwin Lake, the first in a chain of lakes that has formed along the river. The road passes Pine Tree Lake and Cotton Lake before turning westward into the mountains. At Cotton Lake, the forest is interrupted by an extensive burn. A careless camper ignited the blaze in 1982, and it blew up into a major conflagration. Cotton Lake is the put-in point for canoeists taking a Class II float down the Dease River to Boya Lake Provincial Park. The river flows through the core of the mountains, passing through outstanding moose habitat and visiting the historic ruins of McDame Post.

Meanwhile, the Cassiar Highway jogs westward, following the glacier-carved valley of the Cottonwood River into the heart of the Cassiar Mountains. The verdant forest of lodgepole pine sweeps upward to soaring peaks cloaked in alpine tundra. The road soon abandons the river and climbs through a pass to the north, from which stunning views of the peaks unfold on all sides.

The high country is filled with beautiful lakes. Simmons and Twin lakes are the first ones you will see. After skirting around the base of Needlepoint Peak, you will come to Lang and Vines lakes, from which you will have good views of Needlepoint.

At Jade City (population 12), the building east of the road is the ore-crushing mill for the Cusak Gold Mine. Gold was discovered in the mountain to the east, and the ore is processed here. Jade City is also a processing and trans-shipment point for the Princess Jade Mine 130 kilometers (80 miles) to the east. Much of the jade is sold to Oriental markets, where it is highly prized for jewelry, carving, and medicinal purposes. Just north of town, a short spur road leads to the abandoned Cassiar Asbestos Mine. Once a thriving company town, the mine closed in 1992 and now houses only a skeleton security staff. Visitors are discouraged.

As the road continues northward through the mountains, it enters the heart of the historic Cassiar placer-mining district. Most of the gold-panning and sluicing activity occurred between 1872 and 1878, with the richest deposits found along McDame Creek. Watch for piles of gravel along the streambanks that indicate past placer mining. At Kilometer 131, the highway reaches the former site of Centreville, once a boom town of 3,000 souls at the upstream limit of paying gravel on McDame Creek. The largest solid-gold nugget ever found in British Columbia showed up on a nearby claim in 1877. It weighed 72 ounces.

Wildlife-viewing opportunities abound on the approach to Good Hope Lake. Stone sheep are often spotted along the road on the descent into town, and you may be able to see mountain goats on the slopes of Mount Pendleton across the lake if you use binoculars or spotting scopes. On the southern outskirts of town, a gravel road winds around the south shore of Good Hope Lake, bound for the standing ruins of McDame Post, built by the Hudson's Bay Company during the heyday of the fur trade. To reach the post on the Dease River, you must drive 15 kilometers over rough ground and across shallow creek fords. Four-wheel drive is recommended, and you should avoid the road altogether during wet weather.

The town of Good Hope Lake is a center of Kaska Indian settlement. This formerly nomadic tribe ranged all the way into what is now the Northwest Territories. Early explorers knew them as the Nahanni Indians. You will have more opportunities to look for Stone sheep as the highway passes Mud Lake on the way out of town. Although similar in appearance to the bighorn, the Stone sheep is a thinhorn variety. Biologists classify it as a subspecies of the all-white Dall sheep that lives farther north.

The Cassiar Mountains dwindle as the road runs north from Good Hope Lake. A side trip to Boya Lake Provincial Park yields a view of the scenic Horseranch Range. A portage trail leads from the lake to a canoe take-out point on the Dease River. As the highway leaves the mountains, lodgepole pines make way for the white spruce more typical of the cold subarctic regions. Forest stretches away in all directions, and the low mounds of the French Mountains are visible to the west. At Kilometer 204, the Blue River heralds the beginning of a land of tiny woodland lakes. As you rise in

Mt. Pendleton is one of the most spectacular peaks that rise above the McDame Post Road.

elevation, you will enter a bleak forest of stunted black spruce. If you drive the Cassiar in May, you have a good chance of seeing woodland caribou in the vicinity of the British Columbia-Yukon border. The Cassiar Highway joins the Alaska Highway 3 kilometers north of the border and about 20 kilometers west of the town of Watson Lake (see Drive 5).

Nass River Forest Road Sidetrip

This rugged logging road follows the Cranberry River westward through heavily logged country. After 46 kilometers, the road passes Dragon Lake, and a short spur leads to a primitive Forest Service campground on its north bank. The Nass River Road continues westward, passing junctions with trunk roads that run north to Alice Arm. (You should bear left.) It finally reaches the Nisga'a Indian village of New Aiyansh in the lower valley of the Nass River.

Across the river is the original settlement of Old Aiyansh, an impressive collection of Victorian buildings that had to be abandoned due to flooding. If you wish to view this ghost town, stop at the Nisga'a Tribal Center in New Aiyansh for permission to cross the private land that leads to the riverbank.

Just west of New Aiyansh are the great fields of lava that comprise Nisga'a Lava Beds Memorial Park. The lava flowed from a cone east of Lava Lake in 1917, damming several creeks to form a new river, the Tseax. During this cataclysmic eruption, several Nisga'a villages were buried. According to Nisga'a tales, the eruption was a form of natural retribution that occurred after some native children treated the pink salmon with disrespect and cruelty.

The road cuts directly through the lava flow and then follows it southward along the Tseax River. The seemingly barren volcanic surface is covered with lichens, a pioneering form of fungus that will create soil for future plants. You can hike across the lava surface, but be forewarned: the rocky landscape hides unstable stones and is prone to cave-ins.

The south end of the park encompasses Lava Lake, where a private campground offers spectacular views of Oscar Peak to the south. Just south of the lake, you can pick up the paved Nisga'a Highway, which leads southward to the town of Terrace and forms a sort of loop with the beginning of the Cassiar.

2

Glacier Highway

Official Designation: British Columbia Highway 37A
Description: A paved highway from a junction with the Cassiar to Hyder, Alaska; 66 kilometers (41 miles)
Recommended Maximum: 40 kph/25 mph (Granduc Road only)
Hazards: Granduc Road too narrow for RVs or trailers
Distance Markers: Kilometer posts count westward from Meziadin Junction
Information Sources: Kalum Forest District, Stewart-Hyder Chamber of Commerce

 The Drive

The Glacier Highway is a short, well-paved spur road that connects the Cassiar Highway with Stewart, British Columbia, and Hyder, Alaska. The highway crosses the Coast Mountains, and you can see more than twenty glaciers from the road. The Bear Glacier descends almost to the roadside and is considered by many to be the highlight of the trip. Stewart and Hyder are quiet villages on one of the long fjords that carry salt water from the Pacific far into the mountains. There is a weekly ferry that links Stewart with the Alaska Marine Highway system. From Hyder, an improved gravel road climbs high into the mountains, revealing magnificent glacial vistas and visiting old silver and copper mines.

The Glacier Highway runs west from Meziadin Junction, following the north shore of Meziadin Lake. A vigorous growth of forest hides the turquoise water, which owes its striking tint to a suspension of fine glacial silt. The silt refracts the light that enters the water, and the light that escapes is limited to the blue-green part of the spectrum. There is a picnic area near the head of the lake at Kilometer 8. The peaks of the Cambria Range crowd the head of the lake, and the road crosses Sunrise Creek and ascends gently toward Bear Pass. Several hanging glaciers in the peaks to the south are visible from this section of the road. As the highway drops into an alpine valley beyond Bear Pass, be on the lookout for mountain goats.

The Bear Glacier originates in the Cambria Ice Field and pours down toward the road between Mounts Disraeli and Strohn. Its surface is fissured

Glacier Highway

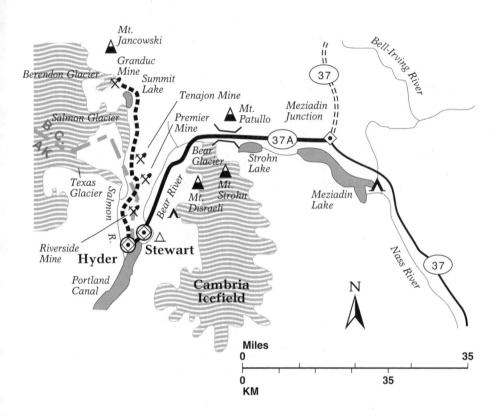

with deep crevasses that glow with an ethereal blue light. The glacier has been retreating in recent years; it once crossed the valley floor to meet the far slopes. Look uphill to spot the old roadbed, built when the glacier crossed the valley. As the glacier retreated, it left a deep basin that later filled with meltwater to form Bear Lake. From time to time, great slabs of ice calve off the glacier and slide into the lake to form icebergs.

The Bear River carries the glacial meltwater toward the coast, and the road follows its westward descent. Watch for avalanche chutes dropping from the steep slopes that surround the valley. Periodic snow slides have cleared these tracks, and they are often populated by specialist shrubs, such as slide alders. Unlike stiff-trunked conifers, which snap under the force of an avalanche, these shrubs can bend without breaking.

The road drops quickly into the lowlands, and the trees return in the form of a lush coastal forest. Sitka spruce, hemlock, and cedar thrive on the abundant rainfall and frequent fog that typify the northern coastline. Numerous tributaries join the Bear River during the course of its descent, and it soon becomes a tangle of braided channels wandering across a gravelly flood plain. As the highway approaches the town of Stewart, watch for the gossamer waterfalls that grace the steep slopes high above the valley floor.

Stewart is a mining town at heart, and it has suffered the boom-and-bust fate so typical of this industry. There has been little mining activity in recent years, giving the town a quiet and restful aspect. Stewart is situated at the end of Portland Canal, a narrow, 150-kilometer (90-mile) fjord that forms the southern border between Alaska and British Columbia. The town has a small historical museum that specializes in displays of old mining equipment. Ask here about the several historic buildings in town. There are also several stonework storehouses built by the U.S. Army in 1896 at Eagle Point, on the international border. You can view spawning salmon in the clear water of Rainy Creek on the northern end of Stewart; pink salmon run in September and October, while the silvers spawn during November. Ferries run once a week from Stewart to Ketchikan, Alaska, linking the community with the Alaska Marine Highway system.

From Stewart, the road winds around the north end of the fjord, crossing an unguarded border to reach the Alaskan town of Hyder. Because Hyder is so isolated from other Alaskan communities, it has forged close ties with

Snowy crags rise above Glacier Highway.

The Salmon Glacier pours down from the heights of Mt. White-Fraser.

its Canadian neighbor. There is no customs house, and Hyder businesses accept only Canadian currency, since the only bank in the vicinity is in Stewart. The two towns hold a combined celebration of Canada Day and Independence Day that lasts from July 1st to the 4th. Hyder bills itself as "The Friendliest Ghost Town in Alaska" and offers a rollicking and popular nightlife. If you are adventurous, ask about becoming "Hyderized," a ritual of some local notoriety.

Granduc Road Sidetrip

From Hyder, you can can follow the Granduc Road deep into the mountains to visit old mining sites. The road is steep and winding. It can be negotiated by most passenger cars but should not be attempted by RVs or vehicles pulling trailers.

The road begins by following the Salmon River northward through a deep valley flanked by steep mountains. After 7.6 kilometers, the road crosses Fish Creek, which is known for supporting the largest run of chum salmon in the world. Specimens weighing 35 pounds and more have been recorded, and the clear waters of the creek make for ideal viewing. The run begins in late July. The spawning salmon also attract the coastal brown bear, a larger relative of the grizzly. This magnificent animal is the lord of its domain. Do not approach, taunt, or attempt to feed it! Enjoy the bears only from the safety of your car.

The Granduc Road continues along the river, passing the Riverside Mine site just before reaching the Canadian border. This small mine was active during the early 1900s, but now only rusting equipment and scattered timbers remain. Soon after crossing into British Columbia, the road climbs into a side valley and passes beneath the enormous Westmin Premier Mine, which produced gold and silver between 1919 and 1954. It now employs only a skeleton staff. You can get the best view of the enormous tailings heaps, produced by decades of hard-rock mining, from the far side of the leaching pond.

The road soon climbs around a hillside and returns to the Salmon River drainage. It charts a precarious path across the steep slope of Big Missouri Ridge, named for another of the prominent local mines. The road winds high above the valley floor and offers views of the Munro and Texas glaciers cupped in folds on the wall of the opposite valley. You can barely see the old Westmin Tenajon Mine above the road, and the Salmon Glacier in the valley below.

The Granduc Road tops out at a lofty summit. From this point, you can view Salmon Glacier in all its glory as it descends from the heights of Mount White-Fraser to a low pass, where the flowing ice splits and pours down both sides of the Coast Mountains divide. Watch for mountain goats in the alpine meadows along the top of the ridge.

As you begin to descend, the murky waters of Summit Lake appear below, dotted with the ice floes calved from the northern lobe of the Salmon Glacier. Above the foot of the lake sits the ore mill of the old Granduc Copper Mine. The mine itself is 8 kilometers to the northwest, and ore was transported to the mill through a tunnel blasted beneath the glaciers. Mining activity is thought to have changed the hydrology of Summit Lake. It once drained northward into the interior, but it now drains coastward beneath Salmon Glacier, causing annual August flooding in the valley of the Salmon River. The road dead-ends near the Granduc mill at Kilometer 36, amid a spectacular and barren landscape.

3

Telegraph Creek Road

Official Designation: Telegraph Creek Road
Description: Improved gravel road from Dease Lake on the Cassiar Highway to Telegraph Creek; 119 kilometers (74 miles)
Recommended Maximum: 55 kph/35 mph
Hazards: Steep grades may be slippery after rains; no guardrails
Distance Markers: Kilometer posts count westward from Dease Lake
Further Reading: *Trail to the Interior* by R.M. Patterson
Information Sources: Cassiar Forest District

 The Drive

This improved gravel road links Dease Lake on the Cassiar Highway with the historic settlement of Telegraph Creek, at the head of navigation on the Stikine River. The road has some steep and narrow sections with incredibly tight curves. Passenger vehicles should be able to negotiate it without difficulty in dry weather, but rain turns the surface to slippery mud and some of the grades may become impassable. The road is too narrow and winding to accommodate RVs or vehicles pulling trailers. The road was built in 1922, making it one of the oldest auto routes in the Far North.

The Telegraph Creek Road runs westward from the town of Dease Lake, passing an airfield as it follows the course of the Tanzilla River. Low ridges flank the narrow river valley, and a boreal aspen forest clothes the hillsides. These trees provide a spectacular display of color as they prepare to shed their leaves in September. The valley ultimately opens into a broad basin, and the road finds its way to the crest of a narrow ridge that separates the Tanzilla and Tuya river valleys.

After 63 kilometers, the road enters the Stikine River Recreation Area, and a pullout on the right provides access to a trail to the Tuya Viewpoint. This short footpath climbs to the grassy brow of a high bluff, offering spectacular views in all directions. Below is the rugged gorge of the Tuya River, while to the east the prominent peak is Mount Meehaus. Meehaus is a corruption of the Tahltan word *Me-hah-zie*, which translates as "calving place." The local woodland caribou migrate to the high slopes of Mount Meehaus each spring to bear their young. To the south, the volcanic cone of Mount

Telegraph Creek Road

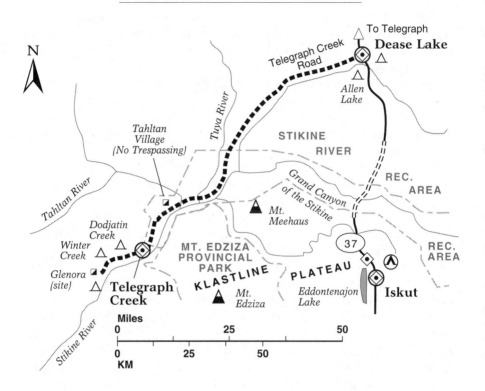

Edziza rises from the barren wastes of the Klastline Plateau, with Eve Cone visible in the foreground. This peak also can be seen from a roadside viewpoint atop a grassy summit a few kilometers farther down the road. Look at the vegetation on the ridgetop; it is the result of an old forest fire.

The Telegraph Creek Road continues along the crest of the finger ridge, and just before reaching its end you will have a stunning view of the jagged peaks far down the Stikine River to the southwest. The road snakes down a treacherous grade to reach the Tuya River. Tuya means "deep water" in the Tahltan tongue.

The road now enters the Stikine River valley. The grassy meadows and log cabins south of the road are part of the Day's Ranch. A steady climb leads to the top of the next ridge, a narrow promontory covered by an ancient lava flow. From this high point, you can get your first look at the Grand Canyon of the Stikine River; only the lower reaches are visible. At its narrowest point, the canyon constricts the current to a passageway only 2.5 meters (8 feet) wide.

The road crosses the Tahltan River at Kilometer 97. Notice the traditional pole smokehouses beside the road. Before the arrival of European explorers, the river was the focal point of Tahltan culture. The entire tribe would congregate here to fish for salmon during late summer, then scatter far and wide for the rest of the year as they pursued a nomadic hunting and gathering lifestyle.

The Tahltans developed a special breed of dog to help them hunt bears. Known as the Tahltan bear dog, it had a bushy tail like a fox and was one of the rarest breeds in the world before it became extinct in the middle of the twentieth century. After the arrival of Anglican missionaries, the Tahltans built a small village of permanent cabins around the chapel at the top of the hill. You can see this abandoned settlement from the road near the top of the next grade. It is privately owned and is not open to visitors.

About 3 kilometers beyond the old village, a bridge over Eight Mile Creek offers a view of a waterfall that plunges into the gorge of the Stikine. The creek was named for its distance from the town of Telegraph Creek, a quaint frontier community that has changed little in almost a century. Surveyors on the ill-fated Collins Overland Telegraph Project blazed a trail through the future townsite in 1865. This telegraph line was to link North America with Europe via an undersea cable across the Bering Sea. However, cable was successfully laid across the Atlantic before the Collins line was completed, and so the northwest telegraph route was abandoned. At the end of the nineteenth century, a new telegraph line was built to reach the Klondike gold fields. It followed the abandoned Collins route, and Telegraph Creek became a major construction camp for the northern end of the line. Maintenance cabins were spaced "a long day's walk"—from 50 to 80 kilometers—apart. This line operated until 1936, when it was replaced by more modern communications systems.

Although gold was never found in the vicinity, Telegraph Creek became a major transportation hub during the various gold rushes. Prospectors who had seen the lower Stikine rush of 1864 come and go followed the river as far into the interior as it would take them and then struck out overland to seek the elusive metal in the Cassiar rush of 1873. Even the distant gold rush in the Klondike caused a boom at Telegraph Creek. Canada held the right to ship goods up the Stikine duty-free, and Telegraph Creek was the starting point for a grueling overland route across Canada to the Klondike gold fields. Travelers on this route had to cross miles of blown-down timber and endless bogs that swallowed their pack animals. They found little forage for their pack stock. Thousands of would-be prospectors headed up the Stikine by steamer, but few would ever make it as far as the Klondike gold fields.

The lower reaches of the Grand Canyon of the Stikine.

More successful, perhaps, were the efforts of the Hudson's Bay Company, which built a trading post on the upper Stikine near Glenora in 1898. The company hoped to trade for furs with the Tahltans without having to go through the middlemen of the coastal tribes. This structure was moved to Telegraph Creek in 1903 and now serves as a rustic lodge and general store. Saint Aidan's Church was built here in the 1920s, and many of the other clapboard cabins in town were built during the same period. The town has a charming and graceful aura despite old age and disrepair. It has been spared the ravages of modernization by its remoteness. Always a jumping-off point, Telegraph Creek now serves as a gateway to the remote and rugged wilderness of Mount Edziza Provincial Park.

The road continues for another 20 kilometers to the former site of Glenora, which was a thriving tent city of 3,500 souls during the height of the Klondike gold rush. Along the way are primitive campgrounds at Winter and Dodjatin creeks. The road ends at the old Glenora townsite, where little remains to mark the heyday of the gold rush. An old cabin or two sits on a weedy flat along the river, and there is an overgrown cemetery on a terrace to the east of it. The area is now used as a fish camp by the Tahltans, and public camping is also allowed.

4

Alaska Highway

Official Designation: British Columbia Highway 97
Description: Paved highway from Dawson Creek, British Colum-
bia, to Delta Junction, Alaska; 2,238 kilometers (1,390 miles)
Recommended Maximum: Highway speeds
Distance Markers: Kilometer posts count historic distance northward
from Dawson Creek. (Actual distance is shorter since road was straight-
ened and signposts were not changed.)
Further Reading: *Maps and Dreams* by Hugh Brodie, *We Like It Wild* by
Bradford Angier
Information Sources: Fort Saint John Forest District, Fort Nelson For-
est District, British Columbia Parks (Fort Saint John office), Peace River
Alaska Highway Tourist Association

 The Drive

The Alaska Highway is still the most popular route to the North Country, and it is impossible to drive to Alaska or the Yukon from the south
without traveling at least part of it. The highway is paved along its entire
length, but expect to encounter some extensive gravel sections where the
road is being rebuilt. Highway construction is an ongoing process in the Far
North, where the extreme weather is hard on roadways. Services are available at frequent intervals.

Because of the length of this highway, its description will be presented
in three separate segments corresponding to the geographical divisions of
this book: the Southern Approaches, the Yukon, and Alaska.

The Alaska Highway was born of military necessity during World War
II. Alaska occupied a strategic location on the North Pacific, but it had few
military bases and no secure supply line to the rest of the United States.
Military planners feared that Japan would gain a foothold in Alaska and use
it to stage a full-scale invasion of the United States. (These fears proved
correct when Japanese forces landed in the Aleutians in June 1942, captur-
ing the islands of Attu and Kiska.)

The Alaska Highway was envisioned as an all-weather road that would
provide a vital supply link to the few bases in Alaska. Three routes were

Alaska Highway

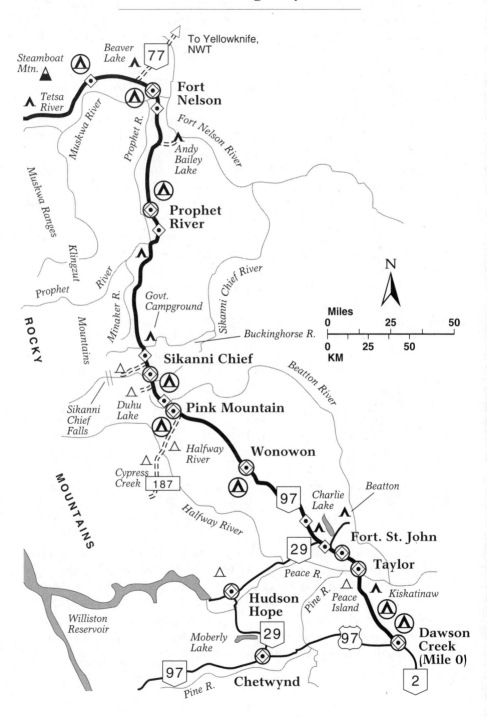

considered: a western route along the edge of the Coast Mountains, a central route through the Rocky Mountain Trench and into the central Yukon, and a prairie route that would follow the Rocky Mountain Front. The coastal route was shortest and was the peacetime favorite of the Canadians. The route following the Rocky Mountain Trench had already been surveyed and would be easiest to construct. The prairie route had little to recommend it, as it crossed vast tracts of muskeg that would pose an engineering nightmare.

But a final consideration played a pivotal role in the route selection: a chain of airfields called the Northwest Staging Route had been constructed through northern Canada and eastern Alaska to ferry warplanes to the Soviet Union, where they would be used to fight Nazi forces on the Eastern Front. Only the prairie route provided access to the airfields of the Northwest Staging Route, and so this route was selected to become the Alaska-Canada (or Alcan) Highway. It is now known as the Alaska Highway.

Canada and the United States cooperated in the venture, with the U.S. government bearing construction costs and the U.S. Army providing the initial manpower. Construction of the original grade, which became known as the "Pioneer Road," began in March 1942 and took 8.5 months. Workers bladed the road through the permafrost which, because of the disturbance, melted into a mucky gumbo when the temperature rose. Bulldozers had to pull the trucks through the worst of the mudholes. After the Pioneer Road was completed, civilian contractors moved in to bring the new highway up to all-season standards. The completed highway stretched more than 1,200 miles through some of the most remote and inhospitable terrain on the continent.

After the war, the gravel highway was turned over to the Canadian government. Early travelers found it to be an adventurous drive, with winding turns, no guardrails, and service stations hundreds of miles apart. Travelers had to take extra fuel, spare tires, and supplies in case of a breakdown. The highway has since been paved, most of the curves have been straightened, and there are services at regular intervals. The highway may not be as dangerous as it was in the early days, but it has lost little of its romance and adventure.

The Alaska Highway begins in the prairie country of the Peace River Basin and soon enters the vast belt of boreal forest that encircles the Northern Hemisphere. After skirting the mountains, the road penetrates the northernmost ranges just before entering the Yukon. Attractions in British Columbia include views of the Rocky Mountains, outstanding wildlife-viewing opportunities in Stone Mountain and Muncho Lake provincial parks, and outstanding natural hot springs at Liard River.

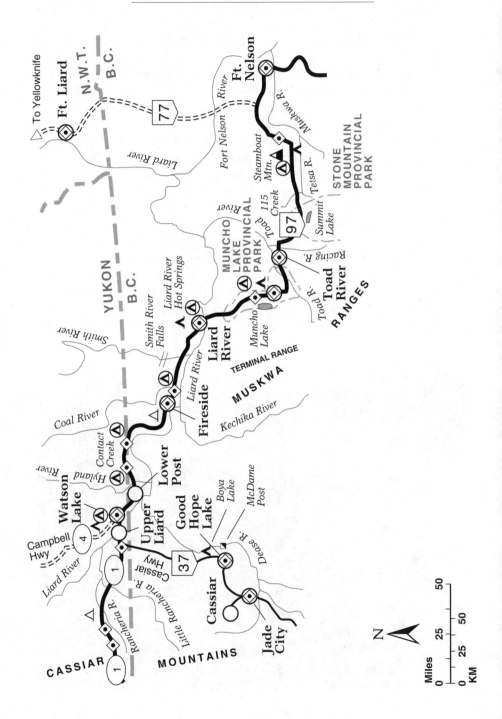

The Peace River Country

The Alaska Highway originates in Dawson Creek, a prairie city that is a hub of railroad and highway commerce. Dawson Creek prides itself on being the "Mile 0 City" on the Alaska Highway, and a large milepost in the center of a roundabout commemorates the construction of the route. Grain elevators rise above the town, storing tons of canola seeds and cereal grains that are raised in the surrounding fields. Before the coming of white settlers, this area was known as "The Beaver Plains" and was an important buffalo hunting ground for the Beaver and Sarcee Indians. The Peace River Basin was opened to homesteading in 1912, and proceeds from land sales helped to pay for the construction of the Canadian Pacific Railroad. The first settlers carved their fields from a vast and trackless forest. Early farmers supplemented their income with trapping during the winter. Today, the fields of grain, hay, and canola are separated by narrow stringers of aspen and poplar, remnants of the boreal forest.

The highway soon climbs into the rolling hills, which are all that remains of the Alberta Plateau. This great tableland rose up during the formation of the Rocky Mountains 55 million years ago. Since then, streams have carved valleys into the plateau, and thousands of years of weathering are responsible for the rolling uplands that exist today.

In ancient times, this country was repeatedly submerged beneath a shallow sea. Sediments became the shales that form the bedrock of the Alberta Plateau, and rich beds of organic matter became pockets of oil and natural gas. Today, oil and gas have become major contributors to a vigorous and growing economy.

Hay fields dominate the landscape as the highway continues northward, and at Kilometer 32, a section of the old Alaska Highway splits away to the east to reach Kiskatinaw Provincial Park. The park was built around a semicircular bridge constructed as part of the original Alaska Highway. It is the only original timber bridge from the original Alcan that remains in use today.

The new highway continues northward and descends a long grade to cross the Peace River, which got its name as a result of fierce intertribal warfare that raged in the eighteenth century. The Cree Indians, who had acquired muskets from fur traders, pushed westward into the lands of the Beaver people, who had only bows and spears. The Beavers were pushed steadily westward to the edge of the Canadian Rockies, and they in turn pushed the smaller tribes that lived there into the mountains. In 1781, the Crees were decimated by a smallpox epidemic, and the Beaver warriors attacked and defeated them at the Battle River. The two tribes then signed a peace treaty along the waterway that flows beneath the highway, and so it became known as the Peace River.

Alexander Mackenzie was the first known explorer of European descent to visit this remote corner of the continent. He and his voyageurs traveled up the Peace River by canoe, laying the groundwork for a network of North West Company trading posts. In 1793, Mackenzie reached the Peace River canyon, just upstream from the route of the future highway. He described the pristine landscape as follows: "Groves of poplars in every shape vary the scene, and their intervals are enlivened with vast herds of elks and buffaloes." Mackenzie continued westward across the mountains, reaching Bella Coola on the Pacific Ocean on July 22, 1793 (twelve years before Lewis and Clark made the "first" crossing of the continent). Soon white settlers eradicated the buffalo and drove the elk deep into the mountain wilderness to the west. Today, the banks of the Peace River are dominated by the natural-gas refineries and pulp mills of Taylor, one of the region's most industrialized towns.

The highway climbs back into the uplands and continues northward through a pastoral landscape of hay fields and pastures. Watch for deer along the roadsides in the morning and evening. The road passes Fort Saint John at Kilometer 74, and an access road runs eastward into the heart of the city. In 1794, a North-West Company trader named John Finlay built Rocky Mountain Fort at the mouth of the Moberly River. In 1821, the Hudson's Bay Company absorbed the North West Company, and for the balance of the century, Fort Saint John was the major fur-trading post for the Peace River country. One of the early factors of the post was Frank Beatton, known to his contemporaries as "a grizzled and hard-headed Orkneyman." The nearby Beatton River bears his name. Fort Saint John continues to be the commercial hub for the region, providing a center for oil and natural-gas exploration on the Alberta Plateau.

As the highway continues northward, it follows the approximate route of the Sikanni Trail, which connected Fort Saint John with Fort Nelson far to the north. This pack trail was blazed in 1920 by Joe Apsassin, a Cree from the Blueberry Reserve, along with a white trapper named Glen Minaker.

At Kilometer 86, Highway 29 joins the route from the west. It leads to Hudson Hope, W.A.C. Bennett Dam, and Williston Lake. Originally called Hudson's Hope, this settlement was a trading post built by the Hudson's Bay Company in 1803 to compete with the rival North West traders at Fort Saint John. As the Alaska Highway continues northward from the junction, the hay fields give way to a long stretch of clearcuts between Charlie Lake and Wonowon, which you will reach at Kilometer 162.

North of Wonowon, the highway enters a large tract of boreal forest. This forest stretches around the globe, encompassing the northern half of Russia and the Scandinavian countries. This ecosystem is remarkably similar throughout its worldwide range: unbroken forests of spruce, birch, and poplar are inhabited by moose, wolves, and caribou. Patches of permafrost, or permanently frozen ground found from 6 inches to 2 feet beneath the surface, crop up in the midst of the forest. They are characterized by the growth of spindly black spruce rising from peat bogs. This plant association is known locally as muskeg. It was a major obstacle for settlers on their way west, as wagons would become mired to the axles in the rich, black mud lying atop the frozen soil.

The highway follows the old overland gold-rush trail from Edmonton. The trail was touted as an "all-Canadian" route that would spare travelers the customs and duty fees charged for passage through the Alaskan routes of Chilkoot Pass and White Pass. It was blazed by a North-West Mounted Police inspector named John Moodie in 1897. About 1,600 stampeders headed north via this "trail," which was little more than a series of blazed trees. The muskeg was too boggy for horses, the rivers were too swift for canoes, and fallen timber barred the route. Only about 725 of the stampeders reached Dawson. The rest died or turned back.

At Kilometer 215, the highway enters country that was burned in the 1983 Blair Fire. The blaze was ignited by a camp garbage incinerator, and it blackened 8,840 hectares (34 square miles) of the best timber in the district. About a third of the burned trees were harvested in a salvage logging operation.

Agriculturals lands of the Peace River country, near Dawson Creek.

The highway reaches the settlement of Pink Mountain at Kilometer 226 and then descends to cross the Beatton River valley. Forest Road 192 runs westward along the south bank of the Beatton River, and by bearing right at the forks, you can reach the top of Pink Mountain after a journey of 30 kilometers. This alpine setting features outstanding wildflower displays and is a gathering place for arctic butterflies. On the highway, historic Kilometer Post 148 commemorates "Suicide Hill," a treacherous downhill grade that once ended with a sharp curve. During icy weather, heavily laden trucks slid off the road with alarming frequency. Waggish truck drivers posted a sign on the grade that read "Prepare to meet thy Maker." The highway has since been straightened and rerouted away from this dangerous grade.

You will cross the swift Sikanni Chief River 13 kilometers north of this point. The "drunken forest" that flanks the road was created by slow-moving mudslides in the unstable clay soils. The landscape beyond is dominated by tracts of muskeg. The Russians called this the *taiga*, or "land of little sticks." Moose often wander along the highway during the twilight hours, so drive cautiously.

A privately maintained gravel road leads westward for 17 kilometers from Kilometer 271, passing through oil fields to reach an overlook of Sikanni Falls. A short stroll leads to the overlook, which commands views through the trees of a spectacular cataract on the Sikanni Chief River. A population of wood buffalo has been reintroduced to the area west of the falls, but these animals rarely range far enough east to be seen from here.

The ragged peaks to the west are the Klingzut Mountains, a rugged arm of the Rocky Mountain chain. You can see them periodically as you continue northward along the escarpment of the Trutch Plateau. Here, a tabular layer of resistant sandstone has formed a landscape of extensive mesas and flat-topped buttes. This area is an important winter range for the wood-land caribou that summer in the Klingzut Mountains.

The highway passes through the settlement of Prophet River at Kilo-meter 365, and 8 kilometers north of it the road climbs to a hilltop that offers the last westward views of the Klingzuts. After passing the northern palisades of the Trutch Plateau, the road continues northward across an unbroken stretch of black-spruce muskeg. The arrow-straight corridors through the trees were cleared for seismic lines in the search for oil. Dyna-mite charges were set off at regular intervals, triggering vibrations in the bedrock that could be measured to reveal underground pools of oil and natural gas.

You can see a natural-gas processing plant from the highway 18 kilo-meters south of Fort Nelson. As the road approaches this boom town, the black-spruce muskeg gives way to a rich forest of aspen and birch, the legacy of extensive wildfires that burned throughout the region a century ago. The timber industry has established a major particle-board mill to take advan-tage of this abundant supply of wood, and the world's largest chopstick factory has been built here. The chopsticks that are mass-produced at this plant wind up in fast-food restaurants in Japan and other Asian countries.

The road crosses the muddy Muskwa River just before reaching the center of Fort Nelson. Muskwa is an Athapaskan word meaning "bear;" the river valley supports a large population of black bears. This area has always been a focal point for Athapaskan settlement. The Slavey Indians were driven from their homeland along the Great Slave Lake in 1775 by the Crees, who had acquired firearms from the fur-trading companies. The refugees settled in this area and called it *Thikanni Qua*, or "People of the Rocky River's House," in reference to the Sikannis who already lived here.

The North-West Company established a fur-trading post here in 1805 and named it in honor of Lord Horatio Nelson, a British admiral who had just defeated the French fleet at the Battle of Trafalgar. The fort was later relocated, and in 1813 it was burned to the ground by angry Indians, who murdered its inhabitants. The site was abandoned for more than 50 years until the Hudson's Bay Company built a third Fort Nelson in an effort to stifle competition from free traders, who were offering higher prices for pelts. This post was flooded in 1890 and rebuilt on the west bank of the Fort Nelson River.

The present townsite, at Kilometer 465 on the north bank of the Muskwa River, is thus the fifth incarnation of Fort Nelson. The town remained a center for trapping until World War II, when an airfield was built here as part of the Northwest Staging Route. The Alaska Highway soon arrived and replaced the river system as the town's link to the outside world. In the early days, Fort Nelson was considered "Mile 0" on the highway because the Canadian government had built a primitive road to the community. You will find historical displays at the Fort Nelson Heritage Museum in the heart of town. Also on display is a mount of a rare white moose.

Through the Canadian Rockies

As the highway runs north from town, it passes through land that has recently been cleared to create summer pasture for beef cattle. The livestock is brought by rail from the south and is returned to southern markets in the autumn. These fields disappear behind you as the Alaska Highway reaches a junction with the Mackenzie Highway, which runs north to Yellowknife in the Northwest Territories.

The Alaska Highway turns southwest here, passing through a lush forest that is occasionally interrupted by sloughs and small wetlands. You will encounter the first outlier of the Rocky Mountains about 80 kilometers west of Fort Nelson. This is Steamboat Mountain, a flat-topped peak that, like the buttes and mesas to the south, is the remnant of an ancient plateau long since divided by the carving of streams and rivers.

The road struggles up the south slope of Steamboat Mountain in a series of hairpin curves. From the top, a spectacular panorama unfolds to the south, encompassing the rugged backbone of the Muskwa Ranges. This mountain chain is made of sea-floor sediments that turned to stone and rose up during the mountain-building period in which the Rockies were created The wilderness that stretches away to the west and south is part of an immense wildlife preserve, the Muskwa-Kachika Wildlife Management Area. Here, herds of elk, deer, caribou, and Stone sheep wander across a primeval landscape undisturbed by humans. Wolves and grizzly bears reign supreme here, as they have for centuries.

As the road rounds the western face of Steamboat Mountain, the craggy profile of Indian Head Mountain rises ahead. A 12-kilometer trail to Teetering Rock, which you can see on the horizon, begins at a pullout at Kilometer 584. This weathered remnant of sandstone teeters atop a pedestal of weaker rock that has been whittled away by centuries of wind and rain. The

Stone sheep in Stone Mountain Provincial Park.

highway then makes a long descent to the valley floor, bottoming out at the Tetsa River campground. The road follows this rushing mountain stream upward through a scenic valley, as the foothills grow into rugged peaks.

Eventually, the road climbs away from the river and enters Stone Mountain Provincial Park, which offers a number of fine day-hiking trails. Longer routes for extended wilderness journeys stretch southward into the neighboring Wokkpash Recreation Area.

At the top of the grade, the blue waters of Summit Lake stretch out below the rocky summit of Mount Saint George. The highway traces the lakeshore through alpine country that is 1,295 meters (4,250 feet) above sea level. This is the highest point along the entire route and is just below the timberline. Naked summits of limestone rise on all sides, offering a windy and inhospitable habitat for alpine plants. A small pond just beyond Summit Lake has a mineral lick that is visited frequently by woodland caribou and Stone sheep. There is a second lick at Kilometer 570, where a pullout overlooks the deep valley of MacDonald Creek. Stunning peaks rise around the head of the valley, and the stream brawls across a floodplain of bare gravel.

The road glides down to the valley floor and then follows MacDonald Creek to its confluence with the Racing River. The highway is surrounded by grassy shoulders in this area, and mule deer are a common sight during the morning and evening hours. The road follows the river upward and crosses a bridge that offers a spectacular vista of the knife-edge ridges that rise far to the south.

The highway then crosses through a low gap and enters the valley of the Toad River. The Toad once ran northward into Muncho Lake, but it has been "captured" through headwaters erosion by the Racing River, and it now drains into the Liard River. There are few amphibians in this mountainous habitat, but toads are said to be abundant on the lowlands where the river pours into the Liard.

After passing a small group of homesteads at Toad River (Kilometer 672), the highway follows the aquamarine waterway into the heart of the mountains. Massive peaks of white limestone flank the narrow canyon. The rock is made of ancient seafloor sediments, the accumulated calcareous remains of millions of shellfish. The rock folded and faulted as it was pushed skyward to form the mountains, and you can easily see the distortions in its layers from the road.

After you cross the river, Centennial Falls appears to the south. The highway soon turns northward, offering views of the jagged peaks that surround the headwaters of the Toad. Upon reaching a high pass, you will see the sawtooth peaks of the Sentinel Range to the east, while those to the west are part of the Terminal Range.

The road descends gradually to Muncho Lake, the centerpiece of Muncho Lake Provincial Park. Muncho means "Big Lake" in the Athapaskan tongue, and the Kaska people have come to hunt and fish along its shores for millennia. Boat tours depart from several lakeshore lodges, featuring guides who explain more about the history and ecology of the area. Woodland caribou and Stone sheep are common along the shoreline. The woodland caribou is a smaller and darker version of its barren-ground counterpart. It travels in small bands and does not undertake lengthy migrations. The gray Stone sheep resembles the Rocky Mountain bighorn, but it is a subspecies of the all-white Dall sheep of Alaska and the Yukon.

The segment of highway that follows the shoreline of Muncho Lake was one of the most difficult and expensive construction efforts of the entire Alcan project. The roadbed had to be blasted out of sheer mountainsides that rose above a deep abyss of frigid water. Pack horses hauled away the rubble. On several occasions, machinery plunged from the narrow road grade into the azure depths of the lake.

Spectacular mountain scenery surrounds the lake, as the Sentinel and Terminal ranges march northward to form the final tier of the Canadian Rockies. The road follows the lake to its foot and then follows the Trout River to its confluence with the mighty Liard. The mountains fall away as

Limestone peaks guard the Toad River valley.

the Trout River plays out onto the narrow floodplain, and the highway follows the muddy Liard westward. A suspension bridge spans the river at Kilometer 796, leading to the settlement of Liard River and its famous hot springs. Wood buffalo have been reintroduced downstream from the bridge, and you may get to see them as they expand their range up the Liard River.

Liard River Hot Springs are among the great natural wonders of the Far North, and they have been developed for recreational use with a tasteful eye toward preserving the wild and natural character of the surroundings. A plank boardwalk leads to the two hot pools, where small changing huts have been constructed. The hot springs pour into their natural, shale-bottomed basins, and birch trees lean out over the water.

The hot water escaping from the springs feeds a series of warmwater fens that was known in the 1940s as the "Liard Tropical Jungle." The fens support a diverse population of exotic plants and animals, such as orchids, ostrich ferns, sundews, and sandworts. The lake chub thrives in the waters of the fens, separated by a thousand miles from other populations of its species. The mineral-rich aquatic plants attract moose that may occasionally be spotted at twilight.

The description of the Alaska Highway continues with Drive 5.

THE YUKON
TERRITORY

The Yukon is a wild country of boundless forests, isolated mountain ranges, and arctic tundra. It is a young land, both in terms of geological time and human settlement, and caribou still outnumber human inhabitants by a substantial margin. Its stark beauty inspired writers such as Jack London and Robert Service, who immortalized the Yukon gold rush in their stories and poems.

The Yukon has been a cultural watershed for Canada, defining the frontier spirit of the country much as the Wild West defined the United States. The gold rush brought an incredible influx of prospectors, who built scattered cabins and ramshackle towns, who blazed trails through the forest and over the passes, who found fortunes in gold dust and squandered them in town, gambling, carousing, and drinking. It was this colorful and lawless period that spawned the North-West Mounted Police, later called the Royal Canadian Mounted Police and popularly known as the Mounties. They brought justice to the boom towns and patrolled the bush by dog sled. Their red serge uniforms came to symbolize integrity and order in the Far North.

The Athapaskans have inhabited the Yukon for more than 10,000 years. In perhaps no other part of the Western Hemisphere have the native peoples had such a defining influence on modern culture. During the gold-rush era, Athapaskans were at the forefront of discovery. "Skookum Jim" helped blaze trails over the Coast Mountains and into the territory, and "Tagish Charlie" discovered the gold fields of the Klondike and the Kluane. In many parts of the Yukon, native peoples still pursue their traditional subsistence lifestyles. Their hunting, gathering, and fishing practices harmonize with natural cycles, and their lives provide a vivid demonstration of how humans can partici-pate in their natural ecosystem without destroying it.

The landscape of the Yukon is both rich and varied. To the south, the Coast Mountains crowd a district of large lakes that are world-famous for trophy lake trout. The center of the territory is defined by a great plateau that has weathered into rounded, forested hills. This is the land of the moose and the wolf, and it is also rich in fur-bearers such as the lynx, marten, and fox. Craggy ranges rise north of Dawson City and stretch east and then south along the border of the Northwest Territories. Beyond these ranges is the vast expanse of the arctic tundra, where great herds of caribou migrate hundreds of miles each year. This is a place where the summer sun shines throughout the night, and northern lights play over the snowbound winter landscape.

The Yukon has not yet achieved recognition as a full-fledged Canadian province, and its territorial infrastructure is run by the national government. The capital of Whitehorse and the gold-rush city of Dawson are its only urban areas, and the remainder of the region is characterized by isolated bush communities. Most of the population lives along two paved arteries: the Alaska Highway and the Klondike Highway. The White Pass Route and Haines Highway are the other two paved thoroughfares in the territory, and each passes through the spectacular Coast Mountains to reach a port city on the Alaskan coast.

Travelers in search of solitude can find it on roads that penetrate the bush: the Campbell Highway, Canol Road, Silver Trail, Nahanni Range Road, and Dempster Highway. The latter is Canada's highway to the Arctic, and it provides access to the land of the Inuit along the Beaufort Sea.

5

Alaska Highway

Official Designation: Yukon Highway I
Description: Paved highway from Dawson Creek, British Columbia, to Delta Junction, Alaska; 2,238 kilometers (1,390 miles)
Recommended Maximum: Highway speeds
Distance Markers: Kilometer posts count northward from Dawson Creek, British Columbia, marking the historical distance. They are no longer accurate
Further Reading: *Edge of the River, Heart of the City* by Yukon Historical and Museums Association, *Another Lost Whole Moose Catalogue* by Lost Moose Collective, and *The Legacy of a Taku River Tlingit Clan* by E. Nyman and Jeff Leer
Information Sources: Watson Lake Forest District, Whitehorse Chamber of Commerce, Kluane National Park, Tourism Yukon

 ## The Drive

West of Liard River Hot Springs, the Alaska Highway follows the British Columbia-Yukon border westward, crossing it seven times before reaching the town of Watson Lake. After traversing a broad lowland, the road passes through the northern end of the Cassiar Mountains and enters the Lake District of the southern Yukon. Large lakes dot the route to Whitehorse, which is the territorial capital and largest population center in the Yukon Territory.

The highway continues westward, finally turning northward along the boundary of Kluane National Park and following the mountains into Alaska. The Alaska Highway is the transportation backbone of the Yukon Territory, providing access to such routes as the Campbell Highway at Watson Lake, the Cassiar Highway at Upper Liard, the Atlin Road at Jake's Corner, the Klondike Highway and White Pass Route at Whitehorse, and the Haines Highway at Haines Junction.

Across the Southern Yukon

From Liard River Hot Springs, the highway follows the Liard River westward through a short and narrow canyon flanked by stony peaks. These soon open onto a series of rolling hills clothed in a mixed forest of spruce

Alaska Highway

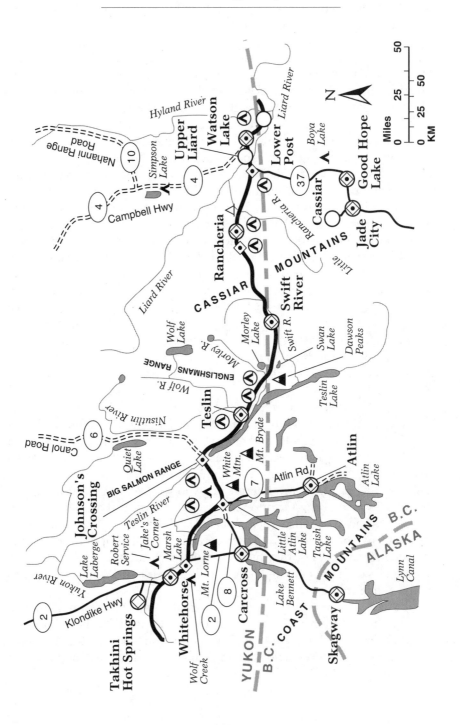

and birch. A bridge spans the Smith River at Kilometer 827, and a narrow spur road follows the west bank of this river for 2 kilometers to reach Smith River Falls. Here, the water pours over a sheer drop-off and plunges into a foaming pool.

The highway continues westward along the Liard, reaching the Coal River at Kilometer 858. An exposed seam of coal is located 10 kilometers upstream from the bridge, and chunks of coal regularly drop into the river, to be washed up on gravel bars downstream. The Coal River marks the eastern boundary of the massive Egnell Lake Fire of 1982. This fire burned an estimated 200,000 hectares (772 square miles) of timber, and its aftermath will dominate the landscape for the next 62 kilometers.

Forest fires are a normal and beneficial occurrence in northern British Columbia, because lightning tends to strike during the driest part of the year. Weather patterns create a severe drought about every thirty years, and it is during such years that the largest fires rage. Almost all of northern British Columbia and the Yukon interior have burned in the past 150 years, and so stands of timber that are older than 200 years are extremely rare. Forest fires can benefit wildlife populations by destroying unproductive stands of older trees and liberating minerals into the soil to sustain a flush of new growth that provides valuable forage for herbivores. Following the Egnell Lake Fire, the marten population fell dramatically, causing hardships for local trappers. However, within a few years, the snowshoe hare population exploded, and the number of lynx rose with the abundance of their favorite prey. The result was a string of fur harvests that proved among the most lucrative in the region.

The Alaska Highway ultimately swings away from the Liard River for a short time, and when it returns, it passes such landmarks as Whirlpool Canyon and Cranberry Rapids. Early-day voyageurs feared the Liard, and with good reason: more than twenty boatmen are known to have perished on its waters during the fur-trading era. The Hudson's Bay Company had difficulty finding paddlers and interpreters who were willing to travel up the brawling waters of the Liard to reach trading posts in the Yukon interior. Voyageurs had to negotiate such obstacles as Hell's Gate, the Grand Canyon of the Liard, the Gates of the Damned, and Devil's Portage. To bypass the most dangerous rapids, they used overland portage routes, carrying enormous bales of trade goods and furs, as well as their heavy canoes, over steep and winding trails.

The highway leaves the burned area at Kilometer 925 and enters a climax forest of spruce. The road soon crosses Contact Creek, where roadbuilding teams working northward from Edmonton linked with crews working southward from Whitehorse, completing the southern half of the Alaska Highway in late 1942.

Smith River Falls.

The next major waterway you will cross is the Hyland River at Kilometer 975. This river drains south out of the forbidding Mackenzie Mountains, which rise along the border between the Yukon and Northwest Territories. The river marks the beginning of another fire, which was ignited in the Lower Post dump on July 31, 1982, the windiest day of the year. Fire crews had their hands full with the much larger Egnell Lake Fire to the east. The Low Fire, as the new fire was called, burned approximately 10,000 hectares (39 square miles).

The road exits the smaller burn just before reaching Lower Post, a Kaska Dené village on the banks of the Liard River. There are no services here. This spot marks the confluence of the Dease and Liard rivers. Rufus Sylvester established a fur-trading post here in the mid-1870s after a disappointing try at placer mining during the gold rush in the Cassiar Mountains to the south.

The road then climbs to the top of a rolling plateau that marks the final approach to Watson Lake. On the way into town, the highway passes the Liard Canyon Recreation Site. Lucky Lake, the local swimming hole, is located here.

The first settler in the area was Frank Watson, who came north on the overland trail from Edmonton during the gold rush and built a small lakeside cabin from which to trap and prospect. An airfield was built beside Watson Lake after his death, and it was expanded during World War II into a military airbase along the Northwest Staging Route.

With the coming of the Alcan Highway in 1942, Watson Lake became a major supply depot and construction camp. Homesick GIs posted distance markers to their hometowns here, and this tradition grew into the Signpost Forest, a collection of more than 20,000 signs of all descriptions. The collection grows each year as travelers add signs of their own. A visitor center is located beside the Signpost Forest at Kilometer 1022, and it offers interpretive displays on the Northwest Staging Route and the construction of the Alcan. The Campbell Highway runs northwest from the visitor center, providing the most direct route to Dawson City and the gold fields of the Klondike.

The Alaska Highway runs westward from Watson Lake, traveling across a vast lowland robed in white spruce and lodgepole pine. It crosses the Liard River for the final time at Kilometer 1033, passing the Kaska village of Upper Liard on its far bank. Its junction with the Cassiar Highway is 5 kilometers beyond the bridge.

Signs of civilization fall away as the Alaska Highway penetrates the unbroken forest. It crosses the Little Rancheria River at Kilometer 1079, and 27 kilometers later it crosses the Rancheria itself. These rivers were named by a party of prospectors who moved through the area in 1875 following the Cassiar gold rush. Veterans of the California gold fields, the prospectors applied the Spanish term rancheria to describe the small family compounds of Kaska Indians that they found along these rivers.

After crossing the Rancheria, the highway follows the rushing river into the northern fringes of the Cassiar Mountains and passes through an area burned in 1958. At George's Gorge (Kilometer 1129), you can see rugged mountains rising south of the river. The river bottoms are dotted with shallow lakes, and old spruces that survived the fire lean over the shorelines and riverbanks.

Soon after passing the tiny settlement of Rancheria, the highway leaves the burn and enters taller timber. This forest, too, has a history of frequent wildfires. The prevalent tree species is the lodgepole pine, which has cones that are sealed with pitch. The heat of a forest fire melts the seal, and after the fire has passed, the cones break open and release their seeds onto the newly charred soil.

The road reaches Rancheria Falls Recreation Site at Kilometer 1157, and a short interpretive trail leads to a spot where the river pours through a bottleneck in a resistant ledge of granite. Water ouzels dive into the torrent near the falls. The trail is wheelchair-accessible and is an easy 15-minute trip.

Just west of the falls, the highway crosses the river and climbs a watershed divide. Streams to the east drain into the Mackenzie River and from there into the Arctic Ocean. To the west, the Swift River pours into Teslin Lake, which empties into the Yukon River drainage. The Yukon flows west into Alaska before pouring into the Bering Sea.

You will cross Seagull Creek at Kilometer 1180, and the rounded hills open briefly to reveal ragged summits to the north. The road passes through the settlement of Swift River and climbs onto a wooded bench that overlooks Swan Lake. A final view of the sharp pinnacles of the Cassiar Mountains stretches to the south. The mountains fall away as the highway enters a broad, forested basin. The road climbs to Morley Lake, where stunted black spruces replace the lodgepole pines. The highway soon crosses the Morley River and follows it to the shores of Teslin Lake. To the south, the jagged summits of the Dawson Peaks rise in isolated majesty from the surrounding lowlands.

At Kilometer 1295, the highway crosses a long bridge over Nisutlin Bay, revealing a first glimpse of Teslin Lake. The name of the lake derives from the Tlingit words *Deisleen Aayi* which mean "long, narrow waters." The Taku band of Tlingits were drawn inland by the abundant game and fish found here, and they left their home on the coast to settle along Teslin Lake before the coming of the first white prospectors.

This band lived a nomadic existence, following traditional travel routes in pursuit of fish, game animals, and edible plants. Summer brought a strong run of king salmon, which made a freshwater journey of more than 3,200

Along Teslin Lake.

kilometers (2,000 miles) to spawn in the lower reaches of the Nisutlin. In late August, hunting parties headed high into the mountains in search of woodland caribou. During the winter, the pelts of fur-bearers came into their prime, and the Tlingits dispersed into the lowland forests to trap them. Springtimes were spent hunting beaver and migratory waterfowl on the delta of the Nisutlin River, which pours into Nisutlin Bay to the east.

The Nisutlin Delta is still a wetland of critical importance to waterfowl. From October through July, the water level in the lake drops, exposing the fertile soils of the delta. These sediments support a lush growth of aquatic plants that provide forage for migrating waterfowl. All three subspecies of Canada geese can be found here seasonally, as well as mallards, pintails, wigeon, Barrow's goldeneye, and green-winged teal. In spring and autumn, tundra swans use the delta as a stopover on their long migration to and from nesting grounds in Siberia.

The first known white visitors to the area came with the Klondike gold rush. Teslin Lake lies at the end of the overland trail from Telegraph Creek. The 150-mile route crosses a forbidding stretch of muskeg bogs and blown-down timber. In 1898, it was traveled by the Yukon Field Force, a party of 500 North-West Mounted Police that headed north to enforce law and order in the tumultuous days of the gold rush. It took a month for the Mounties to reach the shore of Teslin Lake, where they could build boats and float the remaining distance to the gold fields.

With the gold rush came trading posts such as the one built at Teslin Village in 1903. These trading posts soon became focal points for native settlement, and the Tlingits ultimately abandoned their nomadic ways and settled along the shores of Nisutlin Bay.

The Tlingits have always been known for their shrewd business sense, developed over centuries of trading shells and candlefish oil to the inland Athapaskans for furs, meat, and hides. Particularly notable are the entrepreneurial exploits of George Johnston, the son of Taku chief Kowakha. Johnston imported the first automobile to Teslin in 1928, long before the Alaska Highway was built. He constructed 6 kilometers of road along the lakeshore for his new car, a Chevrolet sedan. In the summer, he ran a taxi service, and in the winter he painted the car white and drove onto the ice-covered lake to hunt wolves. Johnston was also a noted photographer, and his pictures of early Teslin are on display in the village museum, along with his famous "Teslin Taxi."

From the village of Teslin, the highway runs north along the lakeshore, offering periodic views of the glittering water. The north end of the lake is crowded with low but rocky summits, the tail of the Big Salmon Range. At Kilometer 1344, the Canol Road climbs into these mountains, following the course of a World War II oil pipeline to the border of the Northwest Territories. The pipeline linked the oil fields at Norman Wells, Northwest Territories, with a small refinery at Whitehorse, Yukon. From there, the oil could be transported to the Alaskan Front to support troops fighting the Japanese. However, by the time the pipeline was completed, Japanese invasion forces had long since been driven from the Aleutians, and the threat to Alaska was over. Historians view the Canol project as a spectacular engineering feat and a total waste of money and resources.

The Alaska Highway crosses the Teslin River where it pours from the lake. Early entrepreneurs salvaged surplus materials from pipeline- and road-construction camps to build roadside lodges such as the one at Johnson's Crossing on the west side of the bridge. This particular lodge was constructed without insulation in the attic, so for many years the hoarfrost would build up above the ceilings and create indoor rainstorms when warmer weather arrived.

The highway climbs westward, passing through a gap that contains Little Teslin Lake to the south of the road and Salmo and Squanga lakes to the north. Salmo is the Latin term for trout, while Squanga is an Athapaskan name for the humpbacked whitefish. This fish was an important food source for the Athapaskans, who caught them in nets woven from spruce roots. Squanga Lake is a nesting site for ospreys, and moose frequent its shorelines.

Mountains flank the valley, and to the south, the limestone palisades of White Mountain soar into the sky. If you view White Mountain from the west, you will notice that it resembles the profile of an elephant's head. Mountain goats were transplanted here from Kluane National Park, and a thriving population travels along the cliffs. As the mountains open onto a broad basin, the highway reaches a junction at Jake's Corner (Kilometer 1392.4). The Atlin Road heads southward to a picturesque resort village on Atlin Lake (see Drive 9), and the Tagish Road splits away from it to join the White Pass route at Carcross (see Tagish Road Sidetrip toward the end of this chapter).

The Alaska Highway runs northwest, parallel to the shore of Marsh Lake. A wall of trees hides the lake initially, but you should be able to see the water about halfway down the lake. You will have good views of the isolated mountains beyond the water. Pyramid-shaped Mount Landsdowne is visible to the south, and the bulkier summit of Mount Lorne rises farther to the northwest. Marsh Lake holds the collected waters of Atlin, Bennett, and Tagish lakes, and the broad flow that leaves its foot is the Yukon River.

The M'Clintock River flows into Marsh Lake near its foot. This sluggish, sandy stream forms a rich delta where it enters the lake, and this wetland provides habitat for thousands of tundra and trumpeter swans in April and May. Coyotes, wolves, and bald eagles venture onto the edge of the ice during this time in hopes of snagging a swan dinner. At the foot of the lake, the road follows a sluggish estuary known as the Lewes River Marsh, where beavers and moose are occasionally spotted. The area is a haven for canvasbacks, common mergansers, pintails, and wigeons during the vulnerable period when they moult their flight feathers.

The road crosses a bridge over the Yukon at Kilometer 1442. From this point, the river flows westward for almost 2,000 miles to reach the Bering Sea. Athapaskans knew the waterway as Duicke-on, or "Great River." A short distance downstream from the bridge is a hydroelectric dam. In the heyday of the gold rush, a wooden dam was built across the river at this point. The water was released in great floods to float steamboats over shallows and rapids during periods of low water.

The highway climbs to the bluff tops that rise above the south bank of the river and tracks a course through the forest just out of sight of the water. At Kilometer 1454, the White Pass Route (Klondike Highway 2) heads southward, bound for Skagway, Alaska. The main highway continues westward and enters the Whitehorse city limits. The city itself is still 15 kilometers away, but it sprawls in all directions from its urban core, encompassing 421 square kilometers (162 square miles).

A spur road runs northward from Kilometer 1466 to reach a bluff-top overlook of Miles Canyon. U.S. Army Lieutenant Frederick Schwatka passed through this area on a covert reconnaissance of the Yukon River. Schwatka undertook his expedition without the knowledge or consent of the Canadian government. His official order was to determine the friendliness of the Athapaskan tribes along the Yukon River. Given the expansionist policies of the United States and the controversy over the location of the Alaska-Yukon border at that time, Canadian officials were understandably alarmed.

Schwatka's real love was exploration itself, and he named every land-mark he encountered with an arrogant disregard for existing names used by the local residents and natives. He named this canyon after his commander, General Nelson Miles. The general had earned fame leading cavalry forces in the Indian Wars of the Great Plains and the Desert Southwest.

The canyon has since been flooded by the dam that created Schwatka Lake, but the sheer walls of basalt once rose 100 feet above raging rapids. Boaters who shot the rapids had to ride a 3-foot-high crest of water down the center of the river between two enormous whirlpools. Many boats were lost and prospectors drowned in the attempt to negotiate this stretch of whitewater. In the spring of 1898, enterprising Whitehorse businessmen built small railway trams to bypass the rapids along the bluffs on either side. Some of the stampeders shipped their supplies around the rapids and floated through in unburdened boats, while others packed even their boats onto the tram to bypass the whitewater entirely.

The highway now runs along the bluff tops above Whitehorse, and access roads run into the city from Kilometer 1470 and Kilometer 1476 (see Whitehorse Sidetrip toward the end of this chapter). The airport lies be-tween these two roads, and beside it is a transportation museum and the Whitehorse Visitor Reception Centre. This new facility offers an outstand-ing slide show covering the heritage and natural wonders of the Yukon Ter-ritory.

On the way out of town, the highway passes through the district of Kopper King, which derives its name from a copper mine that once oper-ated in the area. Just west of town, the Klondike Highway runs northwest toward the gold-rush city of Dawson.

The Kluane Country

As the Alaska Highway leaves Whitehorse, it winds through a verdant forest of spruce. About 12 kilometers west of its junction with the Klondike Highway, it enters the Takhini Burn of 1958. The Yukon was especially dry that year, and forest fires raged throughout the territory. This one destroyed 630,000 hectares (2,340 square miles) of climax spruce forest, returning nutrients to the soil to allow a flush of new growth. Near the eastern edge of the burn, dense "doghair" stands of lodgepole pine sprang up after the blaze. Farther west, quaking aspens and grassland replaced the spruce forest. The only population of elk in the Yukon Territory lives within the burn, winter-ing on open slopes north of the valley. These slopes receive plenty of sun and thus have less snow. Mule deer also inhabit this area, and you may see them in the mornings and evenings.

Before long, the bluffs of the Takhini River appear to the north of the road, and an interpretive sign at Kilometer 1508 marks the spot where the

Peaks of the Boundary Ranges rise near Kusawa Lake.

old overland trail from Whitehorse to Dawson City crossed the river. This was a winter trail used by horse-drawn sleighs, and it saw its peak use between 1902 and 1907. The highway continues westward, crossing a bridge over the Takhini at Kilometer 1525. The impressive summits of the Boundary Ranges rise south of the valley.

Some 12,500 years ago, a glacier dammed the Alsek River in the heart of the Saint Elias Mountains. The resulting lake was called Glacial Lake Champagne, and strand lines on the surrounding mountainsides mark the locations of its ancient beaches. The water remained for 2,000 years before the ice dam broke. After the lake drained, lake-bottom sediments supported a fertile grassland where steppe bison and primitive horses roamed. Nomadic bands of Stone Age hunters followed the herds, leaving charred campfire remains, small mounds of flint flakes, and a few small stone blades to mark their passage. Later, the Southern Tutchones built long caribou fences near Kusawa Lake and the Aishihik River to aid them in their hunts for these migratory animals. The fences funnelled the caribou into neck snares or corrals, where they could be killed easily with spears.

The Takhini River soon makes a sharp bend as it swings into the lowlands from a cleft in the mountains to the south. A spur road runs southward from Kilometer 1543 to a campground along Kusawa Lake. A steamboat landing at the nearby confluence of the Takhini and Mendenhall rivers marks the beginning of the old Kluane Wagon Road. Freight wagons hauled

Alaska Highway

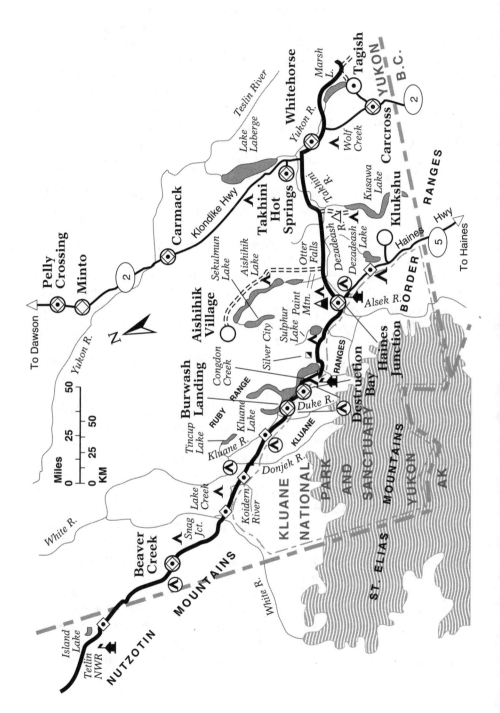

supplies from Whitehorse to the gold fields over this route during a brief spurt of mining activity in the Kluane Mining District. The highway roughly follows this old route into the historic town of Champagne.

Just before reaching town, the highway passes the First Nations Camp at Kilometer 1566.5. This area was known to the Southern Tutchones as *Shadhala ra*, or "Sunshine Mountain Camp." It has been occupied for more than 5,000 years. Here, you can view reconstructions of Southern Tutchone winter and summer encampments, including hide tents, fish traps, caribou fences, deadfall traps, and cache setups. Native guides provide an interpretive account of traditional Southern Tutchone lifeways as they were before the first Europeans arrived.

You will reach Champagne at Kilometer 1568. This tiny settlement of log cabins was originally a way station along the Dalton Trail, which ran from Haines, Alaska, to the Yukon River. The town was christened in 1897, when a group of Jack Dalton's freighters, heading north to Dawson City with a herd of cattle and supplies, stopped to celebrate the end of the worst leg of their trip by liberating a case of French champagne from their cargo.

Harry Chambers opened a trading post and roadhouse here in 1902, and the town became an important crossroads when the Kluane Wagon Road was built through the outpost in 1904. It has become a backwater and is now inhabited primarily by Athapaskan Indians of the Southern Tutchone group. The town sits atop an ancient glacial moraine, which in turn is mantled in stabilized dunes of wind-blown glacial sand.

As the road continues westward through the valley, the granite domes of the Ruby Range loom to the north. Straight ahead, the jagged peaks of the Kluane Ranges offer a preview of the stunning scenery yet to come. At Kilometer 1602.2, the Aishihik Road runs northward to the shores of Aishihik Lake (see Aishihik Road Sidetrip at the end of this chpater). The village of Canyon Creek lies at the bottom of the next grade. It features a replica of the original timber bridge that carried the Kluane Wagon Road over the Aishihik River. The original bridge was built in 1904, and Sam McGee (the legendary protagonist in Robert Service's ballad) was one of its builders.

The Aishihik River drainage holds great significance for native people. It has a history of habitation that goes back to ancient times. Prehistoric bison hunters paused to cook a meal here following a successful hunt 7,200 years ago, and their fire pit has become one of the most important archaeological sites in the Far North.

At Kilometer 1619, watch for evidence of a small fire that burned in 1995. After another 9 kilometers, the road passes the Pine Lake Campground, and Paint Mountain rises to the north. On its crest, beside a microwave relay station, is an extremely sensitive seismograph that can detect tremors deep within the earth's crust. On average, it detects three tremors a day, most of which are too faint for a person to feel.

The Kluane country is one of the youngest and most geologically active landscapes on the continent. The Saint Elias Mountains form its backbone, rising along the western horizon. They began rising only 15 million years ago, a mere eyeblink in geologic time. Mount Logan crowns the range. At 19,519 feet, it is the tallest peak in Canada. Great faults trend northwestward along the front ranges of the Saint Elias Mountains and extend deep into Alaska. As the road approaches Haines Junction, it enters a long basin known as the Shakwak Trench. This broad valley is a *graben*, an elongated depression that forms when a block of bedrock between two faults slips downward.

Haines Junction is a modern town that grew up around the junction of the Alaska and Haines highways. It is the gateway to Kluane National Park, and a Parks Canada visitor center in the town features interpretive displays and park information. The park encompasses the rugged Kluane Ranges as well as the glacier-bound Icefield Ranges, which form the core of the Saint Elias Mountains. This range was named by Vitus Bering, a Danish mariner who explored the North Pacific in the service of the Russian czar. He sighted the unknown continent on the feast day of Saint Elias in 1728, when his crew spotted the snowy crest of the range rising above a fog bank.

If you plan to continue following the Alaska Highway northward, you must turn right at the intersection at the heart of town. The highway straight

Looking down Copper Joe Creek at Kluane Lake, near Destruction Bay.

ahead leads southward to Haines. As you leave Haines Junction, the Kluane Ranges soar skyward to the west. The highway follows the western edge of the Shakwak Trench, climbing over several rolling summits as the forest grades from lodgepole pine to the white spruce more typical of subarctic regions. Views are outstanding all along the way, especially at Kilometer 1694, when the turquoise expanse of Kluane Lake appears ahead. The striking color is caused by fine glacial silt suspended in the water. As sunlight enters the water, its angle of refraction is altered by the silt, and the light that emerges has a bright aquamarine color.

A gravel road leaves the highway here and leads northeastward to the ghost town of Silver City on the shore of Kluane Lake. The sagging shells of log buildings hark back to the days when this town was the supply center of the Kluane Mining District. The original gold strike in the district was made in 1903 on Fourth of July Creek, deep in the heart of the Ruby Range east of the lake. The discoverer was none other than "Dawson Charlie," the same Tagish Indian who had struck gold in the Klondike seven years earlier. Dawson Charlie became an important figure in the Yukon, and in 1904, the Canadian Parliament enacted special legislation making him the first native to be accorded the full rights of Canadian citizenship.

At its height, Silver City boasted a post office, a mining recorder's office, and a detachment of North-West Mounted Police. Freight was shipped here via the Kluane Wagon Road and then loaded onto barges for the journey across the lake to mining settlements scattered along the opposite shore. The gold rush was over by 1907, and by 1915, the town had only one inhabitant.

The highway approaches the lake and then swings westward along its shore, following a narrow arm into the mountains where a bridge spans the Slims River, a river that has run two ways. In ancient times, Kluane Lake was smaller, and it drained southwestward through the mountains into the Pacific via the Alsek River. About 400 years ago, the Kaskawulsh Glacier surged forward and dammed the narrow canyon. Kluane Lake rose until it spilled over the northern rim of the basin to form the Kluane River, which flowed into the Yukon River watershed for a much longer journey to the sea. The Slims now carries a heavy load of glacial silt from the Kaskawulsh Glacier, and on windy days the silt is borne aloft on the breeze.

The silty flats at the edge of the lake were well-known to prospectors for their quicksand. Most men chose to head up the valley and cross the icy glacier rather than cross the flats at the river's mouth. According to local legend, the river was named after a foolish greenhorn who tried to take a shortcut across the flats to reach the gold fields. The man started across the flats with a horse named Slim, but the horse floundered and was sucked into the quicksand.

Small pockets of placer gold were found on Sheep and Bullion creeks up the valley, and they sustained short-lived boom towns before playing out. In 1903, the prospectors who made the Bullion Creek strike found 43 ounces of gold in only nine days. You can see one of the prospector's cabins just east of the Sheep Mountain Visitor Center.

The visitor center sits on the north shore at Kilometer 1707, offering a fine view of glaciated Vulcan Peak to the south. Above the visitor center, the slopes of Sheep Mountain are an important range for Dall sheep, which are most commonly seen along the road in late spring and autumn. These south-facing slopes host vegetation that paleontologists believe is similar to the "mammoth steppe" ecosystem of the Pleistocene epoch. Of particular interest is a rare species of sagebrush, Artemesia rupestris, which is also found in Siberia. Its presence here lends credence to the argument that Alaska and Siberia were once connected by a land bridge.

The highway soon rounds a mountain and follows the lakeshore northward. There are fine views across the water of the Ruby Range. The highway reaches the tiny settlement of Destruction Bay at Kilometer 1743. During World War II, this remote outpost was a convoy relay station where drivers rested and trucks were repaired. It got its name after a severe windstorm destroyed most of the buildings and flattened the surrounding trees like matchsticks.

The highway wanders inland for the next 16 kilometers, with only occasional views of the water. The town of Burwash Landing sits at the north end of the lake in a grove of aspens. The Southern Tutchones called this spot Tlu'an Man, or "Place of Fish." (Kluane itself is a corruption of the Athapaskan term for "lake of the big fish.") Eugene and Louis Jacquot founded a trading post here in 1904. When gold was discovered on Burwash Creek in 1906, the entire population of the Bullion and Sheep creek gold fields pulled up stakes and moved here. The Jacquot brothers stayed on after the gold played out and became famous as hunting guides in the game-rich Kluane country.

After leaving town, the highway crosses the Duke River, and there are excellent views of Mount Hoge from its floodplain. The local natives called this stream Shar Ndu Chu, or "Long Bear Creek." They used it as a migration corridor between berry-picking grounds high in the mountains and autumn fishing areas below Tincup Lake, which lies within the Ruby Range to the northeast. They harvested king salmon below the lake and chum salmon from the Kluane River, which the highway reaches at Kilometer 1791. The autumn run of spawning salmon attracts grizzly bears and bald eagles to the floodplain.

The highway soon leaves the river and begins to climb. It reaches a high overlook of the Donjek River valley at Kilometer 1816. From here, you will have an outstanding view of the Icefield Ranges on cloudless days. The tallest peaks visible from this point are Mounts Wood and Constantine.

The Donjek carries a heavy load of glacial silt out of the mountains. It wanders across a broad outwash plain of loose cobbles, and the shifting gravel causes frequent changes in the river's many braided channels. *Donjek* is an Athapaskan term meaning "white berries water." It refers to a species of pea vine that grows on the floodplain. Grizzly bears relish the roots of this plant, and it is an important staple of their diet in early summer.

From here, the road climbs into a narrow fault valley that bears the clear-flowing Koidern River. Water lilies grow in the many lakes that dot the valley floor, and the rugged peaks of the Kluane Ranges are reflected in the water. Southbound travelers will see the snowy crest of Mount Hoge rising ahead.

The road crosses Long's Creek at Kilometer 1860. To the southwest, you can see a hill with a landslide scar high on its slopes. The rocky brow of a long ridge soon rises east of the road, while the unbroken wall of the Kluane Ranges guards the western side of the valley. The road passes Pickhandle and Reflection lakes in rapid succession; these lakes provide nesting and moulting areas for pintails, wigeon, common goldeneye, buffle-heads, and lesser scaups.

The road then crosses the Koidern River again to reach the old settlement of Koidern. The town was built in 1942 as a telecommunications station. In its day, it had the most modern sewerage system in the territory. It has since been converted into a collection of lodges and service stations.

The Alaska Highway goes on to cross the White River, which derives its peculiar color from thick beds of volcanic ash that were deposited during two great eruptions 1,200 years ago. The volcano was located beneath the Klutlan Glacier, 40 kilometers to the southwest. The eruptions sent separate plumes of ash northward and eastward, blanketing much of the Yukon interior with a thick layer of grit. The ash also covered the toe of the Klutlan Glacier, forming an insulating soil. Today, a full-grown forest of spruce covers the ice of the stagnant glacier. Natives used caribou antlers to dig copper nuggets from exposed deposits along the White River. They fashioned the copper into weapons and cooking utensils and used it to trade with the coastal Tlingits.

The road climbs through a gap containing Moose Lake, continues northwest for 14 kilometers and crosses Dry Creek. Gold was discovered along the Chisana River in Alaska in 1913, and a stampeders' trail followed Dry Creek and then crossed a low pass to reach the gold fields across the border.

Leaving Dry Creek, the road climbs onto an elevated plain of black-spruce muskeg crisscrossed with marshy streams and dotted with small wetlands. Permafrost lies just below the moss mat. Army engineers had great difficulty building the original Alcan Highway across this boggy terrain.

After bulldozers scraped away the insulating mat of sphagnum moss, the frozen soil underneath melted to form a slimy morass that swallowed vehicles up to their fenders. One section of the road became particularly famous as the "Grand Canyon of the Alcan" when bulldozers dug a deep trench through the soil in a vain effort to find solid ground. Ultimately, engineers learned to build on top of the insulating vegetation mat rather than strip it away. They laid a corduroy surface of logs across the muskeg as a base for the roadbed, and some of these original timbers form the foundation of the modern highway.

At Kilometer 1932, the road crosses Beaver Creek, whose clear channels meander across the flats. The hardscrabble sourdoughs who prospected the Kluane District found gold here, and by 1903 there were 1,000 souls working the gravel of Beaver Creek. Supplies had to be poled up the creek in shallow-draft boats since the muskeg flats were considered all but impassable. The placers were soon depleted, and the land was reclaimed by wilderness. The modern town of Beaver Creek, just west of the stream, sprang up after the completion of the Alcan Highway as a customs station.

From Beaver Creek, the road runs northward across the flats. Snag Creek flows lazily through the muskeg, charting a northward course on its way to join the White River. Rumpled hills rise northwest of the basin, and the highway soon winds among them. A forest of white spruce and aspen grows from the well-drained hillsides, but the pockets of lowland among them harbor only peat bogs and malnourished black spruce.

At Kilometer 1966, the highway crosses the 141st Meridian and enters Alaska. A broad swath has been cut through the trees and shrubs to mark the international border. You should set your clocks back an hour here, as the road leaves the Pacific time zone and enters the Alaska time zone. Turn to Drive 16 for a description of the final leg of the Alaska Highway.

Tagish Road Sidetrip

This 54-kilometer road connects the Alaska Highway with Carcross, Yukon Territory, and serves as a shortcut for travelers approaching from the east. It can also be used by westbound travelers willing to make the longer but more scenic drive to Whitehorse.

The Tagish Road runs southward from Jake's Corner, and after 2 kilometers the Atlin Road splits away to the left. The Tagish Road becomes a gravel highway as it veers westward. Spruce forests give way to groves of aspen and balsam poplar. This part of the drive is particularly pretty when trees are decked out in their autumn colors.

After 21 kilometers, the road crosses the Tagish Bridge at the head of Marsh Lake. This is a traditional fishing spot for the Tagish Indians, whose main village is on the west bank of the waterway. The road is paved beginning at this point, and it runs westward across the forested flats for 17 kilometers to reach the eastern end of Crag Lake. Mount Nares rises above the far shore, and you can sometimes spot Dall sheep on its upper slopes. The stark crags of Caribou Mountain soon rise above the road to the north, as the glittering waters of Chooutla Lake slide by. The road drops into a broad valley to intersect the White Pass Route just north of Carcross.

Whitehorse Sidetrip

Whitehorse began as a ramshackle collection of tents and shanties below the rapids of Miles Canyon. The lower rapids had standing waves that reminded travelers of the flying manes of wild stallions, and so it became known as White Horse Rapids. (The rapids have since been submerged by the impoundment of Schwatka Lake.)

The new town marked the head of steamboat navigation on the Yukon River, and it quickly became a bustling transportation hub. The first steamboat to call at Whitehorse, the A.J.Goddard, arrived here on June 21, 1898, after being carried across Chilkoot Pass piece by piece and assembled on the shores of Lake Bennett. The boatyards on the north bank of the river soon produced a fleet of large paddle-wheelers, which plied the waters of the Yukon all the way to Saint Michael, a tiny Alaskan outpost on the edge of the Bering Sea. Each autumn before freeze-up, horses would haul steamboats onto skids on the riverbank. They were launched again the following spring when the river ice disappeared. The S.S. Klondike, one of the largest of the stern-wheelers, has been restored and converted into a riverboat museum at the eastern end of town.

Whitehorse grew in importance in 1900, when rail service arrived from the coastal port of Skagway, Alaska, via the White Pass and Yukon routes. The budding city became the transportation gateway to the Klondike, and each spring the people of Dawson City eagerly awaited the first steamer bearing mail, produce, and returning miners.

Whitehorse enjoyed a second boom during World War II, when it became the headquarters for construction of the Alcan Highway and the Canol Pipeline. Its airfield became an important stopover on the Northwest Staging Route. Whitehorse continues to grow in importance as a mining and transportation center, and in 1953 it replaced Dawson City as the capital of the territory.

Whitehorse has a broad range of tourist attractions, and a visit to one of the information centers (downtown at Third and Steele or beside the airport on the Alaska Highway) will help you get oriented. The city boasts a number of fine museums in addition to the S.S. Klondike. The Yukon Transportation Museum, on the highway beside the airport, focuses on the history of stern-wheel paddleboats and early aviation in the Yukon. The MacBride Museum, downtown at First and Steele, features displays on the natural and cultural history of the Yukon, as well as a collection of pioneer memorabilia that includes Sam McGee's original cabin. The Old Log Church Museum on Third and Elliott houses relics from the missionary days of the Far North. There are a number of other historic buildings in the downtown district, and walking tours conducted by the local historical society begin daily at the Donnenworth House at 3126 Third Avenue.

For outdoor buffs, a system of day-hiking trails crisscrosses the north bank of the Yukon River, passing through the former shantytown of Canyon City. The trailhead is at the Miles Canyon overlook just east of town. You can see migrating king salmon from mid-July through August at a fish ladder that bypasses the north end of the dam that created Schwatka Lake. Several tour companies run boats along the Yukon River, and the longer tours take in the historic ghost town of Hootalinqua. Vaudeville shows are staged nightly at Frantic Follies in the downtown district. A short drive up the Klondike Highway to the northwest of town leads to Takhini Hot Springs Resort.

The Whitehorse area offers campers several options. If you have a tent, you can find space at the Robert Service Campground, a city-run area on the valley bottoms just east of town. There are a number of private campgrounds on the high ground along the Alaska Highway, and most of these cater to RV owners. The Wolf Creek Campground occupies a pleasant, forested site just east of town along the Alaska Highway.

Aishihik Road Sidetrip

This improved gravel road follows the narrow valley of the Aishihik River northward past a string of large lakes. The road begins by running northward through rolling hills that are cloaked in aspen. Watch out for horses, which roam freely across the lower stretches of the road, as well as wood buffalo near Aishihik Lake. At Kilometer 30, the road reaches Otter Falls, a delightful cascade that once was pictured on the back of the Canadian five-dollar bill.

The road runs along the shore of Canyon Lake before climbing the hillsides. The bald domes of the Ruby Range rise all around, their upper reaches clothed in tundra. At Kilometer 41, the road reaches a campground at the foot of Aishihik Lake. Beyond this point, the road becomes narrow and rutted as it follows the lakeshore for another 94 kilometers to the former Athapaskan village of Aishihik at the head of the lake. Four-wheel drive is recommended for this final stretch of road, even during dry weather.

6

Campbell Highway

Official Designation: Yukon Highway 4
Description: Gravel highway from Watson Lake to Carmacks through the Yukon interior; 602 kilometers (374 miles)
Recommended Maximum: 70 kph/45 mph
Distance Markers: Kilometer posts count northwest from Watson Lake
Information Sources: Ross River Forest District, Tourism Yukon

 The Drive

This gravel thoroughfare connects Watson Lake and Carmacks, Yukon Territory, and is the most direct route to Dawson City for northbound travelers. The highway follows the route of explorer Robert Campbell, who was sent into the Yukon during the 1840s by the Hudson's Bay Company to set up trading posts among the Athapaskan tribes. Fur traders had heard tales from the natives of a great westward-flowing river, and part of Campbell's mission was to discover and map this waterway.

Campbell and his voyageurs paddled up the Frances River, portaged over the low divide to the Pelly River, and continued westward to reach the Yukon. Along the way, Campbell named prominent landmarks after his superiors in the fur trade, the factors and governors of the Hudson's Bay Company. Gold-rush stampeders used Campbell's route as they traveled overland from Edmonton. The modern highway travels mostly through forested lowlands, occasionally passing large lakes and offering views of distant ranges.

The road passes the sparkling waters of Watson Lake on the way out of town and soon enters the forest. Lodgepole pine is the dominant conifer, and its presence in pure stands indicates the location of a forest fire in the distant past. Fires are a frequent and natural occurrence in the central Yukon. Biologists estimate that each stand of trees will burn every 50 to 100 years. The fires serve to regenerate the forest, releasing nutrients locked up in the deadwood and allowing new growth to occur.

Areas that have not burned for many years are covered with a mixture of white spruce and aspen. Spindly black spruce indicate the presence of permafrost, or permanently frozen soil, close to the surface. A northern species of larch also grows in these spruce bogs and can be distinguished by pale, scruffy needles that turn yellow and fall off in the autumn. The road-side embankments support a growth of Hedyssarum, or "bear root." Watch for grizzlies and arctic ground squirrels digging for its edible tubers along the road.

Several small lakes can be seen through the trees as the road progresses to the northwest. Narrow spur roads make brief eastward journeys from Kilometers 27 and 37 to reach wetlands rich in bird life. At Kilometer 44, a wide gravel road runs eastward to the Sa Dena Hes Mine.

The Campbell Highway continues to the northwest, and soon a range of bald hills heralds the crossing of the Frances River. This wide, smooth river offers some pleasant canoeing possibilities. Some 25 kilometers beyond the river crossing, an access road runs westward for 2 kilometers to reach a government campground on the shore of Simpson Lake. The lake and the range visible far to the west of it were named by Robert Campbell for Sir George Simpson, who served as the governor of the Hudson's Bay Company for more than 40 years. A lake and river were named in honor of his wife, Frances.

The highway ascends onto rolling uplands, and at Kilometer 110 the Nahanni Range Road departs to the right. This old mining road heads northeast toward the graceful peaks of the Logan Mountains. For a description of the Nahanni Range Road see Drive 7.

The Campbell Highway drops accross a one-lane bridge over the Tuchitua River and then climbs into the uplands again for sweeping views of the peaks to the east. A lower, more massive range of mountains soon looms immediately to the west of the road. This is the Campbell Range, an eastern extension of the Pelly Mountains, which spread throughout most of the Yukon's southern interior. The highway runs through a long stretch of muskeg, where scraggly black spruces rise from peat bogs and pools of stagnant water. The permafrost underlying this area forms a hardpan that prevents moisture from sinking into the soil, creating a swampy environment despite scarce rainfall. The elevated road grade is often the only dry land in sight.

At Kilometer 176, the road crests a rise, revealing a broad panorama of Frances Lake. This large expanse of water is shaped like a giant wishbone, although you can see only the western arm from the road. Look for rafts of surf scoters, scaups, and mergansers on its water. Robert Campbell established the first of his trading posts at the tip of the peninsula between the two arms. The peaks on the eastern horizon are the outlying ranges of the Mackenzie Mountains, which rise along the border between the Yukon and Northwest Territories. The road soon leaves the lake behind, dropping into the valley of the Finlayson River. Massive hills crowd the southwestern edge of the valley, while to the east sharp spires rise in the distance.

Campbell Highway

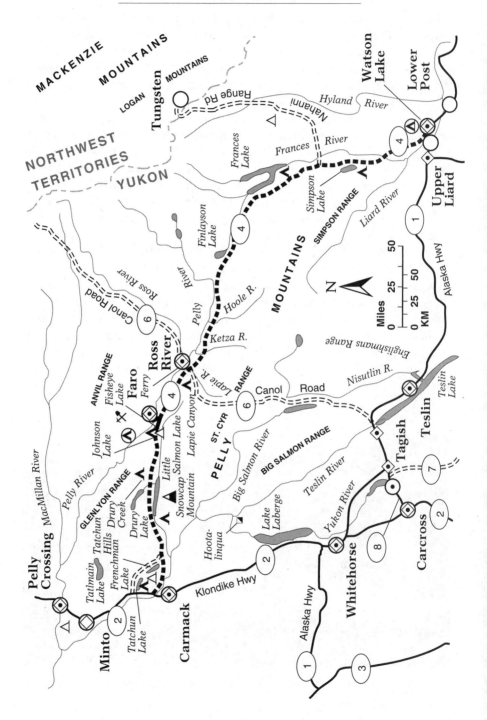

The mountains soon merge with gentle, rolling hills covered in spruce, and the road again climbs to the hilltops for a view of Finlayson Lake. The Kaska people called this lake *Tetl'anejoji Mené,* which means "Chasing into Snares." A population of woodland caribou winters here, and the Kaska hunters once set up neck snares at the narrows of the lake, where caribou could be easily funnelled into the traps and killed. Like all Athapaskan peoples, the Kaska revered the animals and used all parts of those they killed; nothing was wasted.

Far to the east lie the Logan Mountains, where the Finlayson caribou herd spends the summer months. The Saint Cyr Range of the Pelly Mountains presents its sawtooth peaks to the west. Finlayson Lake lies on the Yukon-Mackenzie watershed boundary, and Robert Campbell reported that during floods, water drained out of the lake on both sides of the divide.

The road crosses an imperceptible divide to enter the Pelly River watershed. Its waters flow westward into the Yukon River and ultimately through Alaska to the Bering Sea, while the rivers to the south flow into the Mackenzie River system and then northward to the Arctic Ocean. The buff-colored bluffs of the Pelly River soon appear to the north. Campbell established another trading post near here at a spot called Pelly Banks.

The road follows the river westward, and after almost 30 kilometers it crosses a bridge over the Hoole River. Campbell named this tributary after his half-Iroquois interpreter who, according to Campbell, "could build houses and canoes, make sleds and snowshoes, bring home more meat and fish than anybody else, and serve as an interpreter for trading." This stream joins the Pelly at a point where the larger river flows through Hoole Can-

Sheer bluffs overlook the Pelly River near Hoole Canyon.

yon. This obstacle was impassable by canoe, so the Campbell expedition, like the Kaskas that came before them, had to portage, or carry, their canoes around the canyon.

Campbell had two paddlers named Kitza and Lapie, and at Kilometer 351 the highway crosses the first of two streams named in their honor, the Ketza River. A gravel road runs southward to the Ketza River Gold Mine, a modern hard-rock operation that discourages visitors. The jagged mountains to the west are the Saint Cyr Range, and as the road continues westward, it passes a number of large lakes that reflect these impressive summits. The rounded hills to the north are covered in grassland and aspen stands, a mixture that reminded the Scotsman Campbell of "the green brae-face of the Highland glens." The road runs across a flat to junctions with the South Canol Road (Kilometer 366) and with the North Canol Road 8 kilometers farther. The latter runs through the hills for 11 kilometers to the town of Ross River, which offers all services.

The Campbell Highway continues past the junction, following the base of the hills to a bridge over the Lapie River. This surging stream has carved a deep canyon into the basalt bedrock, and you can see the gorge from a campground here. The road passes several small lakes and follows the Pelly River through the Tintina Trench, a long depression created where the ancestral North American plate meets the smaller, wandering plates called "terranes" that piled up along the edge of the continent millions of years ago. This rift valley is much older than the river that occupies it. The Tintina Trench forms a major flyway for waterfowl bound for the breeding grounds of the Alaskan interior. North of the trench are the massive domes of the Anvil Range, named for their flat tops.

The road crosses streams such as Grew and Buttle creeks, named for trappers who ran their traplines in this area around the turn of the century. They trapped in the winter when pelts were "prime," or at their thickest and most lustrous. They built cabins a day's walk apart, all along the trapline, and stored supplies in elevated caches to prevent raiding by varmints. They would make their rounds, visiting their traps on a cycle that might take as long as two weeks. They stretched skins on specially designed boards and frames and redeemed the prepared furs for credit at a local trading post such as the Nahanni House at Ross River.

At Kilometer 427, a spur road runs northward for 10 kilometers, crossing the Pelly River to reach the modern mining town of Faro. The Cyprus Anvil Mining Company built the town in 1969 to house workers at its enormous open-pit, lead-zinc mine in the mountains. A cataclysmic forest fire destroyed the town the same year that it was built, forcing its residents to start all over again. Since then, the town has waxed and waned as the mine has opened and closed in response to fluctuations in the commodities market. The unpredictable nature of the enterprise is aptly (and perhaps ironi-

Eagle Rock on the far shore of the Yukon River. The formation's two flanks resemble wings.

cally) reflected in the name of the town: "faro" is a French game of chance that involves cards decorated with pictures of Egyptian pharaohs. The mine here is the largest of its kind in the world, and at peak production, it produces more income than any other in the territory, eclipsing even the combined production of the Klondike gold fields.

There are good wildlife-viewing opportunities in the vicinity of Faro. The Anvil Mountains support a substantial population of Fannin sheep, a variety that is thought to be intermediate between the gray Stone sheep and the all-white Dall sheep. The Fannin sheep spend the summer near the Anvil Mine on Mount Mye. During mid-autumn you might spot them on the bluffs along Blind Creek Road. Blind Creek itself supports a spawning run of salmon, and you can see the fish in its clear waters beginning in late August.

The Campbell Highway continues westward from the Faro junction and passes several lakes. An access road departs from Kilometer 428.5 to reach a primitive campground on Fisheye Lake, and there is a government campground 4 kilometers farther on at Johnson Lake. The road soon strikes the Magundy River and follows it down to Little Salmon Lake. Along the way, rugged foothills of granite rise to the north of the road, representing the tail end of the Glenlyon Range.

The pavement ends as the road reaches the head of Little Salmon Lake, a glittering, 35-kilometer (22-mile) long expanse of water hemmed in by spruce-clad mountainsides. The tallest of the peaks is Snowcap Mountain, which pokes its summit above timberline on the far side of the lake. The pavement picks up again as the road leaves the foot of the lake and the mountains fall away to make way for a broad basin. The Little Salmon River flows from the foot of the lake, and the highway follows its clear waters westward toward its confluence with the mighty Yukon River. Near this confluence, there is a cutoff road that runs northwest past Frenchman and Tatchun lakes before joining the Klondike Highway some 27 kilometers north of Carmacks.

The main highway turns to gravel as it continues westward along the Yukon and soon enters the Eagle Rock burn. The fire burned in 1989, consuming almost 5,000 hectares (19 square miles) of timber. After crossing the burn, the road climbs to a lofty bluff top in the Tatchun Hills. There is an overlook here with views of Eagle Rock on the far side of the Yukon River. Eagle Rock was a prominent landmark for paddle-wheel steamboats that plied the Yukon during the gold-rush era.

An interpretive sign commemorates the fiery end of the stern-wheeler Columbian, which exploded near this point in 1906. The steamboat was headed northward carrying three tons of blasting powder for the coal mines at Tantalus Butte when someone spotted a flock of ducks off the bow of the boat. A deckhand rushed forward with a small-caliber rifle to get a shot at the birds, but he tripped and fell, discharging his gun into the powder kegs. The ensuing explosion destroyed the bow of the boat and injured several crew members, but the captain somehow grounded it and sent several teams overland, portaging and paddling borrowed canoes to get help at the Tantalus Mine. By the time the rescue party arrived, it was too late to save six crew members, including the deckhand who had smuggled the contraband firearm aboard the boat.

The road descends from the heights and follows the Yukon River through forested lowlands for the remaining 27 kilometers to Carmacks. You can see the green river from the road at frequent intervals during this final stretch, and there are one or two primitive camping spots along its bank. The Campbell Highway ends where it intersects the Klondike Highway just north of the town of Carmacks.

7

Nahanni Range Road

Official Designation: Yukon Highway 10
Description: Improved gravel road from Campbell Highway to Hyland River valley; passable for 132 kilometers (82 miles)
Recommended Maximum: 55 kph/35 mph
Hazards: No gas stations; road not maintained beyond Kilometer 132
Distance Markers: Kilometer posts count northeast from Campbell Highway junction
Information Sources: Watson Lake Forest District

 ## The Drive

This road was built to provide access to the Cantung Mine, deep in the heart of the Mackenzie Mountains. The mine workings are located on the largest deposit of scheelite (a high-grade tungsten ore) in the Western Hemisphere. Tungsten is used to harden steel, and the resulting metal is used to manufacture military armaments. The mine closed in 1986 and is unlikely to reopen as long as the current climate of détente continues.

The road is poorly maintained and should be driven only by the adventurous. It is suitable for passenger vehicles for the first 132 kilometers. The remaining 69 kilometers to the tungsten mine are obstructed by washouts, and you will need four-wheel drive to negotiate them. Gas and other services are not available at any point on this road. If you drive it, carry enough extra gas in jerry cans to make it either to Ross River or Watson Lake.

The road branches off from the Campbell Highway at Kilometer 110 and runs eastward across the highlands with fine initial views of the outriders of the Logan Mountains. After crossing a bridge over the Frances River, the road winds into a gap between Mount Billings to the north and Mount Murray to the south. The westernmost peaks of the Logan Mountains tend to be the most inspiring, and as the road follows a lake-filled valley eastward, they are replaced by rounded, tundra-clad summits. After passing Long Lake and crossing Dolly Varden Creek, you will enter the glacier-carved trench occupied by the Hyland River. The rocky backbone of the Mackenzie Mountains stretches in an unbroken wall above the far side of the valley.

Nahanni Range Road

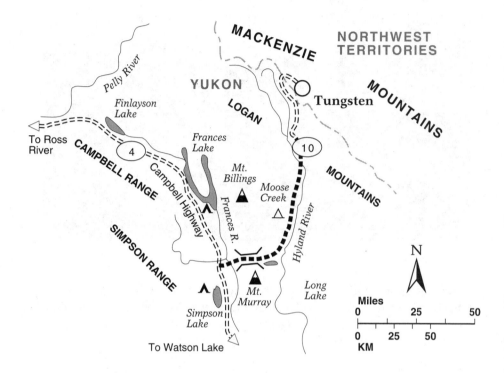

The road turns northward to follow the river toward its source, and there are several spots where you can view its aquamarine water. A number of crystal-clear tributaries pour into the river from the mountains to the west. Perhaps the most picturesque of these is Conglomerate Creek at Kilometer 74. It features a small waterfall that is visible just upstream of the bridge.

Some 10 kilometers beyond this stream, at the point where North Moose Creek pours into the Hyland River, there is a primitive, user-maintained camping area. As the road continues northward, majestic chains of rocky peaks guard both sides of the valley. A substantial tributary of the Hyland pours through a break in the mountains to the east, and the road crosses a bridge over the Hyland River just above this confluence. At Kilometer 132, the road passes a small pond where an outlet stream has washed out a culvert.

Travel beyond this point at your own risk. A sign posted here absolves the Queen and all her underlings of any responsibility for your safety. You

Looking down Conglomerate Creek in the Logan Mountains.

should attempt the next section of the road only in dry weather, and a four-wheel-drive vehicle is a must. The road penetrates deep into the mountains, running another 69 kilometers to the tungsten mine, which is staffed by a skeleton security force and is not open to the public.

8

Canol Road

Official Designation: Yukon Highway 6
Description: Improved gravel road from Teslin Lake on Alaska Highway to Northwest Territories border; 463 kilometers (287 miles)
Recommended Maximum: 70 kph/45 mph on South Canol; 55 kph/35 mph on North Canol
Hazards: North Canol too narrow for RVs or trailers
Distance Markers: Kilometer posts count north from Alaska Highway
Further Reading: *A Walk on the Canol Road* by S.R. Gage
Information Sources: Ross River Forest District, Tourism Yukon, Sahtu Tourism Association

 The Drive

Like the Alaska Highway, the Canol Road was conceived during the early stages of World War II as a means of supplying strategic military outposts in Alaska. Previously, fuel oil had to be shipped to Alaska via the Inside Passage, a lifeline that could easily be cut by Japanese submarines. Military planners envisioned a pipeline stretching from the oil field of Norman Wells, Northwest Territories, to a refinery in Whitehorse, Yukon. From there, the fuel could be shipped overland to the Alaskan front.

The Canadian Oil Pipeline, shortened to "Canol," was built with four-inch pipe along native travel routes through the heart of the Mackenzie Mountains. A gravel road paralleled the pipeline, bearing convoys of construction workers and maintenance staff. In all, the project cost more than the construction of the Alaska Highway and was completed long after the Japanese threat to Alaska had abated. Only a trickle of fuel ever flowed from the newly built refinery, and the entire project is now regarded as an expensive boondoggle.

This road through the wilderness has been opened to tourist traffic as far as the border with the Northwest Territories. Beyond the border, it is managed as a Heritage Trail suitable for backpackers, mountain bikers, and horseback riders. The Canol Road is described here in two sections, the South Canol from the Alaska Highway to Ross River, and the North Canol, which extends northward from Ross River to MacMillan Pass on the Northwest Territories border. The latter is open only in the summer. Visitor services are located at Johnson's Crossing on the Alaska Highway and at Ross River. If you are bound for MacMillan Pass, you would be wise to carry extra fuel.

The northern section of the road is winding, making for slow travel. One-lane bridges cross most of the streams. The North Canol is not suitable for RVs or trailers. Along its course, you may chance upon old vehicle dumps and structures that date to the route's wartime beginnings.

South Canol

The road leaves the Alaska Highway near the north end of Teslin Lake and climbs steadily through a boreal forest of white spruce and quaking aspen. It soon reaches the alpine valleys at the summit, which is surrounded by the massive domes of the Big Salmon Range, a great syncline, or upfolding, of limestone, slate, and schist. Subalpine fir is the most prevalent tree in this timberline ecosystem, and you can identify it by its blunt needles and its slender, spirelike shape, which helps the tree shed snow in the winter. The floors of these high basins are covered with low-growing willows that make excellent moose habitat.

After cresting the Big Salmon Range, the road descends to the hilltops above the Nisutlin River. This broad, slow river is a favorite with canoeists. At Kilometer 49, a spur road departs to the right, bound for a primitive camping area on Sidney Lake. You can glimpse the glittering river through the trees for the next 20 kilometers. An access road runs eastward to the riverbank at Kilometer 68, and the Canol Road swings away from the river on its way to Quiet Lake. It takes four days, a gentle float, to reach the village of Teslin.

There is a government campground at the south end of this large lake, at the end of a short spur road to the left. The road passes through some exceptionally tall timber for these latitudes and reaches the lakeshore about halfway up the lake. The impressive wall of the Big Salmon Range rises beyond the lake, which was named in 1887 by John McCormack. He was one of a party of four miners who prospected the entire length of the Big Salmon River from its headwaters at the foot of the lake to its confluence with the Yukon River. They found some small placer deposits, but none that were extensive enough to be worth mining.

After passing a picnic area, you will leave the lakeshore and climb over a tall hill. From its crest, you can see the Rose River valley and Pelly Mountains stretching away to the north. The road descends a long grade, and there is a one-lane Bailey bridge over the Rose River at Kilometer 105. Combat engineers used Bailey bridges during World War II; they could be loaded onto tracked carriers and positioned over small rivers during assaults. Note

Canol Road

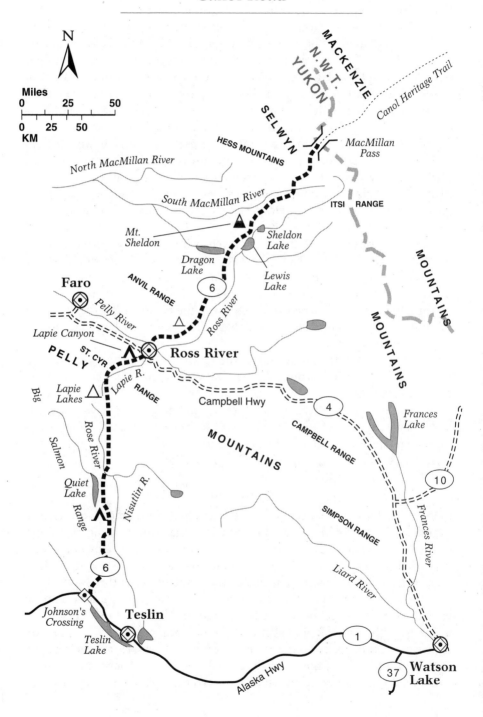

that the river is broad and sluggish here, meandering across the flat, sandy floor of the valley. After the road climbs over another hill, it returns to the river, which splashes vigorously through a steep, boulder-strewn channel.

The road follows the river into the jagged Pelly Mountains, which are not one of the loftier ranges in the Far North but stand out because of their steep faces and knife-edge summits. Lodgepole pine is the dominant tree at lower elevations. Here, it is near the northern limit of its range. The river leads to Rose Lake, which sits in an alpine parkland dotted with wildflowers. A spur road leads to a primitive campsite on the lakeshore.

The main road continues northward, crossing a barren summit pocked with kettle ponds. There is another unimproved camping area along the Lapie Lakes, which reflect the graceful summits to the south. The Lapie River issues from these lakes, flowing slowly through long glides and deep pools that harbor husky grayling. The river is surrounded by lush meadows, and stately peaks line its valley.

The roadway follows the river closely as the valley constricts to form the narrow Lapie Canyon. Here, the water has cut downward through layers of basalt to form a picturesque gorge that you can see when the road descends from wooded slopes to cross the Lapie River at Kilometer 213. The surrounding country burned in 1994. From the bridge, scan the slopes to the northwest for Stone sheep, which use this area as a lambing ground during the late spring.

Watch for eroded landforms at the mouth of the canyon. Beyond it, the road runs into a flat basin and winds through a dense woodland of young aspens and past several lakes before joining the Campbell Highway. To continue the Canol Road drive, turn left onto the Campbell Highway and follow it for 8 kilometers to its junction with the North Canol, which leads into the town of Ross River. The Lapie Canyon campground is just 2 kilometers west of this junction on the Campbell Highway.

North Canol

From the Campbell Highway, the North Canol climbs steadily into rounded hills covered in vegetation similar to that found on the mammoth steppes that covered the interior of the Yukon during Pleistocene times, more than 9,000 years ago. Small lakes occupy the hollows among the hilltops, and you may see seams of coal in the roadcuts along the way.

After 11 kilometers, the road enters the village of Ross River, populated principally by people of the Kaska nation. The site of this village was formerly on the far bank of the Pelly, where a trading post known as Nahanni House once stood. A free ferry carries northbound vehicles across the Pelly River during banking hours, with a break for lunch. There is a pleasant walking trail along the north bank of the river that runs eastward through

Lapie Canyon.

the aspens to the former village site. Only a couple of sagging, abandoned cabins remain.

From the north bank of the Pelly, the Canol Road runs eastward and then swings to the north into the narrow valley of the Ross River. The riverbank is crowded by steep and rocky slopes; watch out for fallen boulders. The roadway then moves inland and begins to climb. Views on the way up are obscured by dense brush. Openings in the shrubs provide growing room for wild raspberries, which ripen in late July.

At the top of the grade, the road reaches a high shelf that holds a number of cold lakes. The Marjorie Lake Fire swept through this area in 1994, burning 52,000 hectares (200 square miles). The following year, morel mushrooms sprouted from the charred soil and their harvest created an economic windfall for the Ross River area. A narrow dirt road runs north to Marjorie Lake from Kilometer 263.2, and 10 kilometers farther along, the road passes Orchie Lake. Low, bald peaks rise to the north of the lakes.

Beyond the lakes, the road begins a long descent into the lowland that borders the Ross River. Isolated ranges and single peaks in the distance give scale to the vastness of the landscape. On the valley floor, the road crosses marshy habitat for moose and beaver. Most of the streams contain populations of small arctic grayling. This distant relative of the trout has an enormous, lobe-shaped dorsal fin that is speckled with purple and aquamarine spots.

The road now enters a burn that occurred in 1989. It stretches northward for the next 10 kilometers. In the wake of the fire, dense brush has grown up to provide ample forage for moose and snowshoe hares. Watch for caribou here in the autumn. The burn peters out as the road climbs from the flats onto a series of steep hills that rise above substantial but nameless lakes. There are many steep ups and downs on this section of the road; proceed with caution. Note that tall white spruce cloak the well-drained hillsides, while the boggy flats below contain only ragged black spruce.

The hills become gentler as the road passes south of Dragon Lake, which drains northward into the MacMillan River system. Primitive camping is permitted at a pullout on the lakeshore at Kilometer 333.7, and the blueberry picking can be especially good in mid-August. The ruins of an old trading post stand about halfway down the north shore of the lake. Straight ahead, the distinctive peak that rises in solitary majesty is Mount Sheldon.

The road crosses the flats and passes a government airfield (no public access). To the east stretches Sheldon Lake, which you can reach via a narrow spur road that leaves the Canol at Kilometer 357.5. A canoe trip down the Ross River from this point takes three to four days, including a portage around Prevost Canyon. Floaters should be sure to visit the old Hudson's Bay post at the foot of the lake, which is accessible only by water.

Beyond the lake, the stark mountains to the east are outliers of the vast Selwyn Mountains. Early reports by fur traders and explorers indicate that some of the local natives believed the headwaters of the Ross River to be inhabited by a race of giant, evil spirits.

The road soon climbs over a range of low and brushy ridges and enters the watershed of the South MacMillan River. During the ice ages, this valley was glaciated all the way to its confluence with the Pelly River. The road stays in the uplands as it follows the river. Views of the somber ranges to the north are afforded along the way. There are several old supply dumps in this general area, where World War II trucks and heavy equipment were abandoned. If you have sharp eyes, you might spot rusting sections of the old 4-inch oil pipeline in the ditches beside the road.

After a steep descent, the road reaches the valley floor at Kilometer 375 and begins to follow the riverbank. The river bottom is robed in brushy tundra and open swales of sedges. An access road runs westward to the river from Kilometer 388.2; this road is the favored access for floaters bound down the MacMillan River. It takes a week to float to Pelly Crossing.

The Itsi Range soon appears ahead, rising to spectacular heights east of the river. *Itsi* is an Athapaskan word meaning "windy." At Kilometer 412.8, the road makes its first crossing of the South MacMillan River via a one-lane Bailey bridge. It then runs into the heart of a circular basin ringed with mountain crags. Joseph Keele made a reconnaissance of this area for the

The last resting place of the Canol Convoy.

Geological Survey of Canada in 1907-08. He made the following comment about the confusing naming of the ranges: "The names Selwyn range and Ogilvie range have been applied in former reports and on previous maps, to cover a considerable portion of these mountains. It has been impossible to define the limits of these subdivisions, on topographic grounds, hence the name Mackenzie mountains has been given to the highlands as a whole."

The basin floor is dominated by a brushy tundra of dwarf birch and willow and a few isolated spruce trees. Scan the tundra for grizzly bears, which are occasionally spotted in this area. Caribou are often spotted during the fall.

After crossing the basin, the road follows the river into one of the many finger valleys that radiate into the mountains from the basin. The tallest peaks in the Mackenzie Mountains are composed of granitic intrusions, and these peaks tower above the lesser sedimentary crags.

After a sharp turn to the north, the valley constricts into a U-shaped glacial trench, with walls that sweep upward to razorback ridges and sharp pinnacles. The floor of this valley is free of trees—a sort of reverse timberline dictated by the prevalence of permafrost and saturated soils on the valley bottom. There is another large vehicle dump at the mouth of this valley. You can still read the painted inscriptions on the truck doors, and a number of old grading rigs are scattered along the roadway.

As the valley swings to the northeast, it passes several recent mining sites. The Jason claim contains zinc, lead, silver, and barite in quantities that have yet to be determined. Not far beyond, the road passes below the Tom mining claim, owned by Hudson Bay Mining and Smelting.

After crossing MacMillan Bridge Number 3, look to the southeast for a fine view of an active rock glacier. Rock glaciers are great lobes of loose rock debris knitted together by a matrix of ice and creeping downhill. Rock glaciers typically arise from a circular amphitheater and flow downhill, but at a rate even slower than that of conventional glaciers.

The peaks recede as the road climbs the final grade to reach MacMillan Pass, on the Northwest Territories border. The road is not maintained beyond this point, so you should turn around here. The valley of the Tsichu River stretches into the distance, clad in open tundra with not a tree in sight. The pervasive yellow ground cover is reindeer moss, a form of lichen that is a staple of the caribou's winter diet.

The road stretches onward from "Mac Pass" as a Heritage Trail, suitable for mountain bikers and backpackers. Many more vehicle dumps and old maintenance stations dot the way, adding historical interest to an already spectacular wilderness trip. There are several major river fords between the pass and Norman Wells. Backcountry users who plan to hike the entire trail should plan their trip thoroughly and have confidence in their wilderness skills.

9

Atlin Road

Official Designation: Yukon Highway 7
Description: Paved/gravel highway from Tagish Road to Atlin, British Columbia; 94 kilometers (59 miles)
Recommended Maximum: 80 kph/50 mph on gravel sections
Distance Markers: Kilometer posts in Yukon and mileposts in British Columbia count southward from Tagish Road
Further Reading: *Atlin, the Last Utopia* and *Taku* by Allison Mitcham, *Atlin: The Story of British Columbia's Last Gold Rush* by Christine Dickins, *Atlin Gold* by Peter Steele
Information Sources: Atlin Visitors Association, North by Northwest Tourism Association

 The Drive

The Atlin Road runs southward from the Alaska Highway, passing through one of the prettiest parts of the Yukon's southern lakes district. It winds up in an isolated corner of British Columbia, at the old gold-rush town of Atlin. The pace of life is appreciably slower in Atlin, a lakeside village off the beaten track. It has been billed as a little Switzerland, and it sits amid such stunning scenery that it became a major holiday destination for the wealthy during the early part of this century.

Several roads out of Atlin lead to scenic wonders and historical sites. The town is well-known for its excellent fishing; anglers should bear in mind that British Columbia fishing licenses are required south of the Yukon border.

From Jake's Corner on the Alaska Highway, follow the Tagish Road southward 2 kilometers to a junction with the Atlin Road. The Atlin Road runs southward beneath the rugged limestone slopes of White Mountain. Mountain goats were transplanted here from Kluane National Park, and they have flourished. There are several pullouts where you can get out your binoculars and look for them on the slopes above the highway.

The Atlin Road soon reaches the shoreline of Little Atlin Lake, which is little in name only. The road follows its shoreline for the next 18 kilometers, occasionally yielding views of the water. Beyond the south end of the lake, an unmarked spur road departs from Kilometer 22 and descends to the west to the Lubbock River. This short waterway connects Atlin and Little Atlin lakes and is popular with fishermen.

Dense stands of lodgepole pine soon line the road, indicating the location of a wildfire that burned here in 1958. The road passes Snafu and Tarfu lakes, two meres with government campgrounds along their shorelines. They were named after military acronyms by the Canadian Army Engineers who built the road. Snafu stands for "Situation Normal, All Fouled Up," while Tarfu means "Things Are Really Fouled Up." The mountains have receded to form a broad basin, but they soon return as the road climbs high onto the shoulder of a hill.

You will get your first view of Atlin Lake from this lofty vantage point. Atlin is a corruption of the Tlingit word *At-len*, which means "big lake." It is the largest natural lake in British Columbia. Black Mountain is the flat-topped peak immediately to the south. The pointed summit of Halcro Peak rises behind it. Mount Minto rises in monolithic solitude across the water. Keep an eye out for Stone sheep, which often wander down to the roadside in this area.

As the road runs southward, it stays well inland, so there are few views of the water. The basin broadens once more, and the mountains recede into the distance. Guest ranches dot the countryside, and grassy pastures interrupt the aspens and spruces of the boreal forest. On the final approach to the town of Atlin, the road passes several small lakes. Davie Hall Lake is a favorite with bird watchers, who can spot waterfowl here.

At Mile 51.5, the Ruffner Mine Road heads eastward into the Gladys Valley. The road reaches MacDonald Lake after 2 miles and then becomes progressively rougher as it penetrates another 60 kilometers into the wilderness. The road passes Como Lake, which has been stocked with rainbow trout. About 3 miles beyond this lake, the road reaches a T-intersection. Turn right for the town of Atlin. The road to the left becomes the Discovery Road (see Discovery Road Sidetrip toward the end of this chapter), with access to the Warm Bay Road, which continues southward along the shore of Atlin Lake (see Warm Bay Road Sidetrip at the end of this chapter).

The Tlingit Indians are the original inhabitants of the Atlin area, having moved inland from the coast centuries ago. The Tlingits once fished for salmon in the Taku River during the summer, and in the winter they moved to the shores of Atlin Lake, where they snared caribou on the lakeshores. The village of Atlin sprang up during a minor gold rush on Pine Creek, east of town, in 1898. Tales of gold in Atlin lured some of the stampeders who had crossed White and Chilkoot passes on their way to the Klondike. The town of Discovery grew up at the diggings, while the larger town of Atlin was founded on the lakeshore, where steamer access on the lake linked the region with the White Pass and Yukon Railway. The caribou here were deci-

Atlin Road

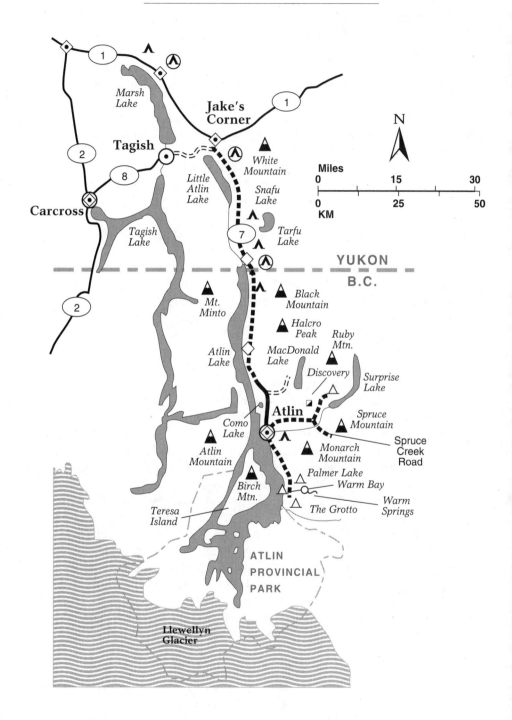

mated by market hunters during the gold-rush era, but the Tlingits stayed on, working in the gold fields and supplying meat and fish to the miners.

After an initial boom, Discovery became a ghost town, and many of its buildings were moved into Atlin. In 1914, a jar of roofing tar left on a woodstove caught fire in a Pearl Street residence, ultimately leveling most of Atlin's waterfront buildings. The town was rebuilt with widely spaced buildings to prevent future fires, but it burned to the ground again two years later.

Gold mining slumped during World War I, when there were not enough men and explosives available to work the placer fields. As the war raged abroad, wealthy North Americans sought vacation destinations close to home, and Atlin became a major resort community. Tourists came by steamer up the Inside Passage and then took the White Pass and Yukon Railway to Carcross on Tagish Lake. Stern-wheelers ferried them across the lake. Then a 2-mile railway across a narrow neck of land just north of Atlin Mountain deposited them on the shore of Atlin Lake. Boats such as the MV *Tarahne* carried them the final distance to Atlin.

The influx of tourists bolstered the sagging economy of the town and prevented it from being abandoned, as were so many other northern boom towns. The gold fields boomed again during the Great Depression, when gold prices fixed at $17 an ounce were deregulated, and the price of the precious metal doubled. Mining has continued on a small scale throughout the century.

There are plenty of things to do in town and on the outskirts. Take a tour of the historical buildings; many have plaques telling about their past. The Atlin Historical Society runs an excellent little museum in the original one-room schoolhouse. The MV *Tarahne* has been restored and is now on exhibit on the waterfront, while the Pioneer Cemetery is just east of town on Discovery Road. This cemetery is the final resting place of Fritz Miller and Kenny MacLaren, who made the discovery strike on Pine Creek in 1898, as well as of many other early prospectors.

Sightseeing from the lakeshore can be rewarding: Atlin Mountain rises directly across the water and a great rock glacier descends between its northernmost peaks. Farther south is Teresa Island, where Birch Mountain rises to 2,060 meters (6,755 feet). Teresa Island holds the distinction of being the tallest freshwater island in the world. Boat tours on the lake are available if you want to see more. Atlin Provincial Park encompasses the south end of the lake. It is a wilderness park with no trails and is accessible only by plane or boat. Finally, scenic drives stretch from Atlin eastward to the site of Discovery and southward on the Warm Bay Road.

Discovery Road Sidetrip

This road runs eastward from the center of Atlin. The pavement ends as the Warm Bay Road branches to the south, and a kilometer farther on, the Atlin Pioneer Cemetery is located across from the airstrip. Gold miners and early aviators are buried here beneath rustic wooden markers.

The road continues eastward into the valley of Pine Creek, where the principal gold strikes were made. At Kilometer 5.5, there is a turnout with an excellent view of Pine Creek Falls. A torrent of white water rushes between the weathered cliffs of a minor canyon. Just beyond it, a spur road departs to the east, following Spruce Creek.

The narrow Spruce Creek Road runs 1 kilometer to a sign advertising for public gold-panning, where you can try your luck on a dormant claim. This stream yielded the 83-ounce West Nugget in 1899. Farther up the creek, you can view an active placer-mining operation from the road.

Meanwhile, the Discovery Road continues eastward for another 3 kilometers to reach the site of the ghost town Discovery. Only a few old cabins and shacks remain here, near the spot where Fritz Miller and Kenny MacLaren first discovered gold in 1898. The town died quickly following its initial boom and was abandoned by 1908. The massive peak to the south is Spruce

The old shacks of the Discovery townsite overlook more recent diggings along Pine Creek.

Mountain, which presides over the heaps of tailings that have accumulated during a century of placer mining.

The road continues to follow Pine Creek upward, passing through rich wetlands where you can often spot waterfowl. The road ends at the foot of Surprise Lake, a large expanse of cold water with ragged peaks crowding its head. There is a primitive campground on the shore. The road continues along the north shore toward Ruby Mountain. This bare peak is thought to be an extinct volcano, 50 million years old. A challenging trail climbs the barren slopes to its summit.

Warm Bay Road Sidetrip

This road leads southward along the shore of Atlin Lake for 26.5 kilometers before ending in the forest. Follow the Discovery Road east from Atlin, passing the highway junction to reach the point where the Warm Bay Road branches to the south. Warm Bay Road passes the Pine Creek Campground, situated on a wooded rise above the fabled gold-rush stream. The forest here is a mix of aspen and white spruce, and it puts on a fantastic color display in early September.

About a kilometer beyond the campground, there are trailheads on both sides of the road. A short path leads westward to the lakeshore, while to the east a challenging track climbs to the top of Monarch Mountain for inspiring views of the surrounding country. From the trailhead, you will have fine views of Atlin Mountain across the lake, and a water pipe just south of the trailhead gushes clear water from an artesian spring.

At Kilometer 11, an overlook offers a magnificent view of the Llewellyn Glacier, which pours from the ice fields of the Coast Mountains in the heart of Atlin Provincial Park. The road then returns to the lowlands and crosses McKee Creek, which has produced substantial quantities of placer gold in its day.

Next, the road swings inland to pass Palmer Lake, a quiet mere whose still waters reflect Sentinel Mountain. There is a primitive camping area here. There are more undeveloped campsites along the road as it descends to Warm Bay, which is fed by thermal springs. The largest of these warm springs is a kilometer up the road in a marshy field east of the road. Its waters are a constant 21 degrees Centigrade (70 degrees Fahrenheit). It warms the soil to create a longer growing season for the plants surrounding it. Early residents of Atlin took advantage of this phenomenon to grow potatoes here.

At Kilometer 16.4, the road reaches The Grotto, where a stream gushes from a mysterious cave. The water is considered a tonic for thirsty travelers. It is clearly healthy for watercress, which grows abundantly in the crystalline, mineral-rich waters. There are several primitive campsites in the forest across the road. The Grotto marks the end of public access. The road deteriorates beyond this point, becoming accessible only by four-wheel drive beyond the O'Donnell River.

10

White Pass

Official Designation: Yukon Highway 2
Description: Paved highway from Whitehorse, Yukon Territory, to Skagway, Alaska; 159 kilometers (99 miles)
Recommended Maximum: Highway speeds
Distance Markers: Mileposts in Alaska and kilometer posts in Canada count north from Skagway
Further Reading: *I Married the Klondike* by Laura Berton, *Life Lived Like a Story* by Julie Cruickshank, *Along the White Pass High Iron* by J.D. True
Information Sources: Skagway Convention and Visitors Bureau, Tourism Yukon, Klondike Gold Rush National Historic Park

 The Drive

The White Pass route follows an ancient travel corridor from Whitehorse, Yukon Territory, to the seaport of Skagway, Alaska. Along the way, it passes through spectacular alpine scenery, and at its end it encounters the breathtaking fjords of the Inside Passage. Thousands of people come each year to retrace the steps of gold-rush stampeders over the storied Chilkoot Pass, which has been preserved jointly by the Canadian and U. S. governments as an international historic park. Skagway and Carcross retain much of their frontier charm; clapboard houses and false-fronted businesses hark back to the rollicking boom years when gold filled the thoughts of every passerby.

The route was first traveled by Tlingit Indians, who traded shells and candlefish oil to the inland tribes for copper, furs, and meat. After the Russians initiated the fur trade in North America, the Tlingits increasingly carried guns, blankets, and beads inland on their "grease trails." The coastal tribes guarded the passes jealously to maintain their stranglehold on the fur trade, but they allowed a party of twenty American prospectors to cross Chilkoot Pass in 1880 with the proviso that the prospectors would not interfere with the Tlingits' fur trade.

When gold was discovered in the Klondike, fortune hunters poured in from around the world, and the Tlingits could no longer maintain control over the passes. Prospectors poured over White and Chilkoot passes and

White Pass

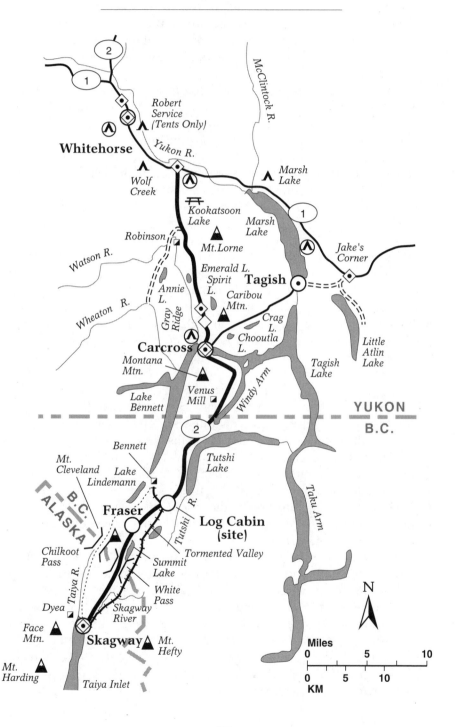

then built a motley fleet of watercraft to float down the Yukon River and its tributaries to Whitehorse. The rails of the White Pass and Yukon Route were pushed through the Coast Mountains on the heels of the stampeders, and the southern sections are still running for the benefit of hikers and tourists. The highway runs beside the old narrow-gauge railroad route for most of the journey.

From Whitehorse, the road runs southward across broad lowlands, and the forest that rises on both sides reveals little of the rounded mountains on the valley's rim. At Lake Kookatsoon, 5 kilometers down the road, you will find a pleasant picnic spot among the trees.

The Annie Lake Road leaves the highway at Kilometer 141 (see Annie Lake Road Sidetrip toward the end of this chapter), in the midst of a rural settlement. A hundred yards beyond this point, a pullout on the west side of the road offers views of the old Robinson train depot. The railroad company named this station after "Stickeen Bill" Robinson, who headed a construction gang that built steamboats and barges on Lake Bennett to ferry in supplies during the construction of the White Pass and Yukon Railway. A roadhouse and several cabins sprang up beside the railway siding as hopes ran high that gold would be found in the mountains nearby. But the local mines never amounted to much, and the roadhouse was abandoned by 1915. Railway service to Whitehorse stopped in 1982 with the opening of the highway to Skagway. The log shells of this frontier outpost still stand beyond the abandoned rails, a short stroll from the highway.

Beyond Robinson, the rocky summits of Gray Ridge encroach from the west, and the rounded top of Mount Lorne can be seen to the east. The highway soon winds between Emerald and Spirit lakes, a brilliantly colored pair of freshwater pools that are a favorite rest stop for travelers. The striking color of the water derives from the light that reflects from the white marl of the lakebed. This marl is a fine sediment of broken shells from many generations of freshwater snails. Depending on the angle of the sun, the water color ranges from a gemlike green to a bright turquoise. The sharp peak of Caribou Mountain rises to the east of Spirit Lake, and as the road continues southward, Montana Mountain and the crag-lined valley that holds Lake Bennett become visible ahead.

At Kilometer 109, there is a gold-rush theme park that has a number of taxidermy mounts and live specimens of local wildlife. As the road approaches Carcross, it passes a small dune field known as the Carcross Desert. When the glaciers retreated from this area 10,000 years ago, they left behind vast outwash plains covered with finely ground rock. The finest dust was blown away by the wind, and it settled in the interior to form deep loess soils. Great sand dunes crept incessantly across the landscape. Eventually, vegetation grew over most of the dunes and stabilized them. However, here on the Carcross Desert, south winds blow off the Windy Arm of Tagish Lake

Caribou Mountain rises behind the dunes of the Carcross Desert.

almost constantly. This keeps the sand moving so that vegetation cannot get a permanent toehold on the dunes. A transitory plant community inhabits the dunes, including sage, common juniper, and kinnickinnick.

At Kilometer 107, the highway passes a junction with the Tagish Road, which runs eastward to the Alaska Highway (see Drive 5). It then drops into the town of Carcross, which occupies a narrow neck of land between Nares Lake and Lake Bennett. Tagish Indians came here to fish and to hunt the bands of woodland caribou that crossed the narrows during their annual migrations. A town sprang up at the end of the 1800s, when prospectors sailed, paddled, and poled their way down Lake Bennett in the mad rush to get to the Klondike gold fields.

The town, then called Caribou Crossing, became an important trans-shipment point when the building of the White Pass and Yukon Railway linked rail traffic with the steamboats that plied Tagish Lake. Anglican Bishop William Bompas chose Caribou Crossing as the center for his missionary activities among the Indians and built Saint Saviour's Church here in 1902. Irritated when his mail was consistently sent to other Canadian towns with the words "Caribou" or "Crossing" in their names, the Anglican bishop ex-ercised his penchant for abbreviation and shortened the town's name to "Carcross."

As the gold boom died out, tourism became the chief industry in the area. Paddle-wheel steamers took affluent tourists to exclusive retreats such as Atlin and Ben-My-Chree, an English-style garden resort on the Taku Arm of Tagish Lake. Carcross is still a fascinating stopover. A visitor center in the old railway depot houses a fine collection of interpretive displays covering local history. A fire wiped out the entire waterfront in 1909, and most of the buildings that stand in the center of town were built in the wake of this blaze. Saint Saviour's Church is one of the few structures of historical note that survived the fire.

Just south of Carcross is a native village inhabited primarily by Tagish and Tlingit families. A side road gives access to a cemetery on the south side of the Nares River, where you may visit the graves of such legendary figures as Tagish Charlie, Kate Carmack, and Bishop Bompas.

As the highway leaves Carcross, it travels along the shore of Nares Lake. Its waters reflect the symmetrical profile of Nares Mountain, which harbors a small population of Dall sheep that are occasionally spotted with binoculars. The road soon begins climbing, and at the top of the grade it reaches a scenic overlook above the Windy Arm of Tagish Lake. The pointed peaks that rise across the water are composed chiefly of limestone inter-spersed with strata of volcanic rock such as argillite, tuff, and porphyry.

Bove Island lies in the water like a giant stepping stone. Its glacier-polished domes of limestone rise from a tapestry of aspen and spruce. The island was named by American explorer Frederick Schwatka during his covert reconnaissance of the Yukon in 1883. Schwatka angered many Canadians by affixing new names to local landmarks, irrespective of the place names already in use among native peoples and local frontiersmen.

As the highway follows the lake southward, Montana Mountain rises above it. Silver deposits were found on its upper slopes during the boom years at the turn of the twentieth century. Mining companies moved in to develop the silver veins, and they built aerial tramways to carry the ore down from the mine shafts high on the mountainsides. At Kilometer 90, a tram tower from the old Montana Mine marks the former lakeshore site of Conrad City, which in 1906 had three hotels, several restaurants, and a mining recorder's office. Steamboats paid regular visits to the lakeshore mining camps and carried ore to the railway depot at Carcross for shipment south. Falling silver prices put an end to the mining boom, and by 1914 Conrad City had been completely abandoned.

Farther up the lakeshore, the old Venus Processing Mill serves as a tangible reminder of the glory days of silver mining. Built in 1908, the mill was used to crush and sort silver ore from the Venus Number 1 and 2 shafts high on the mountainside. The mill had been operating for only six months when it was discovered that much of the silver was being lost in the process. The project was promptly abandoned. A new mill was built just south of the border with British Columbia in 1980, in a short-lived attempt to reopen these shafts for mining.

The old Venus stamp mill rests beside the waters of the Windy Arm of Tagish Lake.

Just after passing the old Venus Mill, the highway crosses into the northwestern corner of British Columbia. Scan the steep slopes on both sides of the lake for mountain goats. At the head of Windy Arm, the road mounts a low pass and then descends to the shore of Tutshi Lake (pronounced TOOSH-i), which reflects the rugged peaks of the White Range. The folds in the rock strata are clearly visible in the peaks that rise above the head of the lake. Across the lake, you may spot bands of Dall sheep. Mountain goats range the slopes immediately above the highway.

The Tutshi River, a sluggish and meandering flow of crystal-clear water, pours into the head of the lake. As the road follows it upward, however, a steep gradient makes for foaming whitewater. The surrounding forest is a mixture of lodgepole pine and subalpine fir, a combination common to the Rocky Mountains as far south as New Mexico.

The mountains fall away here, revealing the broad basin of the Tormented Valley. The valley floor is dotted with numerous lakes, gouged out of the granite by great sheets of ice that filled the basin during the Pleistocene period. Between the tarns, the bare bedrock shows striations that mark the passage of the glaciers. There is hardly any soil here. Only the tortured forms of subalpine firs can grow from the crevices in the bare rock. Winter gales blow through gaps in the mountains and scour the basin, pruning these stunted trees into ragged forms.

The road passes the railway flag stop of Log Cabin at Kilometer 44.

Lakes dot the rocky wastes of the Tormented Valley.

The Tagish Indians once harvested blueberries and lowbush cranberries here. They poured melted moose fat over the berries to keep them from spoiling. With the coming of the gold rush, Log Cabin became the site of a small way camp with a Mounted Police post. During the winter, it was a cozy huddle of cabins and tents, but when the snow melted in the spring, the site turned into a fetid and squalid swamp. Presbyterian minister John Sinclair recorded his impressions as he passed through in 1898:

Such a filthy hole I have never seen as that group of sheds and tents at 'Log Cabin.' Loathsome looking dogs slunk around the tents. They were red-eyed and diseased-looking through gorging themselves on decayed horse-flesh. Greasy and slatternly women, begrimed and ragged children and rough, shifty-eyed men wallowed in a sea of mud and filth.

White Pass Road rounds a mountainside and follows the railroad tracks to the Canadian customs post of Fraser. An average of 24 feet of snow falls here each winter. The border itself lies 12 kilometers to the south, past the slender slip of Summit Lake. The lower reaches of the lake have an opaque aquamarine tint that is derived from the glacial meltwaters borne by Summit Creek, which pours into the lake at its midpoint. The water above the mouth of the creek is clear and crystalline. The stark granite spire of Mount Cleveland rises ahead, guarding the summit of White Pass.

For early fortune seekers, the trail over White Pass to the Klondike was longer than the route over Chilkoot Pass to the west. However, the grade was not as steep, and it could be negotiated with pack horses. By the middle of February 1898, more than 2,500 prospectors had successfully negotiated White Pass. Skagway businessmen dreamed of a railway over the route that would connect the seaport with the gold fields in the interior.

One of the railway boosters was Michael J. Heney, a construction man who was said to have boasted, "Give me enough snoose and dynamite and I'll build you a railroad to Hell." Heney enlisted the aid of British financiers, and construction began in May 1898. The construction continued straight through the winter, with workers making 30 cents an hour per man and working through the worst of winter storms. Many defected to the gold fields, but the White Pass and Yukon Railway still managed to reach Whitehorse in 1900. Upon its completion, the railway was regarded as one of the engineering marvels of its age.

The highway crosses White Pass to the west of the original gold rush route and drops into Alaska. A series of stair-step cascades pours from the glaciers atop Mount Cleveland. This is a good place to look for hummingbirds in June and July.

Rugged peaks near White Pass.

The shallow alpine vale soon opens into a deep canyon robed in a dense coastal forest. An overlook with interpretive signs at Mile 8.8 commands a view of the Skagway River's headwaters. The White Pass and Yukon Railway snakes across the far wall of the valley. You might spot mountain goats on the granite peak that guards the valley's head.

The former site of White Pass City is just visible at the head of the valley. Here, at a checkpoint below the final steep grade, a tent city of 1,500 prospectors waited their turn to climb the last pitch. Around the corner and out of sight is Dead Horse Gulch, where prospectors had to crawl over the corpses of fallen pack animals. The cruelty of the horse packers made a vivid impression on author Jack London, who later wrote,

The horses died like mosquitoes in the first frost and from Skagway to Bennett they rotted in heaps. They died at the rocks, they were poisoned at the summit, and they starved at the lakes; they fell off the trail, what there was of it, and they went through it; in the river they drowned under their loads or were mashed to pieces against the boulders; they snapped their legs in the crevices and broke their backs falling backward with packs; in the sloughs they sank from fright or smothered in the slime; and they were disembowelled in the bogs where the corduroy logs turned end up in the mud; men shot them, worked them to death and when they were gone, went back to the beach and bought more.

The highway descends steadily, passing Pitchfork Falls just above the U.S. customs station. The customs house offers the first views of Mount Harding, which rises beyond the salt-water arm of Taiya Inlet. Coastal vegetation crowds the valley walls, including Sitka spruce, western hemlock, alder, and birch. At Mile 5.2, a pullout overlooks the railway grade across the valley, and you can see Hefty Peak above the head of the East Fork of the Skagway River. You can see the old bed of the Brackett Wagon Road just below the railroad tracks. This road was built as a toll road to the interior, but it was never finished and was ultimately bought by the railroad. The highway ducks into a narrow cleft before completing its descent to the valley floor. At Mile 2.1, the road passes the Pioneer Cemetery and a junction with the Dyea Road (see Dyea Road Sidetrip at the end of this chapter), then enters the outskirts of Skagway.

The town of Skagway lies just across the river on the shores of Taiya Inlet. Tlingit Indians knew this landing as Skagua, or "Home of the North Wind," and they considered it unfit for human habitation. But when William Moore arrived in 1887, he saw endless possibilities. Moore was a veteran of the gold fields, having participated in every major gold rush from California in 1849 to Nome in 1900, when he was 78 years old. Moore had a premonition that the next big strike would occur in the Yukon and that prospectors would need a passable route to reach the gold fields. In the spring of 1887, Moore scouted the White Pass Route with a Tagish Indian named "Skookum Jim," who would later achieve fame as one of the discoverers of the Klondike gold fields. Moore built a pack trail over White Pass, and when the Klondike gold rush brought hordes of adventurers to his doorstep, he made a small fortune with his port facilities.

When the flood of prospectors arrived in 1897, they touched off an unprecedented wave of construction. Shopkeepers rushed in to mine the prospectors. The merchants reaped the benefits of a Canadian law requiring prospector's to bring a year's worth of supplies to gain admittance into the Yukon. Ramshackle buildings sprang up overnight, without regard to building codes or land ownership. Moore, who held a patent on 170 acres of land on his homestead, watched with impotent rage as squatters erected the new townsite on his land. In this frenzy of building, half of the structures were erected below the high-tide mark. As a result, half of the town was washed away by the first spring tide.

Early Skaguay, as it was then called, was a rowdy and lawless place. In 1898, Francis Berkeley reported, " 'Shell games' & bunco devices of every kind were in full swing every where & these merely to ascertain if a man had money. Knowing this, it is simply taken away from him, perhaps on the pretense of a game of chance but often by open highway robbery in broad daylight."

The ringleader of Skaguay's criminal element was "Soapy Smith," a genteel and debonair aristocrat who had a hand in every scheme in town. The Soapy Smith Gang ran crooked gambling parlors, bootlegged whiskey, and participated in robberies and swindles of all sorts. They even ran a telegraph office where messages were tapped out, ostensibly to anywhere in the world for $5, but the company could not receive messages; it had no cable.

Soapy kept up appearances by donating generously to charitable organizations for widows, orphans, and the building of Skagway's first church. On July 4, 1898, the governor of the District of Alaska publicly applauded Soapy's community spirit and offered him a position as federal marshal. Four days later, members of Smith's gang relieved a prospector of his gold, and an angry citizen named Frank Reid organized a vigilante party. Reid confronted Soapy Smith on the Skaguay wharf. Smith was killed and Reid was fatally wounded in the ensuing shootout. The remainder of Soapy's gang was rounded up, and for the first time law and order reigned in Skaguay. The gold rush was over by 1899, but the White Pass and Yukon Railway sustained the town while other communities around it were abandoned.

The modern town of Skagway is a genteel reflection of its rowdy and raucous past. The clapboard buildings that line Broadway have been skillfully preserved as part of a National Historic District. Locals in period costumes roam the streets, lending an air of authenticity to the turn-of-the-century atmosphere. There are several live theater shows that play throughout the summer, and a small museum in the Arctic Brotherhood building preserves gold-rush memorabilia. The Gold Rush Cemetery, located north of town on an extension of State Street, holds the graves of notable gold-rush figures such as Soapy Smith and Frank Reid. Several hiking trails climb the steep-walled peaks that surround the town, yielding spectacular views of fjords and hanging glaciers.

Annie Lake Road Sidetrip

This improved gravel road offers a 26-kilometer excursion for travelers who want to leave the beaten track. It begins by running westward across the valley through an open parkland dotted with stands of lodgepole pine. With its serotinous cones that open after being heated by forest fires, lodgepole an indicator of frequent blazes.

After 11 kilometers, the road enters a circular basin ringed with impressive peaks. Goat Mountain stands to the northwest, Red Ridge and Mount Perkins rise to the west, and Needle Mountain crowns the end of Gray Ridge to the southeast. The road soon turns southward, and the craggy peaks close in around the valley. Beaver have repeatedly flooded most of the bottomlands with their dams.

After a short journey through the marshes, the road reaches Annie Lake. This long slip of water is important habitat for loons, belted kingfishers, and river otters. Just beyond the head of the lake, the road reaches a bridge over the Wheaton River at Kilometer 26. This brawling stream rushes down from the mountains with a heavy load of glacial silt. The bridge is condemned, and vehicle travel beyond this point is not recommended. Hikers and mountain bikers may follow the road deep into the heart of the mountains, where it visits old mines at the base of Mount Skukum.

Dyea Road Sidetrip

This gravel road runs northwest from Skagway for 7 miles to reach the abandoned site of Dyea, a former boom town that marked the beginning of the famous Chilkoot Trail. The road begins by winding high onto a hillside, and at Mile 1.3 it reaches a scenic overlook. Pyramid Peak and the Dewey Peaks tower above the valley of the Skagway River, while Mount Harding and the Harding Glacier rise prominently on the far side of Taiya Inlet. Far to the south, the snowy spires of the Cathedral Peaks rise beyond the waters of Lynn Canal.

The road makes a sharp bend to the north and traces a course around the narrow cove of Nahko Bay. It soon reaches Taiya Inlet, dominated here by Face Mountain across the water. At the head of the inlet, a broad expanse of sand marks the meeting of the Taiya River and the Pacific Ocean. This was the site of the gold-rush port of Dyea, which has long since succumbed to storms and floods.

The town got its start in 1885 as the Healy and Wilson Trading Post. Dyea and Skagway were fierce rivals, each claiming to be the gateway to the Klondike gold fields. Town boosters in Dyea had to build a wharf that stretched a mile from shore to reach water deep enough for ocean steamers. At its peak, Dyea boasted 8,000 residents, but it emptied quickly with the passing of the gold rush, and by 1903 it had a population of one. A few pilings still stand on the mudflats at low tide, and a scattering of concrete foundations mark the once-bustling townsite.

A bridge spans the Taiya River at Mile 7.2. The trailhead for the Chilkoot Trail is on the east bank of the river. This trail follows the old gold-rush route through spectacular scenery. You may even find relics cast off by stampeders. The 33-mile trail has some rugged sections where you may have to scramble over boulder fields. Allow three to five days to hike it one way.

An estimated 40,000 people used this steep route to reach the Klondike gold fields, many of them traveling in the winter. The final pitch was known as "The Golden Stairs," and it took ten trips to haul up the requisite ton of supplies.

On April 3, 1898, an avalanche buried more than 60 prospectors on the Chilkoot Trail. Many of their bodies were brought down to Dyea and buried at the Slide Cemetery, which still exists on a short spur road at Mile 7.4. The Dyea Road continues up the valley for a short distance before narrowing to a four-wheel-drive route just beyond a bridge over West Creek.

11

Haines Highway

Official Designation: Yukon Highway 3, British Columbia Highway 4, Alaska Route 7
Description: Paved highway from Haines Junction to Haines, Alaska; 244 kilometers (152 miles)
Recommended Maximum: Highway speeds
Distance Markers: Kilometer posts in Canada and mileposts in Alaska count north from Haines
Information Sources: Kluane National Park, Haines Visitors Bureau

 ## The Drive

This route was originally one of the famed "grease trails" used by the Chilkat band of the Tlingit Indians to carry rendered candlefish oil, baskets, and seashells inland to trade for caribou hides, moccasins, and birchwood bows made by the interior Athapaskan tribes. Each Tlingit chief had an Athapaskan counterpart with whom he had exclusive trading rights. Trade routes extended as far inland as the site of Fort Selkirk on the Yukon River.

The Tlingits were shrewd businessmen who jealously guarded their monopoly on the interior fur trade. When Robert Campbell established Fort Selkirk on the lands of their trading partners, the Tutchone Indians, the Tlingits organized a raiding party under the warrior chief Koh-Klux and burned the fort to the ground. In 1869, Koh-Klux met with naturalist George Davidson at the chief's home village of Klukwan. Davidson successfully predicted a total eclipse of the sun, and Koh-Klux was so impressed that he drew a map for his guest showing the route across Chilkat Pass and much of the Yukon interior beyond. The map was amazingly accurate.

Before the Klondike gold rush, the old grease trail was developed as a toll road by Jack Dalton, an adventurer and former Indian fighter who first visited this country in 1890 with his partner, E. J. Glave. The Tlingits suspected that these white men had come to take away their land and interfere with their trade monopoly, and so they refused to guide the two adventurers. Nonetheless, Dalton charted a route across Chilkat Pass and through the interior to the Yukon River, and in 1899 he obtained a permit to operate it as a toll road. A single man with a pack had to pay $1 to use the road, while passage for livestock cost $2.50 a head. Although the route never gained popularity with stampeders on their way to the Klondike, it was used for several substantial stock drives. Following the construction of the White Pass and Yukon Railway, the Dalton Trail was abandoned and its proprietor retired as a moderately wealthy man.

In 1903, the Dalton Trail was developed into a one-lane wagon road to the Canadian border. It was upgraded to a gravel highway during World War II and was extended to meet the newly constructed Alaska Highway at Haines Junction in the Yukon. The road also opened a travel corridor for moose and mountain goats to migrate into coastal areas.

The well-paved, modern highway connects the Alaska Highway with the tidewater fjords of Haines, Alaska. Along the way, it passes through some of the most stunning mountain scenery in the Far North as it skirts the edge of Kluane National Park, crosses the spine of the Coast Mountains, and descends through the Chilkat Bald Eagle Preserve to reach its terminus. From here, travelers can link up with the ferry system that serves the Inside Passage of southeastern Alaska.

From Haines Junction, the road follows the foot of the Kluane Ranges through a boreal forest of lodgepole pine and aspen. The Kluane Ranges form the outer cordillera of the Saint Elias Mountains, and they lie within Kluane National Park. The basin stretching to the east drains toward the Pacific through steep canyons in the Saint Elias Mountains. One of these westward-draining rivers is the Dezadeash, which the highway crosses as it leaves Haines Junction.

Several times in recent geologic history, glaciers have dammed the Alsek River, which is the main waterway through the mountains. The resulting impoundments have filled this inland basin with deep freshwater lakes. The most recent of these was Recent Lake Alsek, which formed 5,500 years ago during the "Little Ice Age" and finally drained in 1891. The forest that lines the road has grown up since that time.

At Kilometer 220, a short, paved spur road leads to the shores of Kathleen Lake, which occupies a gap in the Kluane Ranges. The snowbound Icefield Ranges of the Saint Elias Mountains are visible beyond it. This lake with its aquamarine waters and fringe of stately conifers is one of the scenic gems of Kluane National Park. It is inhabited by several kinds of game fish, including the kokanee, a landlocked form of sockeye salmon. The Cottonwood Trail makes a 53-mile loop from the lake-side campground. You will need to get a special permit from park headquarters in Haines Junction. A lodge on the opposite side of the highway sells the last gasoline you can get until the road reaches the outskirts of Haines.

As the highway continues southward, the Auriol Range rises to the west. One of the prettiest of the Kluane Ranges, this chain is known for its rock glaciers. At Kilometer 202, there is a self-guiding nature trail that climbs

Haines Highway

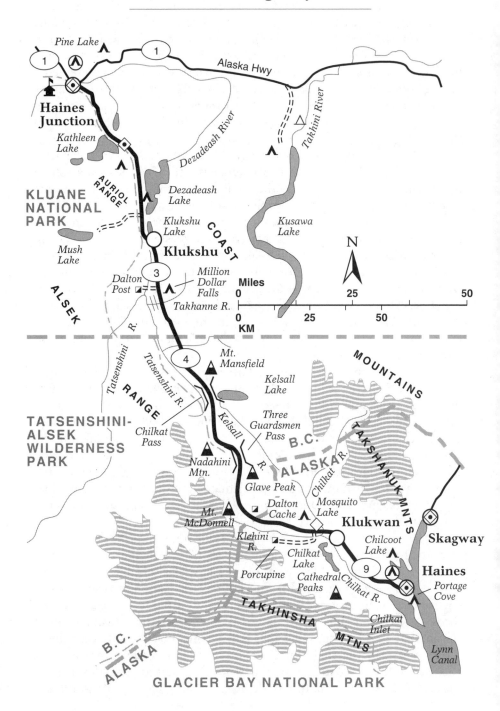

onto the toe of one of these rock glaciers.

The road soon reaches the shore of Dezadeash Lake, a broad and windy expanse of water that is a remnant of the former Lake Alsek. The name Dezadeash refers to an ingenious fishing method employed here by the Southern Tutchone Indians. They sank strips of white birch bark to the bottom of the lake, white side up. When fish swam over the bark, they presented a distinct silhouette and could be speared easily. This is the site of a famous Indian massacre in which Upper Tanana Indians from the village of Snag staged a surprise attack on a village of Southern Tutchones and killed 100 of them.

The rounded peaks east of the lake are part of the Dezadeash Range. A government campground with a boat launch is located on the western shore of the lake, at Kilometer 205 on the highway. Boaters should be aware that heavy winds can rise suddenly on this vast body of water.

At the south end of the lake, the highway passes the abandoned settlement of Beloud Post, and an old jeep trail runs westward to Mush Lake in the heart of Kluane National Park. This area has one of the highest densities of grizzly bears found anywhere; be especially careful along streams when salmon are spawning. Nearby Shorty Creek was the site of prospecting efforts by the "Mysterious 36," a secret party of miners led by a cavalry lieutenant. The group was thought to represent the interests of the Standard Oil Company and eastern Canadian capitalists. It found little gold and abandoned the project.

A short distance beyond Beloud Post, a spur road runs east to the Southern Tutchone village of Klukshu. The name means "Coho Place" in the Tlingit dialect, and the stream that runs past the village supports a strong run of these fish, as well as steelhead and sockeye and king salmon. The Southern Tutchones use traditional fish traps built of poles, which they sank into the streambed to form weirs and corrals. This technology was borrowed from the coastal Tlingit tribe; elsewhere in the Yukon, the Tutchones used a cylindrical form of fish trap. Klukshu is situated on the Dalton Trail and features picturesque cabins and drying sheds. There is also a small museum that is open on an occasional basis.

The highway crosses Klukshu Creek and climbs onto high terraces to meet the Dalton Post Road at Kilometer 169. This gravel road is extremely steep. It leads downward to the site of one of Jack Dalton's old way stations, from which he used to patrol his trail. On one occasion, he caught some cowhands moving a herd of cattle along the trail without paying and turned them back at gunpoint. He shadowed the herd to Haines, making sure it stayed off the trail for the entire 200 miles. Only a couple of tumble-down cabins remain at the site, near the confluence of Klukshu Creek and the Tatsenshini River. Floaters headed down the Tatsenshini and through the Saint Elias Mountains via the Alsek River use this spot as a put-in point.

This is an extremely challenging wilderness float, featuring Class III white water and glaciers that calve directly into the rivers. Floaters need to arrange an aircraft pickup at Dry Bay on the Gulf of Alaska.

The highway sticks to the higher ground, yielding fine views of the Alsek Ranges to the west as it progresses southward. At Kilometer 167, the Takhanne River glides lazily down from its origins among the rounded peaks to the east. Just downstream of the bridge is Million Dollar Falls, where the river plunges 60 meters (200 feet). A viewing platform and walkway have been built atop the basalt walls that guard the violent torrent. Coho and sockeye salmon spawn abundantly below the falls, but they are unable to move beyond this natural barrier.

The road runs along the edge of a great valley, staying close to the timberline as it crosses the border into British Columbia. The low, sinuous hills that flank the road here are eskers, laid down by streams that ran through tunnels under glacial ice. The tundra-clad slopes above the roadway sweep upward to snow-dappled peaks. The trees ultimately fall away, and a vast tundra-clad basin stretches away to the south. Brooding mountains guard its fringes, and many of the inner peaks have been carved into serrated forms by glaciers. Watch for tiny montane glaciers clinging to the flanks of the higher summits.

Alsek-Tatsenshini Wilderness Park stretches west of the road, a trackless expanse of mountain landscape that unites Glacier Bay, Kluane, and Wrangell-Saint Elias national parks into an unbroken block of wilderness that is one of the largest of its kind in the world. This is the home of the "glacier bear," a rare form of black bear that has smoky-blue fur. The broad lowland along the road is Chilkat Pass, the drainage divide between the Alsek and Chilkat watersheds.

Just north of the Nadahini River (Kilometer 109), a small, dull-colored shack stands next to the roadway. This structure was built by a biologist who was studying ptarmigans. It has since become a sort of primitive hostelry used by backpackers, cyclists, and stranded motorists.

The Nadahini drains southward into the Chilkat Valley, but the highway must still cross the low summit of Three Guardsmen Pass before it begins its descent. The pass cradles a barren lake at the foot of Glave Peak, named for Jack Dalton's partner in exploration who died before he could return to the Yukon. As the road begins its descent into the deep valley of the Klehini River, the glacier-clad summits of Mount McDonnell rise ahead in a stunning display of rock and ice. Look eastward from the hairpin curve at Mile 52 to see the Maid of Erin Mine, which produced almost 80,000 pounds of copper between 1911 and 1922.

The road descends steadily into a lush coastal forest that contrasts markedly with the more open stands of white spruce, lodgepole, and aspen

Glaciated peaks stretch southward from Three Guardsmen Pass.

found in the interior. Moisture-loving trees such as Sitka spruce and western hemlock grow tall and thick in this maritime climate. Halfway down the grade, the customs checkpoints are located next to Dalton Cache. The old cabin behind the U.S. customs station (originally called Pleasant Camp) was built in 1896 as a way station, and it still stands in good repair. It boasts a fine view of the Jarvis Glacier's terminal moraine. The glacier carries a steady stream of rock along with its icy flow, and as the ice melts at the toe of the glacier, the rock is deposited to form the great ridges of gravel that are visible here. Take a short stroll northward along the highway from the Canadian customs station to view one of the original bridges of the Dalton Trail. It spans a small stream on the downhill side of the road.

The original wartime road was built on the floodplain of the Klehini despite the warnings of old-timers that it would wash out. Time proved the sourdoughs right; floods soon destroyed the roadbed, forcing its relocation to the slopes above the river. The road completes its descent to the floor of the Klehini Valley, and crosses Big Boulder Creek along the way.

The gold-mining settlement of Porcupine was once located directly across the river from this point. The original strike was made in 1898, and by the following year more than $50,000 in gold had been recovered. A mining town sprang up, featuring a trading post, a hotel, and four saloons. Jack Dalton's Porcupine Trading Company gained control of most of the claims in 1900, and an enormous flume was built to redirect the river away from the gold-bearing gravel. Mining could then progress on a larger scale. Miners netted $150,000 a year in gold. A flood destroyed the flume in 1905, but by that time most of the claims had already been exhausted. Large-scale operations resumed for a ten-year period starting in 1926.

The road soon enters the Chilkat Bald Eagle Preserve. The Klehini and Chilkat rivers are fed by groundwater that surfaces at a constant 4 degrees Centigrade (40 degrees Fahrenheit). The warm water keeps sections of the river ice-free during the early winter and supports a late run of chum salmon. Eagles migrate here from all over the Far North to feast on the salmon, congregating along the river by the thousands from November through January. There is no other place in the world where these beautiful raptors gather in such large numbers.

Just beyond the Chilkat River bridge, a short spur road leads eastward to the Tlingit village of Klukwan. Located at the confluence of the Klehini and Chilkat rivers, this village is the cultural heart of the Chilkat band and was once home to the legendary chief Koh-Klux. There are no visitor facilities here; please respect the privacy of the residents.

The highway crosses the flats of the Chilkat River, where enormous cottonwood trees serve as eagle roosts in the winter. The best eagle viewing is found in this area, and several photographers' blinds are planned with this in mind. The concentration of eagles on these "Council Grounds" begins in mid-November and peaks in January. Travelers who pass through during the summer may see one or two of the great birds. Stopping in the roadway is illegal; if you wish to view the eagles, you should use one of the roadside pullouts, and be careful not to disturb the raptors.

The Takhinsha Mountains rise in lofty majesty to the west of the river, and beyond their crests are the ice fields of Glacier Bay National Park. The most distinctive of these mountains is Mount Emmerich, which can be viewed to best advantage at Mile 8. Scan the slopes above the road for mountain goats and watch the river for fishwheels, used to catch migrating salmon.

The road finally reaches the picturesque town of Haines after a journey of 152 miles. The town sits on a narrow peninsula between Lynn Canal and Chilkat Inlet at a spot known to the Tlingits as *Dei shu* or "the end of the trail." An important portage trail once crossed a narrow neck of the peninsula at this spot, sparing the Indians a 20-mile paddle around the point. Two principle bands of Tlingits inhabited this area, the Chilkat (translated as "basket of many fish") who inhabited the valley to the north, and the Chilkoot ("basket of large fish") who lived to the east along Lynn Canal.

The Tlingits had a rich and complex culture, based on fishing for salmon and trading seashells and eulachon oil inland for furs, hides, and meat. They lived in large dwellings made of cedar planks and were renowned for their artistic abilities. In addition to totem poles, the Tlingits wove intricately patterned baskets and manufactured the distinctive Chilkat blankets, decorated with stylized faces and heraldic crests.

Fishwheels like this research model on the Chilkat River are still used to catch salmon in many parts of Alaska.

Explorer George Vancouver was one of the first Europeans to visit this area, and he named the deep fjord east of town Lynn Canal, after his home port of King's Lynn in England. In 1879, the Chilkats invited naturalist John Muir and Presbyterian minister S. Hall Young to establish a mission and school at the current site of Haines. Muir, who founded the Sierra Club, wrote at length about the glories of Glacier Bay and was instrumental in having it set aside as a national monument.

The settlement soon grew, with clapboard Victorian houses and tidy, fenced yards. The U.S. Army established Fort Seward here in 1903, in part to maintain order along the gold-rush routes and in part to enforce American interests during the boundary dispute with Canada. The fort, later renamed Chilkoot Barracks, was the only permanent Army post in Alaska for 20 years. It was closed in 1946 and now serves as a cultural center. Here, you can watch Tlingit totem-pole carvers at work or perhaps catch one of the several weekly shows of the Chilkat Dancers. The Totem Village is located on the old parade ground of the fort. It features replicas of a trapper cabin and a traditional Tlingit plank house.

Haines enjoys a relatively temperate climate. Winter temperatures never dip below minus 27 degrees Centigrade (minus 17 degrees Fahrenheit). The balmy climate made gardening a popular pastime here, and in 1900 a gardener named Charles Anway developed the Burbank strain of strawberry. This enormous hybrid grows as large as a teacup and is sweet all the way to the center. An annual strawberry festival ultimately grew into the Southeast Alaska State Fair and Music Festival, which is held each August.

In addition to the native artisans at Fort Seward, Haines offers a wealth of other visitor attractions. The Welcome Totems are located at the highway's intersection with the Mud Bay Road on the way into town. The Sheldon Museum, near the waterfront, specializes in cultural and historical exhibits. The American Bald Eagle Foundation operates a free museum that features stuffed mounts of local wildlife. At the end of Mud Bay Road, Chilkat State Park offers beachcombing, excellent views of the mountains across Chilkat Inlet, and a number of hiking trails of varying lengths and difficulties. You can sometimes see humpback and killer whales in the deep waters of Lynn Canal.

Klondike Highway

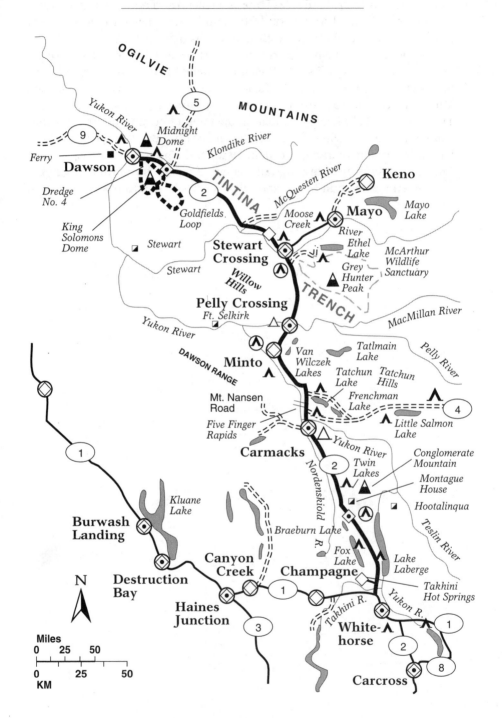

12

Klondike Highway

Official Designation: Yukon Highway 2
Description: Paved highway from Whitehorse to Dawson City in the Yukon; 527 kilometers (327 miles)
Recommended Maximum: Highway speeds
Distance Markers: Kilometer posts count northward from Skagway, Alaska
Further Reading: *Along Alaska's Great River* by Frederick Schwatka, *Carmack of the Klondike* by James Johnson, *The Klondike Stampede* by Edwin Tappan Adney
Information Sources: Tourism Yukon, Klondike Visitors Association, Whitehorse Chamber of Commerce

The Drive

The Klondike Highway is a well-paved route that connects the Yukon capital of Whitehorse with Dawson City and the Klondike gold fields. Fortune seekers followed this same route during the Klondike gold rush of 1898, via stern-wheelers in the summer and overland sleighs during the winter. The modern highway follows the old sleigh route, tracking the mighty Yukon River and crossing the forested uplands of the Yukon Plateau.

Along the way, the road provides access to the history-rich Silver Trail; the Dempster Highway, which runs northward toward the Arctic Ocean; and the Top of the World Highway, with its link to the Alaska highway system. At the end of the road, Dawson celebrates its colorful gold-rush history with false-fronted buildings, museums, gambling halls, and live entertainment.

The road begins by running through ranch country that stretches northward from Whitehorse. Soon after the Klondike crosses the Takhini River, a paved spur road heads 10 kilometers westward to reach Takhini Hot Springs. The thermal pools once found here were well-known to Athapaskans and prospectors. More recently, a small resort has been built around the springs, and the hot water has been funneled into an outdoor swimming pool. The water has a constant temperature of 38 degrees Centigrade (100 degrees

Fahrenheit), and although it is rich in magnesium, calcium, and iron, it lacks the sulphur that gives so many thermal springs their characteristic rotten-egg smell. During the construction of the Alaska Highway, the U.S. Army built greenhouses here and was able to produce bumper crops of fresh produce most of the year.

Beyond its junction with the hot-springs road, the Klondike Highway continues northward through open pastures. At Kilometer 225, the Shallow Bay Road runs eastward, providing access to a working reindeer farm that is open to the public. The road passes to the west of Lake Laberge, although the water remains hidden behind the hills. The lake was immortalized by Robert Service, poet laureate of the Yukon, in his poem "The Cremation of Sam McGee." The Yukon River flows through the lake, which is 64 kilometers (40 miles) long. During the gold-rush era, the ice on the lake was the last to break up during springtime, delaying the anxiously awaited steamboats bound downriver for Dawson City with loads of supplies and mail. To speed the melting of the ice, coal dust was sprinkled across its surface to draw the warmth of the sun.

The highway soon makes its way into the Miners Range, a collection of rolling uplands forested in spruce and aspen. Geologist George Mercer Dawson explored this country in 1887 and named the mountains after the prospectors that he met along the Yukon River. At Kilometer 238, the highway reaches the south end of Fox Lake, which occupies a narrow fold in the hills.

This long sliver of water was one of the many geographic features named by Schwatka, the U.S. Army explorer, in 1883. He named this lake "Richthofen Lake" after a German geographer; Fox Lake was adopted as the lake's official name in 1957.

The road follows the still waters of Fox Lake for 18 kilometers. Beyond it lies Little Fox Lake, a serene woodland pool with sinuous peninsulas and abundant islands that make for excellent canoeing. The road rises to the crest of a high divide that provides a view of the rolling plateau country of the central Yukon. As it descends into the broad basin beyond, you can see Braeburn Lake on the valley floor. The lake is surrounded by thickets of aspen and balsam poplar that sprang up in the wake of an enormous fire that occurred in 1958. The resulting vegetation is favored by woodland caribou as winter range.

A ridge soon rises east of the highway, and its summit is known as Conglomerate Mountain. Conglomerate is a form of rock made from round cobbles cemented together in a matrix of silt and sand. Geologists believe that this particular conglomerate was formed 185 million years ago during undersea mudslides at the edge of the continent. At that time, a great inland sea known as the Whitehorse Trench stretched between the modern towns of Atlin, British Columbia, and Carmacks, Yukon Territory.

The hills soon recede, and the road crosses brushy flats to reach the Twin Lakes, known for their brilliant turquoise color. As you cross a causeway between the two lakes, note the vegetation that covers the island on the western lake. This island was spared from the Braeburn fire, and the old-growth spruce forest that grows here may represent the vegetation that dominated the region before the blaze.

At Kilometer 322, the empty ruins of Montague House stand on the east side of the highway. This structure was one of many roadhouses built in 1899 at 20-mile intervals along the Whitehorse-Dawson winter trail. Horse-drawn sleighs made the 330-mile journey in four or five days, and travelers could get a hot meal and a bed for $2. A detachment of North-West Mounted Police was stationed at Montague House from 1900 to 1905.

Just beyond Montague House, the road finally leaves the old Braeburn burn and enters a forest of full-grown spruce. Flat-topped mountains rise on either side of the basin. The road passes several ponds and wetlands set amid the forest; their margins glow green with a vigorous growth of aquatic vegetation.

At Kilometer 344, a short trail leads eastward to an outcropping of the White Plume agate deposits. Rockhounds can find both agates and geodes (or "thunder eggs") here. The road continues through the valley of the Nordenskiold River, named by Schwatka for an Arctic explorer of Swedish descent. The valley is marshy and choked with brush; the massive peak to the west is Mount Nansen.

At Kilometer 357, the highway reaches the settlement of Carmacks, a traditional fishing site of the Northern Tutchone tribe at the confluence of the Nordenskiold and Yukon rivers. George Carmack, who later was involved in the discovery of the Klondike gold fields, established a trading post here in 1892. The winter trail and steamboat routes crossed at this point, and Carmack's post became an important year-round stopover for stampeders bound for the Klondike.

A hiking trail leaves the south end of the bridge and runs 2.3 kilometers to Coal Mine Lake, a traditional fishing spot of the Northern Tutchones. The trail is a section of the old telegraph trail to Dawson City. Across the river is Tantalus Butte, where seams of coal 6 feet thick were laid down 50 million years ago, when the Tintina Trench was filled with a tropical swamp. The coal once fueled steamboats and the furnaces of Dawson. Later, it was shipped to the hard-rock mines at Elsa and Faro. The tunnels have since collapsed, and the coal seams smolder to this day.

The highway passes to the west of Tantalus Butte and runs north along the Yukon River. At Kilometer 379, there is a viewpoint above Five Finger Rapids, and a boardwalk leads down the long slope to the river's edge if you want a closer look. The rapids were known to the Northern Tutchones as *Tthi-cho Vadezhe*, which means "Rocks (Standing Up) Across the River."

Here, the Yukon River runs swiftly through four "knuckles" of conglomerate stone, creating the five channels that give the rapids their name. It was a major obstacle for steamboat captains. Stern-wheelers heading downstream had to slip through the nearest channel and then turn hard toward the far bank to avoid running aground. Boats going upstream had to use a fixed cable that hung from the rock to winch themselves up through the swiftest part of the current.

The road now follows the banks of the Yukon River, and there are frequent views of the water. During the gold-rush era, wood camps were strung out along the river at regular intervals to keep the paddle-wheelers supplied with fuel. Life was hard in the wood camps. A cord of wood sold for $1. But for many latecomers to the Klondike, it was the only steady money to be had once the paying claims were all staked.

Wildlife is abundant in this area. Ravens and golden eagles nest on the steep bluffs along the river, and you can often see black bears and arctic ground squirrels in the sloping meadows. The south-facing slopes of the Tatchun Hills rise above the river and are covered in sagebrush and grass that hark back to the Pleistocene era. At that time, the central Yukon was an arid steppe populated by saiga antelope, mammoths, cave lions, and steppe bison.

At Kilometer 396, you can pull over to look out over the braided Yukon River as it meanders among dozens of gravel bars and forested islets. The highway then moves inland, and the hills give way to a level upland. The road soon enters the area burned by the Pelly River Fire in 1995. The fire covered about 58,000 hectares (225 square miles), and tendrils of the blaze reached as far north as Rock Island Lake.

A spur road leads 2 kilometers westward from Kilometer 431 to the former site of Minto, a steamboat landing on the banks of the Yukon River. It is a traditional native fishing spot for chum salmon. The Northern Tutchones remember this spot as "Trouble Hill." They warred with a raiding band of Chilkat Indians more than 100 years ago.

Some 22 river miles west of Minto, the ghost town of Fort Selkirk stands along the banks of the Yukon. It is accessible only by tour boat. (Operators are based at Carmacks, Tatchun Creek, and the Minto Resort.) This important fur-trading post was established by Robert Campbell in 1848 for the Hudson's Bay Company. Its construction angered the coastal Chilkat Indians, who until that time had held a monopoly on the fur trade with the Northern Tutchones. In 1852, a raiding party under the Chilkat Chief Koh-Klux burned the post to the ground and sent Campbell and his traders fleeing down the river. The fort was later re-established, and it served as a center for missionary activity and ultimately as a Royal Canadian Mounted Police post.

During the boom years of gold mining on the Klondike, Fort Selkirk was the terminus of the Dalton Trail. Hundreds of head of livestock and tons of freight were brought north on this overland route from Haines, Alaska. Fort Selkirk was completely abandoned by the 1950s, and its turn-of-the-century buildings still stand much as they did during the gold-rush years.

Leaving Minto, the road bears northward across the lowlands between the Yukon and Pelly rivers, passing several lakes along the way. The Van Wilczek Lakes were once the site of a Northern Tutchone winter encampment. Another major winter village was located on Tatlmain Lake, 30 kilometers to the east. The burns found in this area are older, dating from 1969.

The road soon reaches Pelly Crossing, along the banks of the large and silty river of the same name. Long before the coming of the first white men, this spot was a spring fishing camp of the Northern Tutchones, who caught whitefish and grayling with cylindrical fish traps and nets made of sinew.

After crossing a bridge over the Pelly River, the highway climbs a long grade to reach the tops of the Willow Hills. It soon emerges onto a vast area of permafrost covered in stunted black spruce. Frost heaves are prevalent in the roadway here, so drive with caution.

At Kilometer 490, the highway descends to cross Crooked Creek, from which you can see the MacArthur Range to the east. Called *Sedzuan Me Ddhaw* by the Northern Tutchones, these mountains were considered a sacred place of healing and power. They are now protected within a game sanctuary.

From Kilometer 526, a narrow and winding side road leads eastward for 27 kilometers, bound for a primitive campground on Ethel Lake. This large lake is tucked into the heart of the mountains, and camping is permitted on its shores.

The road eventually reaches the village of Stewart Crossing. From here, the Silver Trail Highway runs eastward to the old silver-mining towns of Keno and Elsa. The Stewart River was the site of an early gold strike in 1885. Prospectors jokingly referred to it as the "Grubstake River," because a year's work here yielded just enough gold to buy supplies for the following year.

In 1886, a trading post was built on this site (originally called Frenchman's Bar) by Jack McQuesten, Al Mayo, and Arthur Harper. The three worked as a team under the leadership of McQuesten, one of the greatest entrepreneurs in the history of the Far North. Harper was a prospector who would locate promising gold fields and spread the word. When miners flooded in, McQuesten would give them a grubstake on credit in return for a share of their gold. Mayo was a steamboat captain who piloted McQuesten's New Racket up and down the Yukon, supplying the trading posts along the way.

The highway follows the Stewart River downstream, offering occasional glimpses of the water. At Kilometer 562, there is a bridge over Moose Creek, a major tributary of the Stewart. The creek marks the westward limit of glacial expansion during the ice ages. To the east and south, the central Yukon remained ice-free, even while ice sheets extended as far south as New Jersey and Illinois.

The road soon crosses the McQuesten River, and the Stewart veers away to the west on its way to join the Yukon River. The highway continues northwest into gently rolling country where stands of tall white spruce are interspersed with peat bogs containing its ragged relative, the black spruce. The route here is long and tedious, but a pullout east of the road at Kilometer 620 offers waterfowl viewing opportunities on Gravel Lake. This wetland is an important nesting ground, moulting area, and staging spot for the many migratory ducks that use the Tintina Trench as a flyway.

The scenery improves when the road reaches an overlook of the Tintina Trench at Kilometer 652. This deep valley follows a fault that once marked the edge of the North American continent before "terranes" attached themselves to the edge of the continent, forming most of Alaska and the southwestern Yukon (see page ix). Beyond the trench, the Ogilvie Mountains block off the northern horizon.

The highway descends a long grade, crosses Flat Creek, and follows the south bank of the famous Klondike River. Klondike is a corruption of the Athapaskan Tron Duick, meaning "hammer water." Here, the Hän Indians hammered poles into the riverbed to form fish traps and weirs to harvest the salmon that were once abundant.

The explosion of gold mining in 1896 doomed the salmon runs, as the prospectors overfished and the spawning gravel was buried in silt. Watch for piles of "tailings," or waste rock, that was discarded in order to reach the paying gravel below it. The gold of the Klondike is in "placer" form, ranging in size from dust to nuggets and scattered throughout old river gravel. It originated in veins of quartz in the bedrock but has since been carried far from its source by running water. The source, or "mother lode," of the Klondike gold has never been identified.

The road follows the clear Klondike River through stately groves of spruce that lean over the water. At Kilometer 671, the Dempster Highway branches to the north on its way to Inuvik, Northwest Territories. As the Klondike Highway continues westward, signs of placer mining increase. The long tailings heaps along the river were created by enormous bucket-line dredges, the great floating processing mills that were the hallmark of the industrial age of gold mining. The largest dredges could recover up to 800 ounces of gold a day.

The road reaches Hunker Creek at Kilometer 705. It was in this drainage that Robert Henderson was prospecting when George Carmack arrived

The Klondike River leads travelers into Dawson City.

in the Klondike with his native wife and his in-laws, Tagish Charlie and Skookum Jim. Henderson was a cantankerous Nova Scotian who was prejudiced against Athapaskans. He couldn't stand the prospect of having Carmack's Indian companions around, so he sent the entire party down the river to Rabbit Creek to test their luck. Carmack's party made their big strike on Rabbit Creek, which they renamed Bonanza Creek. Meanwhile, Henderson never found paying gravel and ended up a pauper. Late in life, he convinced the Canadian government to grant him a small pension for his role in discovering the Klondike gold. Albert Hunker filed a discovery claim here in 1896 and attached his name to the stream.

A short distance beyond Hunker Creek is the old company town of Bear Creek, which once supported the gold-dredging operations of the Yukon Consolidated Gold Corporation. Parks Canada has restored the compound, which includes a machine shop, blacksmith shop, and gold assay room. The highway continues westward to cross Bonanza Creek, and the Bonanza Creek Road runs southward to give access to Gold Dredge Number 4 and the scenic Klondike Gold Fields Loop (see Klondike Gold Fields Loop Sidetrip at the end of this chapter).

The road then passes Guggieville, a mining camp operated by the Guggenheim mining interests, and crosses a bridge over the Klondike River. A paved spur road departs to the right, bound for the top of Midnight Dome. This summit offers a fine view of Dawson City and is an excellent spot from which to watch the sun wheel around the horizon on the summer solstice (June 21). The highway continues into Dawson City, and it becomes the Top of the World Highway as it leaves town.

Dawson City is a rollicking frontier town born during the gold rush. It was the seat of territorial government until 1953. Soon after the discovery of gold, a trader named Joe Ladue gained title to the current townsite and divided it into lots. It was a poor place to build. The alluvial delta of the Klondike is marshy and underlain by permafrost, and a levee ultimately had to be constructed along the Yukon River to keep the spring floods out of the streets. The Hän Indians, who had used the site as a fishing camp for generations, were unceremoniously ousted. They had to relocate their village downriver.

Meanwhile, traders from the gold towns of Fortymile and Circle City, farther to the west, poured into Dawson, hastily erecting stores and warehouses to cater to the hordes that were expected to arrive. And come they did, 5,000 strong in the first year, swamping the fledgling town and running through the available stock of food like a horde of locusts. Despite the government requirement that every prospector bring enough supplies to last a year, Dawson City was on the brink of famine by the winter of 1897.

General starvation was averted when a cattle drive reached town in the summer of 1898. The great mass of stampeders arrived that year, swelling the population of Dawson City to 40,000. Most of the best claims had

A view of Dawson City from Moonlight Dome.

already been staked by this time, and many of the newcomers ended up working for wages on the claims of the old sourdoughs. Drift mining was the prevailing method of the time. It involved digging shafts into the frozen ground during the winter and then branching tunnels horizontally or diagonally along the pay streak once gold-bearing gravel was reached. The gravel was piled in big dumps, to be sluiced during the summer.

The permafrost that underlies the Klondike Mining District presented a special challenge to early miners. Initially, they built fires to thaw the soil and dug out the resulting muck. This was a laborious process, and the landscape was soon denuded of trees as they were felled to feed the fires. Later, the miners used steam and hot water and ultimately discovered a cold-water method that was just as effective at a fraction of the cost and effort.

With the dawn of the new century, big corporations began buying the claims to work them on a large scale with hydraulic cannons and floating dredges. Dawson emptied as less manpower was needed, and by 1925 the population stood at 975. Today, the town is enjoying a second "gold rush," as tourists pour in from around the world. The city has responded by restoring old buildings, constructing replicas of fallen structures, and presenting a wide variety of entertainment that harks back to the gold-rush days. Parks Canada has included many of the historical buildings within Klondike National Historic Park.

A walking tour of Dawson features many restored buildings left over from times gone by, as well as structures falling into graceful ruin. Guided tours leave from the Visitor Reception Centre downtown, and interpretive plaques grace many of the buildings for visitors who prefer to explore on their own. The stern-wheeler *Keno* stands along the waterfront, with an interpretive display beside it. One of the highlights of town is the Robert Service cabin, where Parks Canada sponsors a wonderful recital of the Yukon poet's life and works. There is gambling at Diamond Tooth Gertie's, and live shows run nightly there and at the Palace Grand Theatre. The old seat of government has been turned into a museum. It houses displays on the gold rush as well as locomotives from the narrow-gauge railway that once served the gold fields. The old fire hall has also been turned into a museum that depicts the fiery history of downtown Dawson.

Klondike Gold Fields Loop Sidetrip

This drive follows improved gravel roads southward into the heart of the gold fields, making a short loop of 96 kilometers (60 miles) or a longer loop of 164 kilometers (102 miles). Motorists with RVs or trailers should not attempt to go beyond Eldorado Creek because the road becomes steep, narrow, and winding. There are several private claims early in the loop that offer gold-panning for a fee.

The drive begins at Kilometer 714 of the Klondike Highway and wanders up the valley of Bonanza Creek amid massive piles of tailings left behind by dredges. As the road enters the hills, watch for enormous cuts made into the hillsides by hydraulicking. This process involved using huge water cannons called "giants" to wash gravel from the slopes to the valley floor, where it could be processed more easily. The gold-bearing gravel of the Klondike region is part of the White Channel formation, which is dominated by cobbles of quartz. The formation was originally laid down by a slow-moving stream on the floor of a basin. Millions of years ago, the land here uplifted about 200 meters (600 feet) and turned it into a high plateau. The creeks that drained the plateau have cut deep valleys into the bedrock, stranding the ancient White Channel gravel high on the hillsides.

At Kilometer 5.5, you will reach Fullerville, one of dozens of small mining communities that were scattered throughout the hills during the boom years. The Merry Widow Road House once stood here atop Jew Hill, but mining efforts have since erased all signs of the community. However, the Boulder Hill gold dredge is still visible downstream from the first bridge over Bonanza Creek. This was the first gold dredge to operate in the Klondike gold fields. Three kilometers beyond this point, Gold Dredge Number 4 rests in its dried-up basin. It is the largest wooden-hulled dredge ever to operate in North America, and it has been restored by Parks Canada. Nearby is an interpretive center that offers guided tours for a small fee.

Two kilometers beyond the dredge, the road splits. The loop drive takes off to the left, following a narrow road (No RVs or trailers!) along upper Bonanza Creek. The boom town of Grand Forks stood here during the gold rush. This rollicking community of 10,000, which rivaled Dawson as the capital of the Klondike, was completely plowed under by dredges in 1921.

The short spur road up Eldorado Creek is well worth a side trip. It passes a marker commemorating the spot where George Carmack, Tagish Charlie, and Skookum Jim filed the claim that started the Klondike gold rush. Eldorado Creek itself was staked by five prospectors who arrived too late to lay claim to any of the Bonanza Creek gravel. Each of these claims ultimately paid out more than $1 million in gold.

A short distance up Eldorado Creek, you will see Cheechako Hill. Old-timers scoffed at newcomers who began mining high on this hillside. After all, everyone knew that gold-bearing gravel was found only in stream bottoms. The sourdoughs were proved wrong when Cheechako Hill turned out to be one of the richest sites in the Klondike. Interpretive panels along the Eldorado Road tell about prospectors such as Dick Lowe and Albert Lancaster, who pressed ahead in the face of long odds to make fortunes for themselves. Most of the miners were not so lucky and went away penniless.

To continue the loop, follow the narrower road as it climbs steadily through the upper valley of Bonanza Creek. A narrow-gauge railway ran up this grade from 1906 to 1914. This secondary road demands careful driving. It climbs high above treeline onto the slopes of King Solomons Dome. The gold-bearing streams of the Klondike District radiate from this mountain like the spokes of a wheel, suggesting to early miners that a mother lode might be hidden here. Optimistically, they named the summit for a mythical mine of great richness. Today, geologists point out that modern drainage patterns do not reflect the patterns that prevailed when the White Channel gravel was laid down.

Views from the heights are impressive, encompassing the gold-bearing watersheds, as well as the jagged Ogilvie Mountains on the northern horizon. The Quartz Creek Road soon drops away to the south to meet a junction with the Sulphur Creek Road. Travelers opting for the shorter loop should bear left here, while the longer loop (discussed first) follows the Sulphur Creek Road downward.

This road drops quickly to the floor of the Sulphur Creek Valley, which it follows through heavily mined bottomlands overgrown with brush. After 28 kilometers, the road swings northward into the valley of Dominion Creek and follows it toward its headwaters. Kilometer posts count backward from this point to reach 0 at the mouth of Hunker Creek.

There are many signs of modern mining activity here, as well as vestiges from earlier times. Watch for Gold Dredge Number 10 at Kilometer 46. Eleven kilometers beyond it are the huddled cabins of Little Quebec, a tiny community of three families from that province who staked their claims here. The road climbs through the headwaters of Dominion Creek to reach Hunker Summit.

The cutoff road joins the Dominion Creek Road at Hunker Summit, and the two loop drives follow the same route down Hunker Creek. (Kilometers now count distance from the highway). The hollow two-story structure that stands above the intersection is the old Fournier Roadhouse, one of the few of its kind that has survived. The route runs northward as it descends, and at Kilometer 10.5 it passes the abandoned cabins of Bee Gulch. Three kilometers beyond them, the Gold Bottom Roadhouse stands below the road and above the confluence of Gold Bottom and Hunker creeks. Robert Henderson, the first prospector in the Klondike area, is thought to have built his cabin on Gold Bottom Creek. Six kilometers below the roadhouse, you can see Gold Dredge Number 11 west of the road. This is the last feature of note before the Hunker Creek Road merges with the Klondike Highway.

13

The Silver Trail

Official Designation: Yukon Highway 11
Description: Paved and gravel byway from Stewart Crossing to Keno City, in the Yukon; 111 kilometers (69 miles)
Recommended Maximum: 70 kph/35 mph on gravel sections
Hazards: Duncan Creek Road too narrow for RVs or trailers
Distance Markers: Kilometer posts count eastward from Stewart Crossing
Further Reading: *Gold and Galena* by the Mayo Historical Society
Information Sources: Tourism Yukon, Silver Trail Tourism Association

 The Drive

This forgotten byway leaves the Klondike Highway at Stewart Crossing and runs east toward mountainous country that prompted the Yukon's other mining boom—the silver rush. The road is paved as far as Mayo, and then is improved gravel to Keno City. The Duncan Creek Road, which forms the second leg of the loop, is too narrow and winding for RVs or vehicles pulling trailers.

The road begins by following the banks of the Stewart River, where small but paying quantities of gold were found from 1885 onward. Stewart Crossing lies on the Tintina Fault, a zone of lateral (or "strike-slip") movement as the small land masses to the southwest were pushed northward along the North American plate. More recently, a giant glacier filled the Stewart River valley, flowing westward from the ice fields along the Mackenzie Mountains. Look across the river at the slopes of Hungry Mountain. The current timberline is thought to reflect the high-water mark of the ice during the middle period of glaciation, which occurred between 120,000 and 80,000 years ago.

At Kilometer 14, the road enters the site of an extensive burn that occurred in 1948. The fire burned off the insulating ground cover and thawed the upper layers of permafrost, providing suitable growing conditions for lodgepole pine and subalpine fir. You can identify the lodgepole by its round tufts of needles, while the fir is shaped like a spire and has blunt needles. These trees are more typical of the Rocky Mountains, and here they are at

The Silver Trail

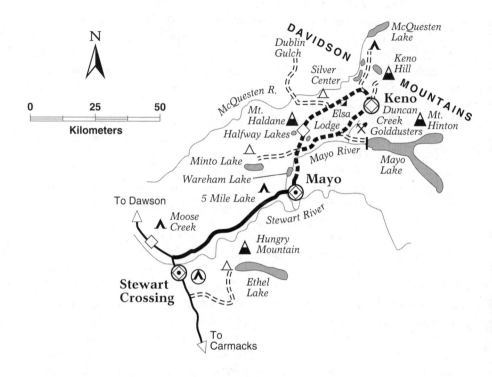

the northern limit of their range. The pine trees found here are particularly cold-tolerant, and their cones have been gathered in the past to ship to Sweden, where the seeds have been used for reforestation.

Beginning at Kilometer 26, the road crosses a series of sand dunes that have been stabilized by the vegetation growing on them. The dunes formed during the most recent glaciation, which ended 14,000 years ago. A melting glacier deposited finely ground rock at its foot, and wind blew away the finer dust and herded the larger grains into dunes. You will cross the terminal moraine that marks the foot of this most recent glacier at Kilometer 33.

The road now crosses terrain that was shaped by the most recent glaciation. At Kilometer 50, there are several large sinkholes south of the road. These were formed when chunks of glacial ice were buried by sediment from a melting glacier. The ice later melted, causing the ground to collapse and form circular depressions.

The road approaches the town of Mayo, and at Kilometer 54 there is a sign for the Mayo Campground. Just east of the sign, a faint trail runs southward into the brush to reach an old Indian cemetery on a high bluff above the river. It commands an excellent view of the old Mayo Indian village, which flooded in 1936 and had to be abandoned in 1954 because of polluted drinking water.

A spur road runs south from Kilometer 57 to reach Mayo at the confluence of the Mayo and Stewart rivers. The town represents the head of navigation beyond which the water was too shallow for steamboats. The lower Stewart River was not navigable some years because of its many shoals and shifting bars. To ply its waters, special shallow-draft steamboats had to be built. They included the Keno, on display in Dawson City. Fully loaded, the entire steamboat drew only 50 centimeters (22 inches) of water.

When word got out that Mayo was being surveyed as a shipping terminal for the Keno Hill silver ore, an entrepreneur named Gene Binet bought the entire townsite. He built a hotel, general store, and restaurant, and made a fortune mining the miners when they came into town to whoop it up. A replica of Binet's residence now serves as an excellent historical and natural history museum and travel-information center.

The main highway continues northeastward, bound for the silver-mining ghost towns of Keno and Elsa. As the last glacier in this area receded, it formed an ice dam, and the country the road now traverses was submerged beneath a freshwater lake. A thick layer of silty sediment covered the lakebed, and when the lake drained, these sediments froze to form a continuous layer of permafrost. From time to time, wildfires or other disturbances remove the insulating mat of vegetation, and patches of permafrost melt away. As the silty soil slumps, the depression fills with water to form a "thermokarst" lake. The water accelerates the melting of the permafrost along the lake margin, constantly enlarging the lake. Look for trees leaning over or toppling into the water; these are the hallmarks of an active thermokarst lake.

The road climbs over a hilltop that looks out over Wareham Reservoir, one of only a few hydroelectric impoundments in the Yukon. At the head of the lake, the road crosses a marsh where the former settlement of Minto Bridge once stood. This was a crossroads town on the Liberal Trail, a winter route to Dawson City. A roadhouse on this site was a stopover point for Keno Hill silver shipments. It has since been flooded by the impoundment of Wareham Reservoir.

At Kilometer 18, the Minto Lake Road runs northward to a primitive campground on Minto Lake and beyond to the placer fields of Highet Creek. This stream was one of the big silver producers of the region, and the Klasco dredge was shipped to Highet Creek in pieces only to be abandoned when the project ran into financial problems. Across the intersection, the Duncan Creek Road comes in from the east. It forms the second leg of a loop drive for small passenger vehicles.

As the Silver Trail Road approaches the Halfway Lakes, you will see the solitary peak known as Mount Haldane rising ahead. Two kilometers beyond the lakes, you will come to a gravel road that leads to a trail to the top of Mount Haldane. There is a forest-fire lookout station on the summit.

The road soon swings into the McQuesten River valley, and Galena Ridge rises to its right. Galena is a compound of lead and silver and is the ore responsible for the silver deposits found here. The road climbs onto the flanks of the ridge, giving you a spectacular view of the upper McQuesten Valley and the rugged Davidson Mountains rising beyond its head. These mountains were created some 330 million years ago from sediment that settled on a continental shelf. The sediment ultimately hardened into sandstone, which was faulted and shattered in the Keno area much later. Tongues of magma seeped into the cracks, carrying with them the lead and silver ores that would form the Keno Hill and Elsa deposits.

At Kilometer 88, the South McQuesten Road branches off and runs northward for 8 kilometers to reach the Silver Centre campground (no fee). Then it continues northward to the gold fields at Dublin Gulch. During their digging, placer miners at Dublin Gulch unearthed the bones of primitive horses, cave lions, and steppe bison dating from 25,000 years ago.

Signs of old silver-mining activity begin to appear as the road approaches Elsa. Below the road, a great pile of tailings covered with a sinuous tunnel of

The abandoned portal of the Elsa Mine.

sheet metal is the Silver King Mine. Prospector H. W. MacWhorter discovered this deposit in 1906, and it became the first active silver mine in the region in 1913. Farther out on the flats, a tall building houses the elevator hoist for the Husky Southwest Mine, which has a vertical shaft sunk into the valley floor. Nearby are several settling ponds, where lime was added to the tailings to neutralize acid mine wastes, thus protecting the South McQuesten River system.

A short spur road leads into the heart of Elsa, a former company town built in 1929 by the Treadwell Yukon Company. The Elsa Mine in the center of town was named for the sister of Charlie Brefalt, a prospector who sold the mine to Treadwell Yukon for $250,000. Treadwell also acquired the neighboring Silver King, Lucky Queen, and Calumet claims. Silver production boomed under the visionary direction of the company's mining engineer, Livingston Warnecke, who is credited with much of the company's success. He died in a plane crash in 1941, and mine production soon declined. The United Keno Hill Mining Company bought the properties in 1946 and turned Elsa into a self-sufficient company town. The mines closed in 1989, but the structures still stand much as they were left. The most interesting is the Elsa Mine portal, where narrow tracks emerge from the shaft and lead into the flotation mill.

The main road continues northwest, rounding the end of Galena Hill. At Kilometer 103, a side road continues past the Hanson Lakes on its way to the shore of McQuesten Lake at the head of the valley. This is the beginning of the Wind River Winter Trail, over which an exploration company hauled oil-drilling equipment to the fields along the Bell River. Too little oil was found to justify the effort, and the company decided it was cheaper to abandon millions of dollars of heavy equipment in the wilderness than to haul it out again.

As the main road drops toward Keno City, you can see the rocky crag of Mount Hinton to the east. Keno City sits atop an old glacial moraine below the foothills of the Patterson Range. The hill behind the town was originally called Sheep Hill by the miners, but excessive hunting soon eradicated the local populations of mountain sheep and caribou. It was renamed Keno Hill after the gambling game.

Louis Beauvette found the first of the silver veins on Keno Hill on his Roulette claim in 1919. A welter of small mining operations soon blossomed here and on neighboring Sourdough Hill to the south. These attracted the attention of the Guggenheim Corporation, which bought many of the claims and began large-scale mining efforts. Keno City boomed from the 1920s to the 1940s, but then mining activity dwindled as silver prices fell.

Keno City is essentially a ghost town inhabited by a handful of people who cherish the quiet and isolation of this beautiful area. There are several excellent hiking trails that visit old mining cabins and traverse the tundra atop Keno Hill. An old saloon and dance hall has been converted into a mining museum, the finest of its kind in the Far North. Pamphlets are available here for a self-guided walking tour of the town, which features false-fronted buildings and log cabins with colorful histories.

Looking southward from the townsite, you can see the Mackeno Mine on the slopes of Galena Hill. The tall structure at its summit is an old radio antenna left over from the Cold War era. The steep and winding Summit Trail Road climbs into the alpine country atop Keno Hill (see sidetrip below). For large RVs and motor homes, this is the end of the drive. Passenger cars can follow the Duncan Creek Road to make a loop trip; a description of the loop follows.

The Duncan Creek Road follows Lightening Creek as it enters one of the most important placer fields in the area. A family of Swedes named Gustaveson made the first strike here in 1898 and mined it for three years in secrecy, without filing a claim. Their scheme ultimately backfired when Duncan Patterson jumped their unfiled claim and staked it legally in 1901. By 1902, Duncan Creek and its tributaries were fully staked.

The Duncan Creek Golddusters operate a modern placer mine 19 kilometers from Keno City. They offer tours and gold-panning opportunities. Just beyond the mine, the Mayo Lake Road runs eastward for 7 kilometers to Mayo Lake, a natural lake that has been enlarged by a hydroelectric dam. Bear right at the intersection to continue the loop drive.

The road follows the historic Silver Trail, along which horses and sledge teams hauled loads of silver ore from the mines at Keno and Elsa. Roadhouses were built at regular intervals where tired horses could be exchanged for fresh ones. Signs mark the locations of some of the roadhouses, but little remains of the structures themselves. This horse-drawn freighting was expensive. It cost more per ton to ship the ore overland to Mayo than it did to ship the ore by paddle-wheeler, rail, and steamship to a smelter in San Francisco. Ultimately, the horses were replaced by "cat trains," which used tracked bulldozers to haul the sledges.

The road crosses slopes that burned for an entire month in 1990. Fall rains finally extinguished the fire. The Duncan Creek Road closes the loop and returns to the main Silver Trail Highway some 69 kilometers east of Stewart Crossing.

Summit Trail Sidetrip

This narrow gravel road snakes up the slopes of Keno Hill for 10.5 kilometers to reach a signpost at its summit. On your way up, you will have excellent views of Mount Hinton and the Keno 700 Mine (last worked in 1978) on the south slopes below the road. The alpine tundra at the top of the mountain is inhabited by hoary marmots and arctic ground squirrels. Outcrops of schist called "tors" stand atop the summit, remnants of bedrock whittled away by frost shattering. Stone nets crisscross the ground, pushed up from the soil and sorted by frost action.

The signpost on Keno Hill was erected during a geosciences conference, and it shows the distances to participating cities around the world. This is another excellent spot to watch the sunset on June 21, the longest day of the year.

14

Dempster Highway

Official Designation: Yukon Highway 5/Northwest Territories Highway 8
Description: Wide gravel highway from Klondike Highway to
Inuvik, Northwest Territories; 741 kilometers (460 miles)
Recommended Maximum: 80 kph/50 mph
Hazards: Sharp gravel between Ogilvie and Richardson mountains causes
frequent flat tires
Distance Markers: Kilometer posts count north from Klondike High-
way in Yukon, reset at zero at Northwest Territories border, and count
northward for remaining distance to Inuvik
Further Reading: *People of the Deer* by Farley Mowat, *The Lost Patrol*
and *The Mad Trapper of Rat River* by Dick North
Information Sources: Tourism Yukon, Western Arctic Tourism
Associ-ation

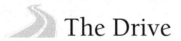

The Drive

The Dempster is Canada's great highway to the Arctic, stretching more
than 730 kilometers (450 miles) north through mountains and tundra to
Inuvik, Northwest Territories. Completed in 1978, the wide gravel highway
retains much of the wilderness quality that has been lost by many of the
more southerly roads. Services are spaced far apart, so you should carry
extra gas and several spare tires. To avoid windshield dings and blinding
dust, slow down when passing other vehicles. Be sure to pull as far to the
side as possible when stopping in the roadway; pullouts are scarce.

The highway begins by crossing the Klondike River, the forested floor
of the Tintina Trench, and, at Kilometer 6, the North Fork Ditch, a project
that channeled water westward from the North Fork of the Klondike to
supply hydroelectric power and water to the gold dredges near Dawson.
The mosaic of forest types and stand ages found on the valley floor is caused
by the interaction of patchy permafrost and frequent small-scale fires.

After 24 kilometers, the road crests a rise that overlooks the North
Fork of the Klondike and its mountain-lined valley. These are the southern
marches of the sandstone Ogilvie Mountains. Heavy timber clothes the bottomlands, but tundra covers the mountain slopes. Watch for beavers and

grizzly bears as the road ascends. You will reach Tombstone Campground at Kilometer 71.4.

The road climbs a low grade to the top of North Fork Pass, and a pullout along the way offers a clear view of Tombstone Mountain. This peak served as a natural landmark for trappers, prospectors, and Mountie patrols, and is still used as a reference point by bush pilots.

The Tombstone Range is a batholith of granitic rock called syenite, which was intruded into the surrounding sedimentary rock as molten magma. Glaciers have sculpted the granite into fantastic spires and walls. A hiker's paradise, the range can be reached via Grizzly Creek at Kilometer 58 or by traveling up the brushy valley of the North Fork from Tombstone Campground. Closer at hand, signs of glaciation surround the roadway. Horn peaks, U-shaped valleys, and low ridges of debris called moraines all testify to the sculpting power of glacial ice.

At the top of North Fork Pass, an old road suitable for hiking or mountain biking leads eastward into the valley of the Hart River. This is the home of the Hart River caribou herd, a small band of mountain caribou that is occasionally seen from the road. Unlike the barren ground caribou found farther north, this animal is a year-round resident and does not undertake long migrations.

The road descends toward the East Fork of the Blackstone River, entering one of the most outstanding bird-watching areas in the Far North. All three species of ptarmigan are found here: willow, rock, and white-tailed. Hoary marmots and arctic ground squirrels are common on the lush swards of tundra, and pikas (also known as "rock rabbits") inhabit the rock slides of the higher slopes. You can occasionally see winged predators such as the gyrfalcon and golden eagle in the skies above. As the road descends, watch the slopes of Anglecomb Peak to the east for the white Dall sheep that use this area as a lambing ground in early summer.

As the road runs northward through the tundra-covered valley, it passes chains of pyramid-shaped peaks. The low mounds that dot the valley floor are "palsas," caused by frost action in the underlying peat. Thaw lakes dot the flats, offering habitat for waterfowl such as the red-throated loon and the oldsquaw duck. This area, known as the Blackstone Uplands, was a traditional fall hunting area for the Gwitch'in, a tribe of Athapaskan Indians who now center their culture at the villages of Old Crow, Fort MacPherson, and Arctic Red River.

Most of the area north of this point and west of the Richardson Mountains was never glaciated and may have been continuously inhabited for more than 20,000 years. The famous Porcupine caribou herd uses the area as a winter range but returns to the edge of the Beaufort Sea each spring for calving.

The peaks ultimately give way to a broad tundra basin flanked by isolated summits. You will reach Two Moose Lake at Kilometer 102.6. It sup-

Falls on Pine Creek are one of the many scenic delights along Discovery Road out of Atlin (Drive 9). .ERIK MOLVAR

Anchorage, Alaska's largest city, basks in the fading twilight of a winter afternoon (Drive 22). ALISSA CRANDALL

The Trans-Alaska Pipeline, one of the world's great engineering marvels, crossing the permafrost basin of the Delta River (Drive 18). JEFF GNASS

Boats in Seward Harbor (Drive 26) ERIK MOLVAR

Strong runs of salmon in coastal rivers like the Chilkat make Alaska an angler's paradise.
FRANK OBERLE

Rainbow in the high country above Sixtymile River, Top of the World Highway (Drive 15). ERIK MOLVAR

The Matanuska Valley's rich soils and almost endless summer daylight combine to produce record-sized vegetables like this cabbage (Drive 22). ROY CORRAL

Pioneer Peaks, one of the principal landmarks along the Glenn Highway, creates a spectacular backdrop for the farms of the Matanuska Valley (Drive 22). JEFF GNASS

Bove Island rises from the Windy Arm of Tagish Lake (Drive 10). ALISSA CRANDALL

Caribou roam freely throughout the uplands and across the open tundra of the Arctic.
JEFF GNASS

Icebergs in Portage Lake, not far from Seward Highway (Drive 26) ERIK MOLVAR

Bald eagles are found throughout the north country wherever there are strong runs of salmon. FRANK OBERLE

Grizzly Bears, not humans, occupy the top spot in the food chain in the Far North.
STEVEN NOURSE

Dempster Highway

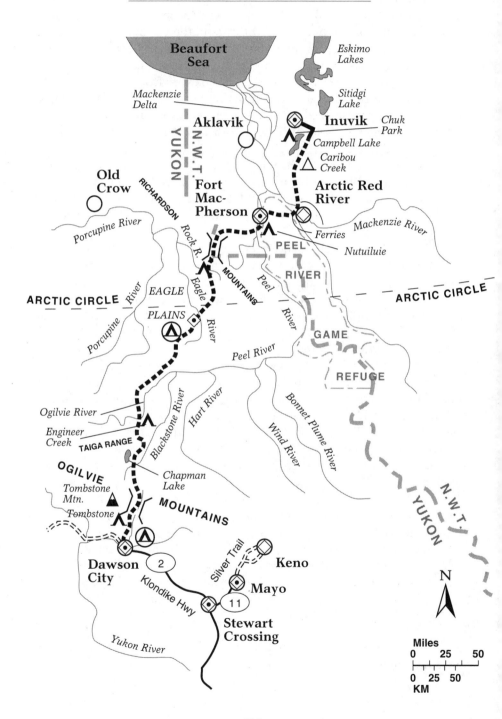

ports a lush growth of aquatic vegetation that draws moose to feed in the late evening. It is also a good bird-watching spot, featuring such interesting species as the harlequin duck and red-necked phalarope on the open water and water pipits and gray-cheeked thrushes in the surrounding brush.

At Kilometer 115, a bridge crosses the Blackstone River, which pours in from a broad valley to the west. Blackstone is a translation of the Gwitch'in *Ttho Zraii Njik*, or "Black Boulder Water." Look west from the rise above the far bank of the river to see two "pingos" about 5 kilometers away. These conical mounds are formed when a core of ice pushes upward from water-saturated sediments. Geologists believe these particular pingos are more than 5,000 years old.

The road soon passes Chapman Lake, which offers nesting habitat to mew gulls and red-throated loons and is occasionally a staging area for tundra swans. To the east, the long, low ridge is thought to be an ancient glacial moraine, marking the eastern limit of glacial expansion from the cordilleran ice sheet to the east.

The former Gwitch'in encampment of Blackstone Village is located near this spot on the banks of the river. The encampment was on a traditional Gwitch'in travel route that extended from the Fort MacPherson area up the Wind River through the valley of the Blackstone and then over Seela Pass to follow the Chandindu River to the present site of Dawson. The Mounted Police adopted this route in 1904 for winter dog-sled patrols, which were led by Gwitch'in guides.

On December 21, 1910, a Sergeant Fitzgerald led a patrol out of Fort MacPherson, after inexplicably hiring a white trapper as a guide instead of one of the Gwitch'ins. The Mounties failed to reach Dawson by February 20, and Corporal W.J.D. Dempster was sent to search for the "Lost Patrol." He discovered their bodies near the headwaters of the Little Wind River and brought them to Fort MacPherson, where their graves can still be seen. Fitzgerald's diary was recovered, and the following entry was recorded for January 17, 1911:

> We have now only ten pounds of flour and eight pounds of bacon and some dried fish. My last hope is gone, and the only thing I can do is return, and kill some dogs to feed the others and ourselves, unless we can meet some Indians. We have now been a week looking for a river to take us over the divide, but there are dozens of rivers and I am at a loss. I should not have taken Carter's word that he knew the way from the Little Wind River.

From that time until the last patrol departed in 1921, the Mounties were required to hire Gwitch'in guides for the winter patrol.

At the far end of the basin, the Taiga Range rises to form a massive wall, its south-facing slopes clad in white spruce. The gray limestone of the peaks is streaked with red and orange, the result of sulphur and oxidizing iron compounds within the rock. The slope of the peaks has been determined by the "angle of repose"—the greatest angle at which rock can keep from sliding down the mountain.

The highway jogs westward to follow a bouldery wash high into the mountains. At the top of the grade at Kilometer 153 is Windy Pass, where dry tundra vegetation is thought to be a remnant of the mammoth steppes that spread throughout the Yukon and Alaska during the ice ages. Several species of rare butterflies and moths are indigenous to this area, including one moth whose caterpillars eat only a certain species of lichen and whose adult females are flightless.

As the road descends into the valley beyond, watch for caribou migration trails on the unstable boulder slopes. Red Creek soon enters the Blackstone from the west, bearing water that is brightly stained by sulphur and other minerals. The Gwitch'ins call this stream *Chuu Tsanh Njik*, or "Stinking Waters Creek," and according to their legends, the mythic hero Willow Man defeated a giant beaver along its banks. This part of the Yukon was actually inhabited by 25-foot-tall beavers during the Pleistocene era, and humans have inhabited the region for at least 23,000 years. This legend may represent one of the oldest cultural memories in existence!

The road continues down the valley, following Engineer Creek. Dall sheep come to the creekside mineral licks at Kilometers 180 and 186 in early summer to ingest calcium and magnesium. Watch for eroded pillars of dolomite, a metamorphosed limestone, rising from the weaker beds of limestone and shale. These "tors" indicate that these mountains remained glacier-free—they would have been sheared away if any glacial ice had passed through the valley.

A distinctive, tor-covered hogback called Sapper Hill rises above the lower reaches of Engineer Creek. "Sapper" is military slang for a combat engineer, and both the hill and the creek were named for the Third Royal Canadian Engineers, who built the bridge over the Ogilvie River as a field exercise. There is a campground where the creek flows into the Ogilvie, and you can sometimes find fossil corals northeast of the bridge.

The Ogilvie River and Mountains were named in honor of Canadian surveyor William Ogilvie, who surveyed the Alaska-Yukon border and helped to settle the boundary disputes that came with the gold rush. According to measurements by modern satellite, Ogilvie's line of demarcation was only 66 meters (218 feet) off the true 141st parallel, a remarkable achievement given his primitive tools and the hostile environment.

After crossing the river, the road follows it downstream beneath a ridge castellated with eroded rock. The mountains surrounding the river often

Tors of dolomite rise from the flanks of Sapper Ridge, in the Taiga Range.

feature symmetrical slopes or rock debris. Churchward Hill guards the spot where the river leaves the Ogilvie Mountains. It is known to the Gwitch'ins as *Chii Akan,* or "Beaver House Mountain." The giant beaver of Gwitch'in legend is said to have lived here.

As the road follows the river through a forested lowland, you might catch a glimpse of the much smaller modern beaver in the water. The Ogilvie River joins the Blackstone far downstream to form the Peel River, which the road will meet beyond the Richardson Mountains.

The road soon begins the long climb to the top of the Eagle Plains. This feature is not a "plains" at all, but a high plateau built of horizontal layers of sandstone. Contrary to its name, eagles are extremely rare here. From the top, there are fine parting views of the Ogilvies as the road follows rounded hilltops clad alternately in open tundra and stunted black spruce forest. Cotton grass unleashes its snow-white "blossoms" in the wet pockets, while fireweed and foxtail grass lend color to the roadsides. The black spruce ultimately closes in around the road, forming an unbroken forest that seems to stretch forever. There are frequent signs of forest fire, a disturbance to which the black spruce is well-adapted.

The road ultimately begins to descend and reaches the Eagle Plains service community at Kilometer 363. You will get your first view of the Richardson Mountains from this area. The Richardsons are a rounded, tundra-covered range with sedimentary origins like the Ogilvies to the south.

The road descends to the Eagle River, where the most dramatic man-hunt in Yukon history ended. Albert Johnson, popularized as "the Mad Trapper of Rat River," was accused of tampering with native trap lines during the early winter of 1931. Mounties confronted him at his cabin, and Johnson killed one of them and escaped into the night. The ensuing chase covered two months and hundreds of miles while the weather hovered below minus 40 degrees. For the first time in the Yukon, an aircraft was used to hunt a man. The Mounties caught up with Johnson just downstream from the bridge over the Eagle River. Johnson saw his pursuers across a narrow neck between river curves and mistakenly assumed that they had gotten ahead of him as well. He made his last stand on the ice, where the Mounties shot him to death. He is buried in the cemetery at Aklavik, in the heart of the Mackenzie Delta.

The Eagle River appears too small and sluggish to have created the large bluffs that line it, and the reason for this odd phenomenon goes back to Pleistocene times. At the height of the ice ages, the Cordilleran Ice Sheet extended as far west as the Richardson Mountains in an unbroken wall thousands of feet high. The ice dammed the Peel River, which rose to form Glacial Lake Bonnet Plume. The lake covered much of the northern Yukon. The water finally found an outlet and drained westward into the Porcupine River

Vast expanses of tundra clothe the Richardson Mountains.

system. In doing so, it carved the bluffs that we see today. When the Cordilleran Ice Sheet retreated, the Peel returned to its original course, leaving only a small stream to drain through the former outlet channel.

At the same time, pre-Columbian peoples migrated across the Bering Land Bridge while ocean levels were low and began populating the northern Yukon interior. Implements from Old Crow Flats, to the west along the Porcupine, have been estimated at 26,000 years old. The oldest undisputed dates come from the neighboring Bluefish Caves, which were inhabited 23,000 years ago. These people were nomadic hunters who made microblade points to hunt the mammals of the mammoth steppe. It is likely that this part of North America was continuously inhabited longer than any other. In recognition of this fact, the Canadian government has designated the Old Crow Flats a cultural heritage park. You must get a permit to fly into the village of Old Crow, home of the Vuntut Gwitch'ins and one of the oldest settlements in the world.

After crossing the Eagle River, the road climbs back into uplands dominated by larch, a conifer that sheds its needles in a fiery fall display and stands dormant throughout the long Arctic winter. You will have excellent views of the Richardson Mountains as the uplands parallel this tundra-clad chain. At Kilometer 405.5, there is a large pullout at the crossing of the Arctic Circle. North of this point, the sun never sets at the height of summer. Watch for white spruce growing as ground-hugging "krummholz" and for frost boils caused by freezing in layers of fine sediment.

The road crosses the tundra at the foot of the mountains as it continues northward, and at Kilometer 445 it reaches the valley of the Rock River. This forested declivity serves as a natural funnel for migrating caribou, and the Gwitch'ins once constructed caribou fences with snares and corrals in this area.

Just beyond the Rock River, the highway turns eastward to cross the Richardson Mountains. The first pass is known as George's Gap, and it leads into a tundra-clad basin that bears the headwaters of the Vittrekwa River. Frost-riven boulders within the soil have come to the surface and been sorted by frost action to form "stone nets."

The highway climbs a long grade to reach Wright Pass on the crest of the eastern cordillera of the Richardson Mountains at Kilometer 465. This marks the Yukon-Northwest Territories border. Kilometer posts ahead count northward from zero beginning at the border, and you should set your clocks and watches to Mountain Standard time. From this point on, watch for "inukshuks" along the side of the road. These stone cairns take the shape of human figures and were originally used by the Inuits to drive caribou. Hunters would stand in a funnel formation, with inukshuks between them to create the impression of greater numbers. The caribou would be driven into the funnel, and at its narrow end spearmen would wait to kill them.

The road drops onto the endless tundra uplands of the Peel Plateau, which was covered by the Cordilleran Ice Sheet during the Pleistocene. The plateau is sprinkled sparsely with kettle lakes, formed when chunks of ice buried by the receding ice melted to form depressions. The largest of these is Midway Lake at Kilometer 44, about halfway between Eagle Plains and Inuvik. It is not known for fishing, but it is the site of a bluegrass festival each July.

Shrubs and dwarfed black spruces begin to encroach as the road approaches the river. An abundance of blueberries and bright-orange cloudberries is available for the picking. Pause at the edge of the plateau for a final look at the Richardson Mountains on the western horizon before descending into the valley of the Peel. You will pass several marshy lakes on the way to a free government ferry across the river at Kilometer 74.

The far bank is a traditional fishing spot for the Gwitch'ins, who net whitefish and inconnu here. They call it *Nutuiluie*, which means "waterfall," for the tributary that enters the river just upstream. Boat tours leave this area for Shiltee Rock, and from there it is only a short hike to a distinctive overlook.

The highway runs north along the riverbank, passing Gwitch'in fishing camps and smokehouses on the way to Fort MacPherson. This frontier post was established by John Bell of the Hudson's Bay Company in 1840. Initially, both the Gwitch'in and Inuvialuit people traded here, but hostilities between the two groups prompted the Inuvialuit to establish their own trading post at Aklavik, the northernmost port of call on the Mackenzie River system. It also served as a northern base for the North-West Mounted Police. Members of the failed Fitzgerald patrol are buried in the cemetery here.

The road now runs eastward, crossing the lowlands of the Peel River Game Sanctuary. Black spruce cover the lowlands, while taller white spruce cling to the few well-drained hillocks. The largest trees in this area are more than 300 years old and yet are only 30 centimenters (1 foot) in diameter.

After 58 kilometers, the road reaches a free ferry at the confluence of the Mackenzie and Arctic Red rivers. The Mackenzie is one of the world's great waterways and one of the few that flows almost entirely through wilderness. Alexander Mackenzie explored the river by canoe in 1784, in the service of the North-West Company.

During periods of high water, the Mackenzie fills with drifting logs. Jack McQuesten floated through in the spring of 1873 and remarked, "We would tie our canoe to a large log, make our fire on the roots to boil our tea kettle and drift night and day."

The ferry will take your vehicle either to the village of Arctic Red River or to the northbound road to Inuvik on request. Arctic Red River is a quaint settlement featuring a red-roofed Catholic mission established in 1868. Its inhabitants fish for whitefish and inconnu and hunt caribou on the Anderson Lowlands to the east. The Dempster Highway makes a beeline to the north, crossing muskeg lowlands with views of the distant mountains to the west.

At Kilometer 178, the road crosses the small Rengling River, which is a lekking ground for sharp-tailed grouse. Males of this species gather at common spots to "boom" and display their feathered finery for the females, which come from miles around to select the most fit and attractive mates.

You will cross Caribou Creek 35 kilometers to the north. It has a free campground on its banks. As the highway approaches Inuvik, the Campbell Hills appear to the northwest. These low bluffs were sheared off long ago by ice sheets. At their foot is the broad expanse of Campbell Lake. The road runs around the north shore of the lake and then crosses through the hills.

The road is paved after it passes a spur to the airport. To the west lies the Mackenzie Delta, an alluvial fan of almost 20,000 square kilometers (7,500 square miles), roughly the size of Massachusetts. It is a labyrinth of channels and lakes, more water than land. It is an important breeding ground for waterfowl, as well as for muskrats. The Mackenzie River warms the soil of the delta, thawing the permafrost and enabling black spruce to grow all the way north to the edge of the Arctic Ocean. Chuk Park, at Kilometer 306, has an observation platform that looks out over this maze of waterways. For a better view, take a boat or "flight-seeing" tour out of Inuvik.

The Canadian government built the town of Inuvik beginning in 1955, as a hub for oil exploration in the high Arctic. The pastel-colored buildings are elevated on stilts so that the permafrost beneath them will not melt and buckle. *Inuvik* is an Inuit word meaning "Place of Man." The Inuits (formerly called Eskimos) and Gwitch'ins both live here. The visitor center also serves as a museum that highlights both cultures. "Flight-seeing" and boat tours leave Inuvik for the Mackenzie Delta and the remote wilderness parks of the Canadian Arctic.

15

Top of the World Highway

Official Designation: Yukon Highway 9
Description: Gravel road from Dawson City, Yukon Territory, to a junction with Taylor Highway in Alaska; 127 kilometers (79 miles)
Recommended Maximum: 65 kph/40 mph
Hazards: Severe washboards and potholes develop following wet weather; no guardrails
Distance Markers: Kilometer posts count west from Dawson City
Further Reading: *Gold at Fortymile Creek* by Michael Gates
Information Sources: Klondike Visitors Association

 ## The Drive

This highway climbs through the high country west of Dawson City, providing an alternate route into Alaska. It follows the route of an old pack trail that once connected Dawson City with the gold-bearing streams around the Sixtymile River. Eventually, the trail was improved and became known as Ridge Road. In 1930, it was punched through to Jack Wade Creek and Chicken, two of Alaska's important gold-bearing sites in the Fortymile drainage. It was not until the late 1940s that the Taylor Highway was built, linking the Fortymile country with the rest of the state via the Alaska Highway.

Most of the road traverses alpine country, offering expansive views in all directions. It is narrow and winding in sections, and guardrails are rare. It is also prone to potholes and washboards, especially after wet weather. Drivers of large RVs or vehicles towing trailers might want to avoid this road. It is not plowed in winter and effectively closes with the first heavy snow.

From Dawson City, the drive begins with a free ferry trip across the broad Yukon River. At the height of the tourist season, you may have to wait several hours to get across. The only way to be sure of a short line is to arrive early at the ferry dock, preferably before 10 a.m.

On the far bank, the road passes the large Yukon River Campground. A stern-wheeler "graveyard" is located on the riverbank a short stroll north of the campground. Here, three paddle-wheelers built in 1898 have been hauled onto dry land and are falling into varying stages of ruin. They are the

Seattle III, the *Julia B.*, and the *Schwatka*. Exercise extreme caution when exploring the ruins: they are both dangerous and fragile.

Across the river from this site is the Hän Indian village of Moosehide, which you can see from the highway as the road begins to climb. This band of river-dwellers was displaced from the region at the mouth of the Klondike River by the construction of Dawson City. Before the arrival of whites, the Häns fished for the chum and king salmon that swam up the Yukon in the summer. They used nets woven from bark and roots, weirs constructed of poles driven into the riverbed, and cylindrical fish traps. They dried much of the catch and stored it in underground caches for winter use. During the autumn, the Häns split into small groups and moved into the mountains to the north to hunt and gather wild berries.

As the road climbs, you will have good views to the south of small farms on the Yukon River bottomland. Moosehide has been inhabited since ancient times; projectile points found here date back 8,000 to 10,000 years.

The road crests the top of a high plateau, and you will spend the remainder of the drive following the ridgetops above timberline. Views stretch away in all directions, initially highlighted by the Ogilvie Mountains to the north. Close at hand, tors rise from the mountaintops, indicating that the highlands were ice-free during the Pleistocene epoch.

At Kilometer 59, a spur road leads 40 kilometers (25 miles) to Clinton Creek, where the ruins of Fortymile guard the mouth of the Fortymile River.

The mountaintop customs stations at Poker Creek.

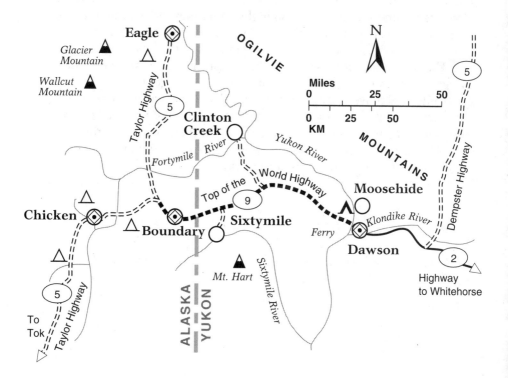

A major gold rush occurred on the Fortymile in 1887, spawning a town that had bakeries, restaurants, blacksmith shops, and two trading posts, as well as the Alaska Commercial Company in town and the Fort Cudahy post on the opposite bank of the Fortymile. In the winter of 1896, George Carmack walked into town with nuggets as "big as beans." The entire population of Fortymile pulled up stakes and rushed to the Klondike. Within a few days, Fortymile had become a ghost town. Mining continued on the Fortymile for many years afterward, but the town never recovered, and it now stands completely abandoned. The access road to Clinton Creek is used as a take-out point by floaters on the Fortymile River system.

In the distance, you can see Wallcut and Glacier mountains, which rise above the headwaters of the Charley River far to the northwest. At Kilometer 86, a gravel road descends to the east, bound for an active gold-mining district on the Sixtymile River that was first mined in 1891. Fortymile is located forty river miles below Dawson City, while the Sixtymile River joins the Yukon sixty miles *above* Dawson. The highest of the peaks visible to the east of this junction is Mount Hart (1,621 meters/5,318 feet). Nineteen kilometers beyond the junction, the highway reaches the mountaintop customs station at Poker Creek, Alaska (population: 2 customs agents).

The road drops into a low saddle and reaches the tiny burg of Boundary. The roadhouse here is one of the oldest in Alaska, and you can see placer workings in the creek bottoms below the lodge. Caribou from the Fortymile herd move through this area in the autumn and commonly block the airstrip runway. The road ends at a junction with the Taylor Highway 16 kilometers (10 miles) beyond Boundary. From there, you can drive north on a road that dead-ends at the town of Eagle on the Yukon River, or you can turn south to meet the Alaska Highway.

ALASKA

Alaska is known the world over as one of the most pristine and beautiful places left on Earth. It is a young land, formed by wandering tectonic plates that over time have collided with the North American land mass. The force of the collisions led to the creation of the lofty Saint Elias Mountains, the Alaska Range, the Chugach Mountains, and the Brooks Range. Alaska's position on the Pacific Rim places it in the heart of the so-called Ring of Fire. Impressive chains of volcanoes form the Wrangell Mountains and the Aleutian Islands. Glaciers have sculpted razor-edge ridges, sharp pinnacles, and deep U-shaped valleys. In parts of the state, vast ice fields crown the peaks, and long valley glaciers pour from the heights and onto the lowlands. Along the coast, these glaciers may calve to create icebergs in the deep and narrow fjords, carved by even greater glaciers during the ice ages.

Twenty thousand years before Columbus sailed to the New World, the forebears of the Alaskan natives walked across the land bridge that joined Alaska and Siberia during the ice ages. At that time, the interior of Alaska and the Yukon was an endless grassland populated by woolly mammoths, giant bison, cave bears, and saiga antelope. The newly arrived nomads had found a rich hunting ground and dispersed throughout the region. Their descendants are the coastal Indians that live along the Inside Passage today, as well as the Athapaskan tribes that inhabit the interior. The Aleuts called their majestic homeland Alyeska, or "The Great Land." Thousands of years later, Inuit people arrived in kayaks and baidarkas made from seal hides. These were maritime people, and they settled along the coastline from the Arctic Ocean to Prince William Sound. Alaska's native population has had a lasting influence on the culture of the forty-ninth state, and in some places they continue to live a subsistence lifestyle much as they always have.

During separate voyages in 1728 and 1741, Vitus Bering became the first European to explore and chart the coastline of present-day Alaska, claiming it for the Russian czar Peter the Great. Bering was looking for a land bridge between continents, a feature that lives on in the oral traditions of the Siberian Eskimos. He found a land much like the Russian ports he had left, and soon fur-trading companies established posts along the coastline to trade with the native peoples.

Russia maintained a presence in Alaska for almost a century, but the Russians never penetrated far inland. When the czar's empire weakened and Alaska became vulnerable to the imperialistic schemes of other world powers, Russia sold the territory to the United States for $50 million. Americans viewed the territory as a barren wasteland inhabited only by Eskimos, but gold strikes soon convinced the populace that this northern frontier was a land of opportunity. It has been attracting pioneers, explorers, renegades, and fortune seekers ever since.

Visitors to Alaska will find a land steeped in frontier history and eagerly straining to embrace the future. In this seemingly limitless landscape of forest, mountains, and tundra, you can find the solitude and peace that is so markedly absent from modern society. Most of Alaska's land is still owned by the federal government and is open to all. Some of the most outstanding areas are being protected within an extensive system of parks, preserves, and wildlife refuges. For hikers, fishermen, hunters, and solitude seekers of all kinds, Alaska represents the last place in the United States where they can pursue their hearts' desire in a land unblemished by commercial development.

The Alaskan road system is a network of paved highways and good-quality gravel thoroughfares. Although the roads penetrate a vast area with outstanding natural features, 75 percent of the state is unaccessible by automobile.

16

Alaska Highway

Official Designation: Alaska Route 2
Description: Paved highway from Dawson Creek, British Colum-
bia, to Delta Junction, Alaska; 1,390 miles (2,238 kilometers)
Recommended Maximum: Highway speeds
Distance Markers: Mileposts count north from Dawson Creek
Information Sources: Tetlin National Wildlife Refuge, Tok Chamber
of Commerce

 The Drive

The final leg of the Alaska Highway traverses the upper basin of the
Tanana River, a region of lake-studded lowlands and distant mountain ranges.
Because the United States has not yet converted to the metric system, distances are now expressed in miles, and you should note that the roadside
mileposts indicate the distance from Dawson Creek before the route was
shortened by straightening out its curves. If you are bound for Fairbanks,
you eventually need to turn to the Richardson Highway description (Drive
18) for the final leg from Delta Junction. The fastest route to Anchorage
turns south at Tok, following the Tok Cutoff and Glenn Highway.

Along the Tanana Lowlands

Beyond the U.S. customs station, the road crosses a boggy lowland
before taking to the hills once more. Watch for rusting sections of a pipeline
built in 1954 to carry fuel from Haines into the Alaskan interior. The Tetlin
National Wildlife Refuge stretches southward from the highway, and it has a
visitor reception center at Mile 1229. Its observation deck looks out over
the lakes of the Chisana River valley. This river rises from the glaciers of the
Wrangell Mountains and works its way northward through a gap in the
smaller Nutzotin Range. Below the visitor center, it bends to the west on its
way to join the Nabesna River to form the Tanana.

The Chisana has carved its own niche in the gold-rush history of the
Far North. In 1913, two miners found a rich placer lode on a small tributary
stream many miles to the south. They named the stream Little Eldorado
Creek, and it is said that they extracted more than 200 ounces of gold from

its gravel in a period of several hours. News of their success brought a stampede of newcomers, but few found riches to compare with the original strike. The gold soon played out and the men moved on, leaving few traces of their presence.

The highway continues to wind among the hills, passing Island Lake within 2 miles of the visitor center. Southbound travelers will get the best views of this scenic gem, which lies nestled in a hollow north of the road. Ten miles beyond the lake, a series of vertical culvert pipes has been embedded in the road embankments. The pipes are designed to dissipate heat from the roadbed into the air, thus slowing the thaw of the permafrost below.

The road reaches the eastern edge of the Tetlin Hills at Mile 1280, and an overlook faces northward for final views of the muskeg. The highway skirts across the southern edge of the hills, which stretch almost all the way to Tok. A broad basin to the south is dotted with lakes and rimmed by the distant crags of the Nutzotin Mountains. The taller of the Wrangell Mountains rise in snow-capped majesty beyond this rocky wall.

The low-lying flats to the south are classified as a "solar basin" because they are much warmer in the summer than the surrounding slopes. Clouds often cling to the mountains, but the high-pressure systems that are so prevalent in the Alaskan interior keep the basins cloud-free. The snow and ice melt comparatively early here, and the long summer days are quite warm.

This is an ideal climate for nesting waterfowl, which breed along the lakes and sloughs that dot the lowlands. Trumpeter swans first colonized the refuge in the early 1980s, and by 1995 the population had grown to more than 400 breeding pairs. In winter, when the waterfowl are gone, cold air flows down from the mountains and pools in the basin, making for extremely cold temperatures. Nonetheless, caribou from the Mentasta and Nelchina herds often winter on these lowlands.

You can see numerous lakes and ponds from the highway as it follows the hillsides westward to reach Northway Junction at Mile 1264. A 7-mile spur road runs southward from this point, crossing marshes, ponds, and sluggish streams to reach the native village of Northway. The Nabesna River flows from its glacial origins in the south, joining the Chisana River near this point to form the mighty Tanana. This great river of the interior swings close to the highway for several miles beyond Northway Junction. The mountains on the horizon form an unbroken line; to the west of the Nabesna River they are the Nutzotin Mountains, while to the east the crags are called the Mentasta Mountains. All are an eastward extension of the great Alaska Range, which rises more than 20,000 feet at its highest point.

The Tetlin Hills die away as the road passes Tetlin Junction (Mile 1302), where the Taylor Highway branches northward toward Dawson City and

Alaska Highway

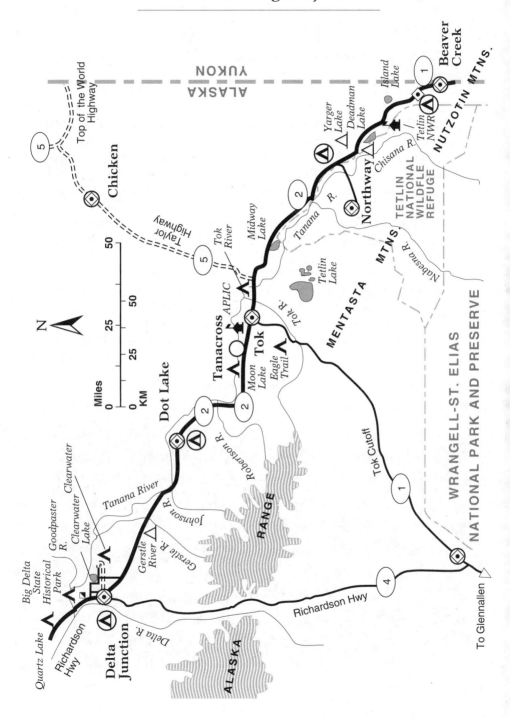

the Fortymile country. After crossing the Tok River, the road runs across lowlands burned during an extensive wildfire in 1989. The following year, mushroom pickers flooded into the area to harvest a bumper crop of morels, which grow abundantly in the wake of forest fires.

The highway enters the crossroads town of Tok at Mile 1314. The town boasts an excellent visitor center, with lifelike mounts of local wildlife. There is also an Alaska Public Lands Information Center, which can provide information about the entire state.

After leaving Tok, the highway runs westward toward the base of some rugged peaks, the outer palisades of the Alaska Range. A spur road runs northward from Mile 1326 to reach the Tanana Indian village of Tanacross, on the banks of the Tanana River. There are extensive sphagnum bogs along the highway in this area, where bog blueberries are ready for picking in mid-August.

The highway skirts the base of the mountains, offering excellent views of the rugged peaks. After crossing Cathedral Creek at Mile 1338, it swings away from the mountains and crosses the Robertson River. This waterway is one of many young, high-gradient rivers that carry rock down from the Alaska Range to be deposited at the edge of the Tanana lowlands. Great fans of gravel have built up below the skirts of the mountains, and this apron of alluvial rubble has pushed the Tanana River against the far wall of the basin.

The highway passes through the tiny burg of Dot Lake at Mile 1361.

Numerous trusses carry the Alaska Highway over the braided channels of the Gerstle River.

Watch out for small planes landing and taking off on the highway. As the road crosses the Gerstle River, there are excellent views up the waterway of the snow-capped crags of the Alaska Range. A bison range stretches south of the highway from the Gerstle River all the way to Delta Junction. The bison were planted here in the 1920s, and their population grew steadily in the years that followed. The Alaska Department of Fish and Game has cleared blocks of the forest south of the road and planted forage crops in an effort to lure the bison away from the barley fields near Delta Junction. This is mostly a winter range, and you will rarely spot bison along this stretch of highway.

On the approach to Delta Junction, there is a homestead museum at Mile 1415.4. Delta Junction was one of the first parts of the state to be homesteaded, and it continues to be the only agricultural area in the Alaskan interior. The Alaska Highway ends at a junction with the Richardson Highway in the center of town. If you plan to continue northwest to Fairbanks, turn to Drive 18 for the Richardson Highway description.

17

Taylor Highway

Official Designation: Alaska Route 5
Description: Winding gravel highway that runs 160 miles (258 kilometers) from Alaska Highway to Eagle, Alaska
Recommended Maximum: 40 mph/65 kph
Hazards: Potholes and washboards possible; too narrow for large RVs or trailers beyond junction with Top of the World Highway
Distance Markers: Mileposts count northward from junction with Alaska Highway
Further Reading: *Coming into the Country* by John McPhee, *Tisha* by Ann Purdy
Information Sources: Bureau of Land Management (Tok Office), Yukon-Charley National Preserve, Eagle Historical Society

 The Drive

This highway runs through the forested domes of the Alaskan interior, passing through the Fortymile gold fields. It follows the route of the old Eagle-Valdez Telegraph Trail, surveyed in part by Lieutenant Billy Mitchell, who was later to become the father of the U.S. Air Force. This area is a mecca for canoeists as it features the Fortymile National Wild and Scenic River and Yukon-Charley National Preserve. About halfway to Eagle, the Taylor Highway joins the Top of the World Highway, which leads to Dawson City, Yukon Territory. There are steep and narrow sections beyond this point, so large RVs and vehicles pulling trailers should not attempt to proceed northward from this junction.

The road reaches a dead end on the banks of the Yukon River, where the town of Eagle is one of the most authentic Alaskan frontier settlements that you can reach by road. The highway is open from March to October and is not maintained during the winter.

The Taylor Highway begins by wandering upward through rounded hills that are heavily timbered in spruce and hardwoods. Permafrost and recurrent forest fires have turned the forest into a patchwork of different plant communities and stand ages. At Mile 4.9, a half-mile trail leads eastward to Four Mile Lake, a popular fishing spot for rainbow trout. Road cuts

Taylor Highway

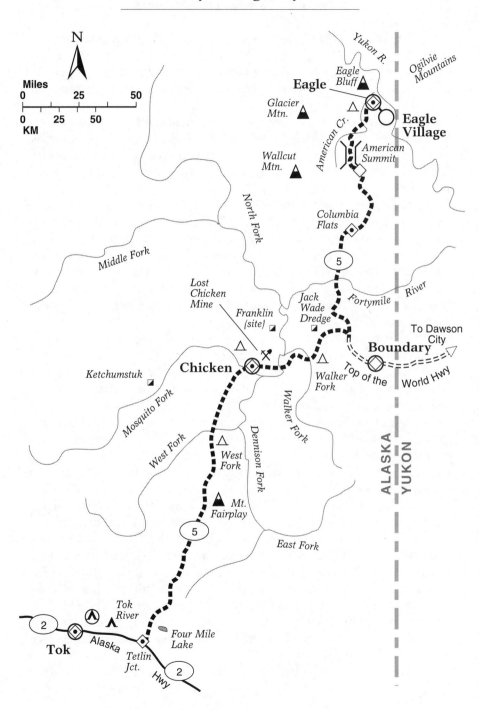

reveal that the initial hillocks are stabilized sand dunes, left over from the ice ages when huge amounts of sandy outwash were deposited nearby by the Gulkana and Chisana glaciers.

The road soon mounts high domes, and the forest thins to reveal views of the Alaska Range and Mentasta Mountains. Straight ahead, the rugged peak that rears its summit above the hilltops is Mount Fairplay, created when molten syenite (a form of granite) intruded into the crumbly metamorphic rock of the surrounding country.

There are additional distant views as the road climbs onto the flanks of Mount Fairplay. Around Mile 31 are several "pingos," or ice-cored mounds. These are formed when ice lenses, lens-shaped disks of ice, build up beneath the tundra at the sites of artesian springs or old, water-saturated pond sediments.

The road soon descends into the folds of the hills, crossing Logging Cabin Creek at the bottom of the grade. This stream was named for an early timber operation located where the creek joins the Dennison Fork of the Fortymile River. Logging Cabin Creek marks the southern boundary of the Fortymile National Wild and Scenic River system. This area, managed by the Bureau of Land Management, was set aside to preserve the remote and beautiful Fortymile watershed, with its many river forks that offer world-class canoeing.

The road soon enters country that burned during the 1967 Chicken Fire, which began with a lightning strike and covered 40 square miles (100 square kilometers) of forest. The fire burned in patches and fingers, pushed into fuel-rich stands of timber by the prevailing winds. Many islands of trees were left standing in the midst of the burn, and these provided a haven for wildlife as well as seed stock for reforesting the burned area. There is a campground at Mile 49.5 as the road crosses the West Fork, one of six major forks of the Fortymile River. After crossing flat bottomlands, the road crosses the Mosquito Fork and enters the placer-mining community of Chicken, Alaska.

The bridge over Chicken Creek stands in the center of "town," if you want to call it that, and the ghost town of Franklin lies just over the ridge to the north. It was at the mouth of Franklin Gulch in 1886 that Howard Franklin found the first gold in the Fortymile country. His claim yielded $60,000 in the first year, and prospectors soon converged upon the site. A rough-hewn mining community sprang up and was dubbed "Dogtown" for its abundance of canines. The miners called a meeting and decided to reduce the size of mining claims so that more gold seekers could work the tiny gulch. Franklin declined steadily after its initial boom, and by 1948 it was totally abandoned.

Chicken's gold rush came in the wake of the Franklin findings, with a

The old Jack Wade dredge stands abandoned north of Chicken.

prospector named Bob Mathieson staking the first claim in 1896. The town grew quickly and soon became the major hub of the southern Fortymile District. Miners originally wanted to call the town "Ptarmigan," after the game bird that was common here at that time. However, no one could spell it, so they settled for "Chicken," the bird's colloquial name.

A two-story roadhouse was built in 1906, and a number of old cabins and former businesses from this era still stand on private land. Tours leave from the cafe. Among the buildings is the school where Ann Purdy taught. It formed the setting for her novel, Tisha. A gold dredge that worked Chicken Creek until the 1960s was abandoned north of the road, but tall brush makes it difficult to see.

The road climbs Lost Chicken Hill, named for a gold deposit or "pay streak" that remained undiscovered for many years and so was considered "lost" in the parlance of the miners. The Lost Chicken Mine is on the far side of the hill, and the bones of numerous Ice Age mammals have been unearthed there. They indicate that humans hunted bison and mammoths in this area as recently as 10,380 years ago.

The road crosses the hillsides to reach the South Fork of the Fortymile and then climbs a long grade above the valley of the Walker Fork. Far below, the river has cut its way downward through several domes of bedrock.

The road ultimately drops from the high country to the banks of Jack

Wade Creek. This stream, named for its discoverers, Jack Anderson and Wade Nelson, yielded one of the richest gold fields of the Fortymile District. The largest nugget washed from its gravel weighed 70 ounces. The Alaska-Yukon border was still in dispute during the gold rush, so miners filed their claims in both Eagle, Alaska, and in Dawson City, Yukon Territory. The old Jack Wade dredge stands abandoned and rusting beside the road at Mile 86. Originally powered by a wood-burning boiler, this dredge was used until 1942. Many of Alaska's mining operations were suspended by law during World War II to free men and heavy equipment for the war effort.

After climbing away from the headwaters of Jack Wade Creek, the road joins the Top of the World Highway just west of Boundary. Beware: steep and narrow sections lie ahead! Bear left to stay on the Taylor Highway, which climbs into the sparsely wooded hilltops for sweeping views in all directions. After a pleasant jaunt through the high country, it makes a winding and perilous descent to cross the main stem of the Fortymile River. A boat launch here is one of the main put-in and take-out points on the river.

The road runs up the valley of O'Brien Creek, which is underlain by shallow permafrost. Stands of white spruce occupy the sunnier south-facing slopes, while the colder north-facing slopes harbor spindly black spruce. Tundra sweeps all the way to the valley floor in places.

There is a lodge with some services at Columbia Flats, a former homestead site at Mile 125. Then the road enters the area of the headwaters of O'Brien Creek, a traditional caribou hunting ground for the Hän Indians who lived along the Yukon River. They built long fences to funnel the caribou into corrals where they could kill them easily. The Fortymile caribou herd still migrates through this area during the autumn. Once numbering more than 500,000 animals, the herd has dwindled to a fraction of its former size.

Eventually, the road begins a long ascent to the tops of tundra-clad domes. It reaches its high point at American Summit, where you will have views of Wallcut and Glacier mountains to the west. These granite peaks rise above the headwaters of the Charley River, a calving ground for the Fortymile herd.

The road ultimately drops down to the Discovery Fork of American Creek. There are a few old miners' cabins scattered along the valley floor. This was a relatively minor gold field, and the efforts of early miners were hampered by flooding of the shafts that they dug into the narrow valley floor. There are still a handful of active placer-mining operations along the main fork of the creek, which the road follows to the banks of the Yukon River. Here it reaches Eagle, perhaps the quintessential Alaskan frontier town.

The settlement began as a trading post called "Belle Isle," established by François Mercier in 1880. The town boomed briefly when gold was discovered in American Creek in 1895 and gained legitimacy in 1901 when Judge James Wickersham chose Eagle as the site of the new federal courthouse. Wickersham's jurisdiction stretched from the Aleutian Islands to the Arctic Ocean, one of the largest judicial districts in American history. During the same year, Eagle became the first incorporated city in Alaska. The Army had a brief presence here at Fort Egbert, a small frontier post that was the northern terminus of the WAMCATS (Washington-Alaska Military Cable and Telegraph System).

The town was briefly famous in 1905 when Arctic explorer Roald Amundsen mushed 1,000 miles to Eagle from his icebound sloop on the Arctic Ocean to tell the world of his successful navigation of the Northwest Passage. By 1911, the population of the town had dwindled away to a few hundred, and it has remained low since. Percy DeWolfe, the "Iron Man of the North," made weekly mail runs by dog sled between Eagle and Dawson from 1915 to 1950. The 210-mile run took DeWolfe four days; with advances in modern technology, the same mail now takes 18 days.

Eagle retains much of its turn-of-the-century charm. Many of the original log cabins still serve as residences, and numerous historic structures have been restored or rebuilt. Structures of note include the Northern Commercial Company store and warehouse, the federal courthouse, a customs house, the Eagle Roadhouse, and a well house that still serves most of the town. The few remaining buildings at Fort Egbert have been restored by the Bureau of Land Management. The Eagle Historical Society conducts walking tours of the historic buildings. They begin each morning at the courthouse. The headquarters for Yukon-Charley National Preserve is also located in town, beside the Fort Egbert parade ground. A short road leads east along the riverbank to Eagle Village, home to a community of Hän Indians.

Eagle sits astride the Tintina Fault, one of the oldest and largest fault systems in the Far North. The Ogilvie Mountains across the river are part of the original North American plate, which in Alaska occupies a narrow wedge of land between the Yukon and Porcupine rivers. South of the river, the hills are part of the Yukon-Tanana terrane, a small wandering plate that rammed into the edge of the continent in ancient times. West of town, the riverbanks are guarded by the craggy face of Eagle Bluff, a slab of volcanic greenstone formed more than 600 million years ago. Peregrine falcons nest on its sheer cliffs.

18

Richardson Highway

Official Designation: Alaska Routes 4 and 2
Description: Paved highway from Valdez to Fairbanks; 364 miles (586 kilometers)
Recommended Maximum: Highway speeds
Hazards: Frost heaves prevalent in Copper River Basin and between Delta Junction and Salcha
Distance Markers: Mileposts count north from old site of Valdez
Further Reading: *An Expedition to the Copper, Tanana, and Koyukuk Rivers in 1885* by Lieutenant Henry Allen
Information Sources: Wrangell-Saint Elias National Park, Bureau of Land Management (Glennallen District), Valdez Convention and Visitors Bureau, Delta Junction Chamber of Commerce, Fairbanks Convention and Visitors Bureau

 The Drive

The Richardson Highway is the oldest road in Alaska. It winds through the spectacular Chugach Mountains, crosses the Copper River basin, and then bisects the Alaska Range before following the Tanana River into Fairbanks. The southern part of the route was pioneered in 1902 as part of the Eagle-Valdez Trail, which followed the route of a military telegraph line. Captain William Abercrombie, who began exploring the Copper River basin in 1884, laid out the southern portions of this route. It became a major pack trail, and gold seekers blazed a spur to the Fairbanks gold fields after traveling inland from Valdez in 1902.

The trail was widened into a wagon road in 1907 by General Wilds P. Richardson, the first president of the Alaska Roads Commission. In the 1920s, it became a gravel road for automobiles, with many rough mudholes and river fords. All of the streams have since been bridged, and the route has become a modern, paved highway.

The highway begins in Valdez, a sheltered harbor on the shores of Prince William Sound surrounded by the snowy Chugach Mountains. The site was discovered by Spanish explorer Salvador Fidalgo in 1780 and was named in honor of the Spanish Minister of Marine. The Chugach Eskimos who once lived along Prince William Sound considered the site too windy and snowy for settlement; the record snowfall for a winter is 46 feet. White settlers largely ignored the spot until gold was discovered in the Klondike.

Following this gold strike, the U.S. government conceived an "all-American" route to the Klondike gold fields that ran over the Valdez and Klutina glaciers and then overland through the Alaskan interior. The first stampeders to land at Valdez found only a huddle of tents above the high-tide mark. They faced a grueling trek through untracked wilderness to reach their goal. The men strung out in long lines up the face of the Valdez Glacier, each hauling a ton of supplies by relays. They died falling into crevasses and were buried by snowslides. They suffered from scurvy because of their poor diet, and they were driven to snow-blindness and madness on the vast expanses of ice. Of the 4,000 fortune hunters who started the journey, only a few hundred even got as far as the Copper River.

In recent years, Valdez has made headlines because of a series of disasters. In 1964, the Good Friday earthquake, recorded at 9.2 on the Richter scale, demolished the old town. As the ground began to shake, the entire waterfront slid into the sea. Then a great wave caused by underwater landslides crashed into the heart of town, completing the destruction. The city was rebuilt on its current site farther west, this time on solid bedrock. Disaster struck again in 1989, when the supertanker Exxon Valdez ran aground on Bligh Reef and spilled 11 million gallons of crude oil into Prince William Sound. Containment efforts failed, and the oil slick spread as far west as Kodiak Island, leaving a trail of dead seabirds and marine mammals in its wake. Cleanup efforts are ongoing, but many of the damaged areas have been slow to recover.

The new townsite is at the mouth of Mineral Creek, on a bedrock shelf that was scooped out of the bedrock by glaciers. The Valdez Museum has displays on the history of the town, including the gold-rush years, and on the Trans-Alaska Pipeline terminal. You can view salmon and birds at Crooked Creek or take a drive on the narrow and winding Mineral Creek Road, which runs 5.5 miles into the mountains to old mine sites set in alpine scenery. Tour boats depart from Valdez to visit the spectacular Columbia Glacier, from which icebergs calve into Prince William Sound.

As the Richardson Highway leaves Valdez, it passes Duck Flat and the Crooked Creek salmon-viewing area. Pink and chum salmon return to this clear stream to spawn from mid-July through September. After emerging from their eggs in spring, the juvenile salmon reside in the brackish waters of the estuary. Bird watching is also popular here, and you may see bald eagles, Arctic terns, gadwalls, mallards, and pintails. The Forest Service maintains an interpretive station on the site.

Four miles from town, the mileposts start counting at zero at the original site of Valdez. Concrete foundations and tall brush are all that remain here. A spur road begins just west of this point and runs toward the moun-

Richardson Highway

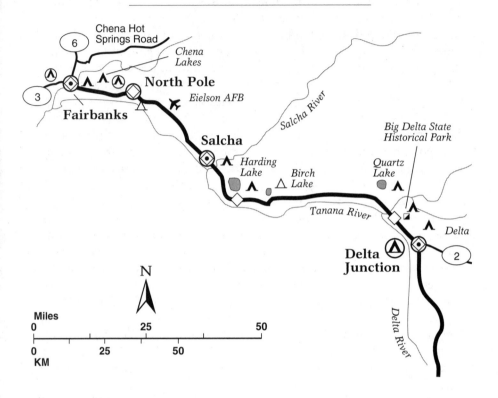

tains, passing the airport and Valdez Glacier Campground on its way to the terminal moraine of the glacier. The glacier has been retreating in recent decades, and a rather rugged hike is required to get a good view of the ice.

The Richardson Highway crosses the Valdez Glacier Stream and the Robe River on its way to a junction with the Old Dayville Road (see Old Dayville Road Sidetrip toward the end of this chapter), which follows the coastline to the Alyeska Pipeline terminal. The Richardson runs inland, following the gravelly channels of the Lowe River.

A lush forest grows on the higher ground that is not affected by annual flooding, and tall Sitka spruce and black cottonwood grow here. As the mountains wall off the head of the valley, watch the slopes ahead to see the old wagon road that led through Keystone Canyon. The canyon was originally considered impassable because of its steep, slippery walls hemming in the glacier-fed torrent of the Lowe. In 1900, Captain William Abercrombie blazed a pack trail through the canyon as he surveyed the southern leg of the Eagle-Valdez Trail. The new trail was a great improvement over the Valdez

Richardson Highway

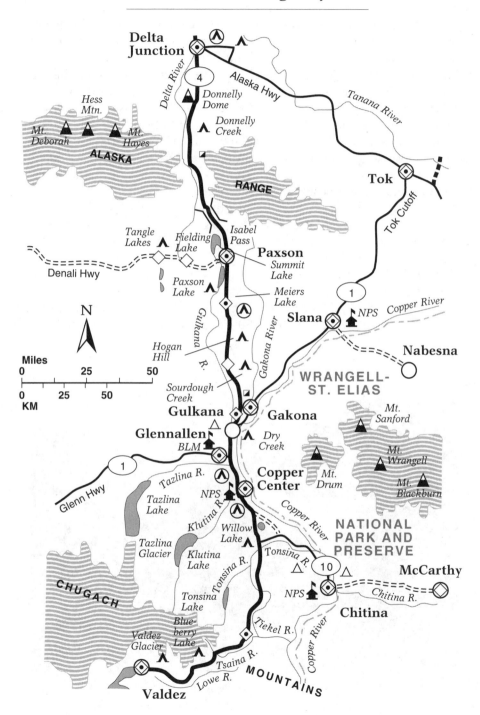

Glacier route, and it became an important travel corridor for prospectors bound for the Fairbanks gold fields in the early 1900s.

The Richardson Highway enters Keystone Canyon at Mile 13 and follows the river through it. Sheer faces of rock rise on both sides. A number of delicate waterfalls grace the canyon walls, the largest of which are Horsetail Falls and Bridalveil Falls. Just upstream of Bridalveil Falls is an unfinished tunnel that was blasted out of the rock to carry a railway to the Copper River basin. Competition was keen between Valdez and rival city Cordova to supply the tidewater rail link to the Kennecott Copper Mine. The Valdez corporation suffered from infighting, and so the Copper River and Northwest Railway was built to Cordova instead. After 3 miles, the canyon widens into a broad valley. Sheep Creek enters via a steep-walled rift to the north, and the road begins to climb toward Thompson Pass.

During your ascent, watch the mountains on the far side of the valley for glimpses of the Worthmanns and Bench glaciers. The road climbs above the timberline, rounds a hairpin turn, and passes Blueberry Lake, an alpine tarn on a tundra-clad bench that overlooks a broad panorama of peaks. The campground here is one of the prettiest in the state, and there are plenty of blueberries to pick nearby.

At Mile 26, the highway reaches Thompson Pass, which holds the Alaskan record for snowfall: more than 80 feet (24 meters) in one winter. The

The Worthington Glacier reaches almost to the highway's edge.

Twentyseven Mile Glacier forms a spectacular icefall immediately north-west of the pass. The road descends into the valley beyond, where the many lobes of the Worthington Glacier pour from the heights of Girls Mountain. A spur road leads onto the glacier's terminal moraine, giving you a close-up view of deep crevasses that emit an eerie bluish light.

The highway leaves the alpine country as it descends toward the Tsaina River. Bark beetles wiped out many of the spruce trees in this area. After crossing a bridge, you will see Billy Mitchell Peak rising to the east of the road. It was named for the young lieutenant in the Army Signal Corps who pioneered the Eagle-Valdez Trail. You will have a good view of the peak's glacier-clad north face from the historical marker at Mile 47.8.

The highway now climbs along the Tiekel River. Its bottomland offers excellent moose and beaver habitat. The beaver is a major architect in re-structuring flood plain ecosystems, as its dams divert the flow of water and its ponds eventually fill with sediment to form meadows. Pump Station Number 12 sits atop the low divide between the Tiekel and Little Tonsina rivers at Mile 65. A jet engine drives the turbines that keep the oil moving through the pipeline. The road descends along the Little Tonsina, and the Chugach Mountains dwindle away. After reaching and crossing the Tonsina River, the road climbs a long grade to emerge on the edge of the Copper River basin.

This spot marks the edge of the Wrangellia terrane, a wandering land mass that collided with North America 100 million years ago. It originated as a chain of volcanic islands off the coast of present-day California and is made up of limestone and volcanic rock. The Chugach terrane piled into its southern margin 35 million years later. The most recent addition is the Yakutat terrane, which arrived 26 million years ago. It subducted beneath the continental plate, and much of its bedrock melted deep in the earth, setting off a wave of volcanic eruptions that gave rise to the Wrangell Moun-tains.

The collision of the Yakutat terrane also caused an uplift of the Chugach terrane, creating a great plateau. Glaciers began carving the Chugach Moun-tains out of this plateau about 6.5 million years ago. Much later, the Copper River basin filled with water when glaciers in the Chugach Mountains dammed the river. The water rose to form Glacial Lake Atna. Its waters finally found an outlet through Mentasta Pass on the northern rim of the basin and flowed west to the Bering Sea by way of the Tanana and Yukon rivers.

The road passes a junction with the Edgerton Highway at Mile 82.6, and soon afterward it finds its way to the shores of Willow Lake. The view across the water is magnificent, featuring the ice-capped volcanoes of the Wrangell Mountains. The farthest to the left is Mount Drum, which was a broad shield volcano before a violent eruption and massive mudflows carried away much of its mass. Glaciers have since been whittling away the core that remains. The largest is the Nadina Glacier, which occupies the amphitheater on the southwest face and has trees and small shrubs growing at its lower end. The second peak to the left is Mount Sanford, and to its right is Mount Wrangell. The latter is the youngest of the volcanoes, and it retains the classic shield volcano form which all of the peaks once possessed. In the past, plumes of steam have been seen rising from its summit. The Athapaskan Indians of the Copper River area knew this peak as K'elt'aeni, or "the One Who Controls the Weather." The snowy pimple to the west of its summit is Mount Zanetti, a cinder cone. On the far right is Mount Blackburn, oldest and loftiest of the Wrangell volcanoes.

There are good views of the Alyeska Pipeline as the road continues northward into the heart of the Copper River basin. This is the land of the Ahtna, or Copper River, Indians. The tribe smelted copper in a primitive manner and used it to make jewelry and implements. One of the first Americans to meet this Athapaskan tribe was Lieutenant Henry Allen, on his epic expedition across the Alaskan interior in 1885. At the village of Taral (near present-day Chitina), Allen was the guest of Chief Nicolai, who was so impressed with the young explorer that he revealed the location of his personal copper deposits. These deposits would later become famous as the rich lode of the Kennecott Copper Mine.

As the highway approaches the Klutina River, a side road leads to the village of Copper Center, on the banks of the Copper River. Stampeders descending from the Klutina Glacier followed the river to this frontier outpost, where many of them spent the winter. More than 300 died of scurvy, and most of the remainder headed back to Valdez to escape the bitter winter cold of the interior. An enterprising local man named Holman bought supplies from the disheartened miners at bargain prices and sold them at a profit to finance the construction of his two-story Holman Hotel. It later became the historic Copper Center Roadhouse, a stopping point on the old Eagle-Valdez Trail. The modern roadhouse was built in 1932 using logs from the original structure, and many of the outbuildings from the 1890s still stand today. There is a small museum beside the roadhouse. Just north of town is the headquarters and main visitor center for Wrangell-Saint Elias National Park.

The highway continues northward, crossing the Tazlina River on its way to Glennallen. Along the way, there are fine views of the Copper River and the Wrangell Mountains. A pullout at Mile 112.5 offers a view of the Klawasi River mud volcanoes on the skirts of Mount Drum. The tallest of these is 150 feet high, and discharges hot water, silt, and carbon dioxide. The Glenn Highway joins the Richardson from the west at Mile 115, and the center of Glennallen lies a short distance down this highway. The Richardson continues northward, passing the Ahtna village of Gulkana at the mouth of the river of the same name. There is a primitive camping area north of the bridge. The road then climbs to Gakona Junction, where it splits away to the left at a junction with the Tok Cutoff.

The highway follows the bluff tops east of the Gulkana River. Most of the Copper River basin is underlain by permafrost that is only 1.5 feet (0.5 meters) below the surface. Black spruce is the primary tree species that grows atop it, eking out a marginal existence in the marshy and acidic soil. This sickly woodland is interrupted by fens and stagnant ponds where cotton grass and water lilies grow. Drier ground is home to a much healthier-looking growth of white spruce and balsam poplar.

You can glimpse the Gulkana River from time to time, flowing through a richly wooded bottomland. Southbound travelers will have fine views of Mounts Sanford, Wrangell, and Drum until Mile 156, when the highway ascends Hogan Hill. From the heights, you will have excellent views of the Wrangell and Chugach mountains, but there are no pullouts where you can stop to enjoy them. Through the trees, you can see lake-studded flats to the south. These rolling uplands stretch westward all the way to the Talkeetna Mountains, forming a vast and empty *terra incognita* through which the Susitna River flows.

The valley to the west of the road soon reveals a string of lakes, offering the possibility of fishing, canoeing, or loon watching. The road passes tiny Dick Lake at Mile 173 and swings close to the Trans-Alaska Pipeline. Sections of the pipe have been raised or buried to permit the migration of the Nelchina caribou herd, which wanders through this area in the autumn.

Paxson Lake soon appears to the west, and the road will follow its sinuous shoreline for the next 8 miles. After the road leaves the head of the lake, a shallow grade leads to the tiny settlement of Paxson and a junction with the Denali Highway at Mile 185.5. Al Paxson established a roadhouse here in the frontier days. The original roadhouse was little more than a collection of tents farther up the river, at a spot known as Timberline Camp. In the winter of 1906, more than 200 people were stranded at this flimsy outpost when a blizzard struck the wagon road to Fairbanks. A log structure was later built at the present townsite, but it burned down on Christmas Eve of 1975. The remains of this structure can be seen to the east of the highway at Mile 185.7.

From Paxson, the road follows the clear-flowing Gulkana River to its source. Red salmon spawn in the river from July through August; its upper reaches are closed to fishing but they offer good viewing opportunities. The highway emerges from the trees and climbs into the alpine country of Isabel Pass. Summit Lake occupies a vast depression scooped from the basin floor by glacial ice, and the road follows the lakeshore for 3 miles.

From the head of the lake, you will have outstanding views of the Gulkana Glacier flowing down the south face of Icefall Peak. The stream that drains this glacier flows northward into the Delta River, and the road follows it through a swampy lowland of brushy tundra. The abundance of willows along the watercourse has attracted beavers; watch for their dams and lodges along the stream.

The road soon reaches the banks of the Delta River, a tangle of channels that weaves across a broad plain of gravel outwash. The great polychromatic wall of Rainbow Ridge rises above its eastern bank. The maroon and green strata are of volcanic origin, while the yellow rock is sedimentary. The road follows the foot of the ridge for 10 miles and then breaks into the open as Miller Creek enters the Delta from the east.

The road now crosses the Denali Fault, a rift along plate boundaries that is a potential earthquake zone. The Wrangellia terrane, to the south of the fault, has been moving westward with respect to the land mass to the north. There is a pipeline viewpoint at the fault crossing. Here, the pipe is mounted on a series of rails, which would allow it to slide with a lateral movement of the ground, distributing the stress along a greater length of pipe. The ground could supposedly move 20 feet laterally without rupturing the pipeline.

At a bridge over the second branch of Miller Creek, you can see the Canwell Glacier to the southeast. The low ridges of gravel just beyond the creek are terminal moraines of the Castner Glacier, which cannot be seen from the road. Scan the rocky peaks on both sides of the valley for Dall sheep.

At Mile 225.4, the road reaches an overlook of the Black Rapids Glacier, which snakes down the mountains across the Delta River. The upper reaches of ice are visible, as well as the terminal moraines. The lower reaches of the glacier are hidden beneath a mantle of broken rock. In 1936, this glacier began to surge forward at a rate of 200 feet a day. The press dubbed it "The Galloping Glacier" and posted a radio announcer at the Black Rapids Roadhouse to report the moment when the glacier crossed the highway and destroyed this historic structure. Fortunately, the glacier stopped before crossing the river. The roadhouse was later incorporated into the Black Rapids Lodge and is now falling into ruin. Later research has shown that the Black Rapids Glacier advanced even farther around the year 1700, crossing the valley and pushing 100 feet up its far wall.

Watch for the Delta bison herd on the river bottoms from this point on, from autumn through early summer. The Delta River carries a heavy load of silt and cobbles washed into the flow by melting glaciers, and these are deposited as gravel bars where the river flows onto the lowlands. Strong winds frequently blow from the south, funnelling through the pass and carrying clouds of silt thousands of feet into the air. The silt is deposited on lee slopes to the north and forms a deep mineral soil called *loess* that is ideal for plant growth. The loess is deepest near the foot of the mountains and becomes progressively shallower as one moves farther from its source. Periodic flooding and shifting channels set the stage for the growth of plants that represent the first stages of forest succession. Among the early colonizers in this area are the grasses that serve as forage for the bison. These animals were transplanted from Montana in the 1920s and their population has since expanded to 450 animals.

A distinctive hillock called Donnelly Dome soon rises ahead, and the road climbs into the uplands to pass below its feet. This geologic feature was surrounded by ice during the height of the glacial advances, and only the top 700 feet were exposed to form a "nunatak," or island amid the ice. The highway passes through hummocky terrain pocked with kettle lakes, a landscape created by melting glaciers. Watch for trumpeter swans and moose in the many small lakes.

As the road runs northward into the great basin of the Tanana River you can still watch the tundra-clad slopes to the south for signs of grizzly bears. A terminal moraine at Mile 253 marks the farthest expansion of glaciers that flowed northward from the mountains. The last stretch of road into Delta Junction is long and straight, passing through a stunted forest of spruce and aspen as it runs through the Fort Greely Military Reservation.

Once a collection of homesteads, Delta Junction is now the main agricultural area in the Alaskan interior. Hay is a major crop, and special cold-weather hybrids of barley have been developed in this area. Local attractions include Clearwater Lake, located off Jack Warren Road, which leaves the Richardson Highway at Mile 268. In the spring, warm chinook winds blow through the passes in the Alaska Range and melt the ice on Clearwater Lake well before other lakes in central Alaska are ice-free. As a result, the lake is a major waterfowl staging area in May and June for an array of birds that includes trumpeter swans, pintails, wigeon (occasionally including the Eurasian species), and diving ducks. The Clearwater River, which flows from the lake, is the first leg of a gentle, day-long canoe float that moves on to the Tanana River and winds up on the Richardson at Mile 275.4. The Clearwater supports a late run of silver salmon in September and October.

From Delta Junction, the highway runs through a mixed forest of white spruce and balsam poplar. At Mile 275, Big Delta State Historical Park is the site of the best-preserved roadhouse in the state. It was originally built in 1909 by John Hajdukovich, an enterprising prospector, trader, guide, and sawmill operator. His many enterprises kept him away from the roadhouse for long periods at a time, and in 1917 he hired a Swedish-born woman named Erika Wallen to manage the business. After a prolonged absence, Hajdukovich returned to the roadhouse in 1923 and sold it to Wallen for $10 and back wages for the previous years. The inn was dubbed Rika's Roadhouse in honor of its new proprietor, who became famous for her fresh produce and cheeses. Near the roadhouse are an old military telegraph station, barn, tack house, and campground.

Just west of the roadhouse, the highway crosses the Tanana River, and there is a fine view of the suspension bridge built to carry the pipeline across the river. A spur road branches off at Mile 278, bound for Quartz Lake. This lake, as well as Birch Lake to the west, were formed when natural berms of gravel were pushed up by the Tanana River, damming the small basins so that they filled with water.

The road then crosses the Shaw Flats, a brushy area where moose are often seen along the roadside. Before long, the highway strikes the broad and tangled channels of the Tanana River. You will have frequent views of the water for the next 13 miles. Far to the south are the snowy crags of the Alaska Range, featuring Mount Hayes (13,832 feet) to the south and the twin peaks of Hess Mountain (11,940 feet) and Mount Deborah (12,339 feet) farther west. The south-facing hillsides in this area are covered in a sage grassland reminiscent of the mammoth steppes of the Pleistocene epoch, when herds of elk wandered freely across the hills of central Alaska.

The road climbs into the Tanana Hills, where a profusion of aspens and poplars makes for outstanding displays of autumn color. These hills are composed of the most ancient rock in Alaska: metamorphic schists that formed 550 million years ago. Birch Lake is nestled among the hills, and the cabins along its shoreline make it a popular summer and ice-fishing retreat for Fairbanks residents. A study of wind-blown pollen in the lake sediments revealed that alpine tundra was prevalent 15,000 years ago, dwarf shrubs moved in 1,000 years later, and the spruce-birch forest arrived 9,000 years ago. The road returns to the Tanana for a final view of the mountains, after which it runs inland onto a broad flood plain. Permafrost is prevalent here, and the black spruce forest that covers it is interspersed with spindly larches.

On the final approach to Fairbanks, the road passes in plain view of the runways of Eielson Air Force Base. During World War II, this airfield was a satellite strip of Ladd Field, which is now part of the Fort Richardson Army Base. The two airfields were located on the Northwest Staging Route, a chain of airstrips used to ferry American bombers and fighter planes to the Soviet Union under the lend-lease program. When relations with the Soviets cooled in the years following the war, this airfield became a strategic base for the jet interceptors that countered the threat of Soviet bombers. Today, you may spot jet fighters, ground-attack planes, and military transports here.

West of the air base, a bridge leads over the Chena Flood Channel, completed in 1981 by the Corps of Engineers to divert floods away from Fairbanks. Disastrous floods struck the town in 1905 and again in 1967. The channel is guarded by a 7-mile long levee, which works by shunting flood water from the Chena River away from town and into the Tanana. During the course of the project, the engineers also impounded the Chena Lakes, which have become a popular recreation spot.

The highway soon passes the town of North Pole, which capitalizes on its unusual name by offering year-round Christmas festivities and specialty shops for kids. The highway then enters the outskirts of Fairbanks, where it meets a tangled array of roadways. Travelers bound for the airport, the University of Alaska, or the Parks Highway should exit at Mile 361. Downtown traffic exits at Airport Way, while travelers bound north on the Steese, Elliott, or Dalton highways should follow the expressway straight ahead.

Old Dayville Road Sidetrip

This paved thoroughfare runs southward from the Richardson Highway, crossing the many channels of the Lowe River. After passing a small jet-fuel refinery, it heads for the coast, where you will have excellent views across Valdez Harbor of the glacier-clad peaks of the Chugach Range. The next cluster of buildings you pass will be a small hydroelectric power plant and a privately run salmon hatchery. Solomon Gulch Falls occupies the spectacular chasm just to the east of them.

Public access ends just beyond Allison Point, a popular fishing spot for the silver and pink salmon returning to the hatchery. The Alyeska Pipeline terminal is at the end of the road; you can book a tour at the Valdez airport. The terminal occupies the site of an old Army post called Fort Liscum, which was active from 1901 to 1922.

Fairbanks Sidetrip

Fairbanks was founded by E.T. Barnette, who traveled up the Tanana by steamboat in 1901 to establish a trading post. Barnette's original destination was the current site of Delta Junction, but because of shallow water and shifting gravel bars, the steamer captain refused to pilot his boat any farther than the Chena River. Barnette and his trade goods were unceremoniously deposited on the banks of the Chena at the present site of Fairbanks. Soon after that, an Italian prospector named Felice Pedroni showed up with gold he had found near the current site of Fox, Alaska. This miner, whose name was shortened to "Felix Pedro" by illiterate frontiersmen, had just discovered the vast gold field that stretched through the valleys of Goldstream and Ester creeks to the north.

The town became the major commercial center for the mining district after Judge James Wickersham moved his federal courthouse there from the town of Eagle in 1903. In return for this boon, Barnette named the budding city for Charles Fairbanks, an Indiana senator who headed the Alaska Boundary Commission and whom Wickersham admired. The city was destroyed by flood in 1905 and by fire in 1906. Its population dwindled somewhat following the gold rush, but the town recovered during World War II when it became an airbase on the Northwest Staging Route. Modern Fairbanks got a major economic boost during the pipeline construction of the 1970s. The current economy is supported by oil, gold mining, two military bases at the edge of town, and the University of Alaska.

There is a tourist information cabin as well as an Alaska Public Lands Information Center in the downtown district. Alaskaland is a theme park on Airport Way, featuring the stern-wheeler Nenana, pioneer and aviation museums, live entertainment in the evenings, and historic buildings moved in from all over town. Admission to the park is free. The University of Alaska Museum has the most outstanding natural and cultural history displays in the state. It also commands the best view in town of the Alaska Range, including (on a clear day) Denali, the highest peak on the continent. You can see migrating sandhill cranes and Canada geese during the spring and fall at the university hay fields below campus and at the Creamer's Field Wildlife Preserve on College Road.

19

Denali Highway

Official Designation: Alaska Route 8
Description: Improved gravel road from Paxson to Cantwell
Recommended Maximum: 35 mph/55 kph
Hazards: Severe washboards and potholes often present
Distance Markers: None; (but the author has counted miles westward from Paxson)
Further Reading: *Frozen Fauna of the Mammoth Steppe* by R. Dale Guthrie
Information Sources: Bureau of Land Management (Glennallen District)

 ## The Drive

This rugged gravel highway connects the Richardson and Parks highways by crossing the high tundra in the heart of the Alaska Range. Before the construction of the Parks Highway in 1971, this road was the only access route to Denali National Park. The scenery along the way rivals that found in the park, without the crowds of tourists and bothersome travel restrictions.

The route follows an old dog-sled trail that once ran between Paxson and Cantwell, providing access to the gold camp at Valdez Creek. The modern highway is wide and fairly level, but it is paved only for the first 21 miles between Paxson and the Tangle Lakes. The gravel portion can be incredibly rough, with long stretches of potholes and washboards. For this reason, some rental-car companies will not permit you to drive their vehicles on the Denali Highway. Lodges on the Susitna River and at Tangle Lakes offer the only gas along the route.

The road begins by crossing the Gulkana River, which is a hotbed of red-salmon spawning activity in July and August. Fishing is not allowed here, but the clear water permits excellent viewing opportunities.

After the road climbs onto the high shoulders of Paxson Mountain, you will see the first of the glacial topography created in Pleistocene times. Summit Lake occupies the broad valley to the north, a basin scooped out by glaciers and dammed by alluvial debris deposited by Falls Creek at the basin's north end. Beyond the lake, the craggy slopes of Icefall Peak are graced by

Denali Highway

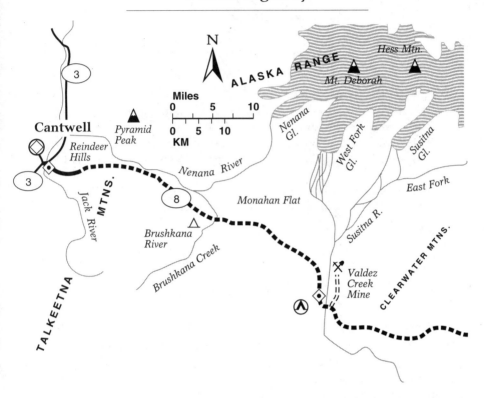

the Gulkana and Gakona glaciers, remnants of an ice field that once filled the basin below them. The summit of Paxson Mountain is littered with glacial erratics, indicating that ice once covered its summit. Much later, a small montane glacier carved a natural amphitheater into the mountain's north slope.

After crossing high, tundra-clad benches, the road swings through a gap occupied by Tenmile Lake. It continues to climb until it overlooks the vast tundra basin known as Hungry Hollow. The extinct volcanoes of the Wrangell Mountains rise in the distance. These are shield volcanoes, which build up layer by layer when lava flowed quietly from fissures in the earth's crust. Glaciers and cataclysmic eruptions have whittled away Mounts Sanford and Drum, while the younger Mount Wrangell between them has retained its original form. It has been known to emit an occasional plume of steam.

The road enters the Tangle Lakes Archaeological District at Mile 15. In this area, prehistoric hunters knapped stone implements from the local chert as they awaited the migratory herds of caribou. The area is important to archaeologists, who have located more than 400 sites. It is illegal to disturb

Denali Highway

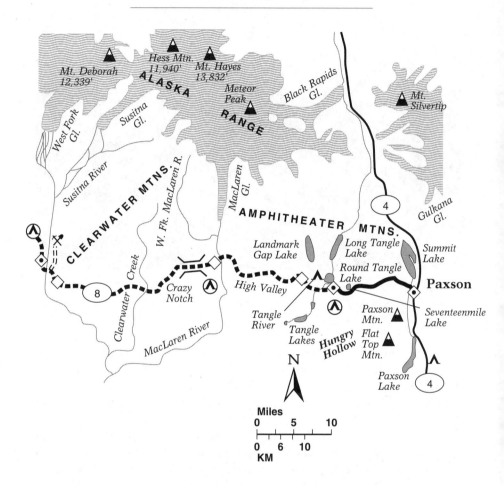

or remove anything of archaeological interest; violators of the Antiquities Act face heavy fines, confiscation of property, and jail sentences. Bands of the Nelchina caribou herd still funnel through this area, which is hemmed in by the craggy mountains to the north and the boggy muskeg to the south.

At Mile 17, you may spot red-necked phalaropes on a lake north of the road. This small waterbird swims in tight circles, creating a vortex that sucks aquatic insects from the muck of the lakebed and brings them to the surface to be gobbled up. The pavement ends as the road passes Round Tangle Lake. This is an outstanding area for bird watchers. Wigeons, goldeneyes, pintails, and trumpeter swans are commonly spotted on the lakes. Harlequin ducks nest along the free-flowing stretches of the Tangle River. The tundra

Landmark Gap.

uplands are home to all three species of ptarmigan, as well as the gyrfalcon, which hunts them. The Tangle Lakes are popular with canoeists and are the put-in spot for a three-day float of the Delta River. The float features predominantly Class II water, with a few Class III riffles and a portage around Black Rapids.

The pavement gives way to gravel as the highway leaves the lakes, and soon the rugged volcanic summits of the Amphitheater Mountains rise to the north. Landmark Gap breaches this range and you can see the snowy peaks of the Alaska Range through this U-shaped passage. The road climbs gently through High Valley, which is dotted with kettle lakes formed when buried chunks of glacial ice melted. MacLaren Summit lies at the west end of the basin and is the highest point in the journey. Trails run in both directions along the summit, heading for the high country where pikas and marmots are often seen. Summit Lake is the large mere to the north, dammed by the terminal moraine of a glacier that once filled the High Valley. Below is the valley of the MacLaren River, and at its head the MacLaren Glacier slides down Mount Hayes, the dominant peak in this part of the Alaska Range. Lesser peaks that are visible from MacLaren Summit include Aurora Peak, Mount Shand, and Mount Geist.

A long grade leads into the MacLaren River valley, and at pullouts along the way you can see mounds on the valley floor called "palsas." These mounds are formed by frost action in deep beds of organic peat. At Mile 40.8, after reaching the valley floor, look for a vegetated mound that rises from a small pond. This is a "pingo," or ice-cored mound, that has begun to melt.

On its way to the MacLaren River crossing, the road runs atop an old terminal moraine left by the MacLaren Glacier at the end of its most recent advance. The glacier extended far to the south during the height of the ice ages, and during that time the ice was 5,200 feet thick at this spot. Watch the kettle ponds for red-throated loons and emperor geese. Grizzly bears and wolves are also common on the valley floor, but the tall brush usually hides them. A lodge at the west end of the bridge is a snowmobiling center in the winter.

The road climbs the far wall of the valley, heading for Crazy Notch. This unusual geologic feature was carved through a ridge of basalt by a stream that flowed from the great ice sheet that occupied the shelf above. After passing through Crazy Notch, the highway continues westward atop sinuous ridges called "eskers." These are formed by streams that flow through tunnels beneath a stationary glacier. The streams continuously deposit cobbles and sediments until the tunnels are filled and the streams are forced to melt their way upward through the ice. When the climate warms and the ice melts, the ridges of sediment remain standing above the basin floor. Some of the larger kettle ponds in this area provide habitat for common loons, trumpeter swans, and beavers. There are more eskers west of Clearwater Creek (Mile 56), and the ragged, volcanic peaks of the Clearwater Mountains soon rise ahead.

The road swings southward around the end of this range, and you can see the Susitna River to the south. It flows through a tapestry of brilliant meadows, shining lakes, and stately stands of spruce. Watch for moose in the tall brush along the roadside; this is one of the few good areas to see them from this highway. The road bears northwest toward a bridge over the river. This area was the site of skirmishes between clans of the Ahtna Indians. These clans defended their hunting and fishing territories and often would starve rather than trespass on the hunting grounds of their neighbors. To the north along the river, the valley of Valdez Creek was known to the Ahtna as C'ilaanaa, or "Place Where Game Abounds." It was later to become an important gold-mining district.

Just before you reach the bridge, you will come to a spur road that runs northward to the Valdez Creek Mine. Gold-bearing gravel along the creek was deposited by a stream before the area was glaciated. That deposit became known as the Tammany Channel. Glacial ice buried the deposit as it leveled the area, and Valdez Creek took a new course. Since then, the creek has concentrated gold from the old Tammany Channel and gravels and from veins in the bedrock.

Gold was discovered here in 1897 by W.G. Jack and a party of miners who had prospected all the way up the Susitna River. They named the stream "Swollen Creek," because their eyes were almost swollen shut from the bites of mosquitoes. The party soon ran out of food and had to leave, and the gold deposit on Swollen Creek became a lost and legendary lode.

The Valdez Creek gold field was rediscovered in 1903 by a party of prospectors from Valdez, who named the stream after their hometown. They sparked a minor gold rush, and prospectors from all over Alaska converged on this remote spot high in the mountains. Many of the local Ahtna Indians moved into the new gold camp to become claim-holders and miners, while other members of the tribe hunted wild game to supply the miners with food. The early days of drift mining in the placer gravels were hard; timber around Valdez Creek was quickly depleted, and logs had to be hauled in from Butte Creek far to the southwest to make mine-shaft timbers, cabins, and firewood.

By 1913, the small drift-mine operations had taken most of the easily recovered gold—a total of $300,000 worth. The Valdez Mining Company bought most of the claims that year and began a succession of unprofitable attempts to mine the gravel on a large scale. In 1925, a prospector named "Laughing Ole" found the mother lode, a vein of quartz in the bedrock that contained gold in its hard-rock form. This started a new flurry of activity, but by 1928 only a dozen miners were working shafts in the bedrock. During World War II, the government shut down gold-mining operations to free men and equipment for the mining of strategic metals such as iron, copper, and tungsten. After the war, mining on Valdez Creek continued on a sporadic basis.

A bridge spans the Susitna at Mile 79, and after crossing it the road follows the west bank of the river upstream. Far downstream lie the impassable rapids of Devil's Canyon, where the river cuts a steep gorge through the heart of the Talkeetna Mountains. Watch for grizzly bears on the gravel outwash plain along the river. Small lakes provide habitat for trumpeter swans, wigeons, and scaup, and the Arctic warbler flits through the riverside brush.

At Mile 82, the road reaches a small lodge at the site of a roadhouse that originally served the Valdez Creek mining camp. The original structure is still standing—a small log cabin that could seat five miners at a time for meals and could sleep twelve on crowded pallets. You can see the Valdez Creek Mine site across the river from here.

Beyond the lodge, the highway climbs to the brow of a hill that overlooks a vast expanse of brushy tundra known as the Monahan Flats. Beyond the flats rise two of the tallest peaks in the area, Mount Deborah (12,339 feet/3,761 meters) to the west and Hess Mountain (11,940 feet/3,639 meters)

Beyond Monahan Flats, the West Fork Glacier pours forth from the Alaska Range.

just to the east of it. The core of the Alaska range is made of metamorphic rock, while the ranges to the south are a mix of volcanic stone and ancient seafloor sediments. The West Fork Glacier pours down Mount Deborah, and you can see its snout clearly from the road. For a better view, climb the small hillock north of the road at Mile 85.

The lowlands are pocked with kettle lakes left over from the last glaciation; hooded mergansers and Arctic loons inhabit the smaller meres, while common loons float on the larger ones. Many of these lakes freeze all the way to the bottom in the winter. Monahan Flats is a winter range for the Nelchina caribou herd, and during the summer you can sometimes spot small bands of caribou in the uplands along the road. The uplands south of the road are home to the golden plover and long-tailed jaeger, and they offer outstanding cross-country hiking possibilities.

The road now crosses an imperceptible but important drainage divide. Runoff to the east flows via the Susitna River to Cook Inlet on the rim of the North Pacific, while to the west of the divide, runoff drains northward into the Yukon River watershed and then to the Bering Sea. Watch the mountains to the north for a glimpse of the Nenana Glacier. The first stream you cross on the west side of the divide is Brushkana Creek at Mile 104. There is a primitive campground along its west bank.

The road then drops gently through increasingly brushy terrain to reach the banks of the Nenana River. Its protected valley is home to a vigorous forest of white spruce, which is the dominant tree of well-drained soils in the Alaskan interior. You can see Pyramid Peak to the north from a turnout at Mile 116. This summit is thought to be the core of an ancient volcano. It gets its rusty color from iron oxides within the rock. A log cabin a mile farther on was built as a shelter by the Alaska Road Commission in the 1920s.

The road soon climbs a rise, passing between Joe Lake (to the south) and Jerry Lake. These lakes mark the divide between the silty Nenana and its clear-flowing tributary to the south, the Jack River. Atop the rise at Mile 130.1 you will have an excellent view of Denali (20,320 feet/6,194 meters), the tallest peak on the continent. If measured from base to summit instead of from sea level, this mountain is taller than Mount Everest.

The northern end of the Talkeetna Mountains rises to the south, while to the north the tundra-covered slopes of Reindeer Mountain provide habitat for caribou in the autumn. Just before reaching the town of Cantwell, the road again becomes paved and drops to the edge of the Jack River's braided, willow-choked channels. During the winter, groups of more than twenty moose have been spotted here. At Mile 134, the highway reaches Cantwell and a junction with the Parks Highway, where it ends.

20

Parks Highway

Official Designation: Alaska Route 3
Description: Paved highway from Wasilla to Fairbanks; 323 miles (520 kilometers)
Recommended Maximum: Highway speeds
azards: Watch out for moose in Susitna Valley
Distance Markers: Mileposts count northward from Anchorage (highway begins at Mile 35)
Further Reading: *A Naturalist in Alaska* by Adolph Murie
Information Sources: Denali National Park, Denali State Park, Alaska Tourism Marketing Council

 The Drive

This paved artery connects Anchorage and Fairbanks, passing through some of the most breathtaking scenery in central Alaska. One of the newest roadways in the state, the Parks Highway was completed in 1971. It was not named for the outstanding nature preserves along the route, but for George Parks, a former territorial governor. The prime attraction along the way is Denali, the continent's tallest peak, which can be seen clearly from several locations along the highway. Bear in mind that Denali is a weathermaker, and during the turbulent summer months, its summit may only be visible one day in seven.

Denali National Park also lies along the highway, encompassing the peak and the wildlife-rich tundra that surrounds it. This national park offers world-class backpacking across the trail-free tundra, while its neighbor Denali State Park has several good routes for hikers who prefer trails. Fishermen will be drawn to the southern reaches of the highway, where the streams of the Susitna River drainage bear abundant runs of spawning salmon.

The Parks Highway begins in the forested lowlands of the Susitna River, country that has been heavily settled in recent years. Wasilla (Mile 42) is the first town you will reach. It was originally a crossroads of the Iditarod Trail and of a wagon road from Knik to the gold fields along Willow Creek. The Iditarod route originally was a winter dog-sled trail that ran more than 1,100 miles between Seward and the gold fields of the Iditarod River and

Peaks of the Talkeetna Mountains line the headwaters of the Chulitna River.

then on to Nome on the Bering Sea. In 1898, three Swedes found gold in the gravel beaches near Nome. As news of the strike spread, the population of the new town ballooned to a peak of 30,000 in 1900.

The Iditarod Trail was blazed in 1908, following a gold strike on the Iditarod River. In December 1911, four dog teams pulled 3,400 pounds of gold dust from the Iditarod gold fields to Seward under the direction of expert mushers Bob Griffiths and Gus Norton. The trail achieved international fame in 1925, when mushers relayed 300,000 units of serum to stem an outbreak of diptheria in Nome. The modern Iditarod dog-sled race traces their route for 1,049 miles between Anchorage and Nome. A dog-sled museum is located in the ghost town of Knik, on the north shore of Cook Inlet 14 miles west of Wasilla by gravel road.

A museum of transportation and industry is located on a spur road that leaves the highway just north of the railroad crossing on the outskirts of Wasilla. The highway continues northward, passing a spur road to Big Lake at Mile 52.3 and crossing the Little Susitna River at the community of Houston. The Little Susitna is known for its strong run of silver salmon in late July.

Farther to the north, the road crosses numerous tributaries of the mighty Susitna River. They support the runs of king, silver, and pink salmon that make this area a popular fishing destination. This was the traditional domain of the Dena'ina tribe of Athapaskans. A spur road runs west to Nancy Lake from Mile 64.5, while the main highway continues north into Willow. This sprawling settlement was conceived in 1976 as the site for a new state

Parks Highway

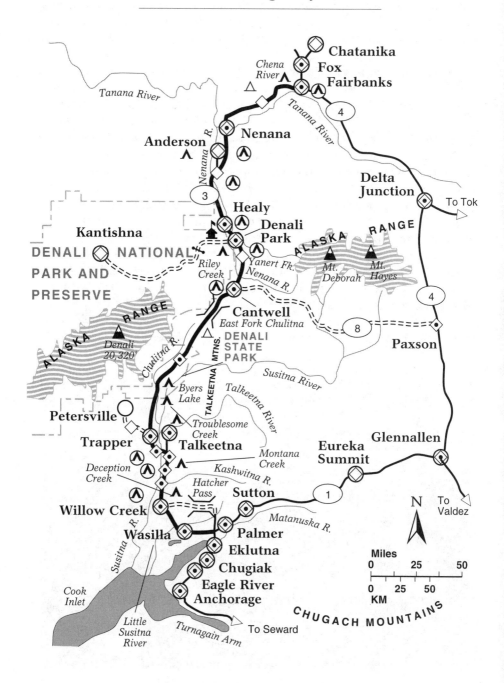

capital because it was more centrally located than Juneau. Land speculators moved in to subdivide the land, sell mountain-view lots, and install electrical, sewage, and water systems. But in 1982, the state legislature failed to fund the project, dealing a devastating blow to investors who held real estate in Willow and to the fledgling community itself.

The Hatcher Pass Road branches to the east at Mile 71.2, in the center of "town." The Talkeetna Mountains rise to the east. A geologically young intrusion of granite forms the core of this range. Watch for moose in the sedge flats near Little Willow Creek and for loons on Kashwitna Lake a little farther on. This area offers the first views of Denali, which at 20,320 feet (6,194 meters) is the tallest peak in North America.

The highway crosses the Kashwitna River and several more salmon spawning creeks before a paved spur road leaves it for Talkeetna at Mile 99. Talkeetna is a pleasant backwater town that features a small historical museum, and its airstrip is the departure point for mountaineers bound for the icebound crags of Denali National Park.

The main highway continues north to cross the Susitna, known to the locals as the "Big Su." The waterway funnels through an impassable canyon in the Talkeetna Mountains before reaching this wide and glacier-carved valley. Then it heads far to the northeast.

The highway continues up the valley, now drained by the silty flow of the Chulitna River. It passes the community of Trapper Creek at Mile 115,

Denali rises in its full glory to the east of Broad Pass.

and the rugged Petersville Road runs west from there to an abandoned mining settlement at the base of the Alaska Range. Eighteen miles beyond this junction, the highway crosses the Chulitna and enters Denali State Park. It quickly climbs onto a high bench above the valley, where a pullout at Mile 135.2 offers a superb view of Denali and the lesser peaks that surround it. The enormous Ruth Glacier flows from the flanks of Denali. This river of ice is 31 miles long and 3,800 feet thick as it squeezes through the Great Gorge. Mount Hunter, known to the Dena'ina as Begguya, or "the Child," rises directly above the glacier. Denali itself means "the Great One" in the dialect of the Kuskokwim Athapaskans. There will be other good views at Mile 162.3 and from Broad Pass.

Along the banks of Troublesome Creek at Mile 137, there is a trailhead from which you can begin a 42-mile hike along the crest of Curry and K'esugi ridges. These ridges, which are great synclines or upfoldings of metamorphic rock, rise to the east of the highway. Their high country offers outstanding blueberry picking. An auto campground at Byers Lake (Mile 147) marks the midpoint of the trail.

Around Mile 156, look west for a view of the Eldridge Glacier, another of the spectacular valley glaciers that cling to Denali. At Mile 164, the road reaches Coal Creek, the northern terminus of the trail system in Denali State Park. The park boundary is 2 miles farther north. At Mile 174, a bridge spans the deep gulf known as Hurricane Gulch.

The road drops gently to cross the forested vale of Honolulu Creek and then climbs again onto the windswept benches. These are the headwaters of the Chulitna River, which splits into three forks. You will have excellent views of the Talkeetna Mountains east of the valley, while the Alaska Range continues to provide spectacular scenery to the west.

The road now enters Broad Pass, carved through the heart of the Alaska Range by glacial ice that was more than 10,000 feet thick. Brushy tundra clothes the pass, and the road passes long lakes gouged out by the moving ice. Look southward for a final view of Denali. To the northeast, Mounts Deborah and Hayes rise beyond the Jack River valley, which enters from the east.

As the highway approaches Cantwell, the tawny slopes of Reindeer Mountain rise ahead. In 1922, a large herd of domesticated reindeer was driven to this area from Goodnews Bay on the Bering Sea. Entrepreneurs hoped that a domestic reindeer industry in this area would make up for sagging railroad revenues. The experiment failed, as reindeer defected to wild herds of caribou or fell prey to wolves. Adding to the problem, the beef industry quashed efforts to market the new meat in the lower forty-eight states.

In Cantwell, at Mile 210, the Parks Highway reaches a junction with the Denali Highway, a broad ribbon of gravel that heads eastward through high tundra to intersect the Richardson Highway. The center of town lies on a short spur road to the west of the Parks, which continues northward, following the banks of the Jack River. The wooded valley bottoms are good moose habitat, and east of the road the open slopes of Reindeer Mountain are an important caribou winter range.

The clear Jack River soon feeds into the strong, silty Nenana River. Watch for glacial erratics on the bluffs beyond the Nenana River bridge. These giant boulders were stranded here by glaciers that had carried them far from their source. Though small compared to the summits of the Denali massif, the peaks that surround the river are craggy enough to lend an air of mountain splendor to the narrow valley.

Beyond Carlo Creek, the highway climbs a rise, and the broad basin bearing the Yanert Fork River opens to the east. Panorama Mountain guards the valley from the south, and the symmetrical form of Pyramid Peak rises to the east of it. Geologists believe that Pyramid Peak is the core of an ancient volcano whose slopes have eroded away.

A chain of rugged peaks skirts the northern edge of the valley. The most striking of these is Mount Fellows, whose craggy summit is castellated with eroded pillars. Look for a rock formation shaped like a musher and dog team along the skyline west of the summit. You can get an excellent view of this valley at a rest stop at Mile 234. Scan the rugged face of Mount Fellows for Dall sheep.

The road soon descends to cross the Nenana River and enters Denali National Park. Watch for moose along the road as the highway climbs over a hill and drops slightly to cross Riley Creek. The Hines Creek Fault runs through this area; bedrock to the south belongs to the Wrangellia terrane, while to the north the mountains are wrought from the much older Precambrian rocks of the Yukon-Tanana terrane.

Just beyond Riley Creek, the Denali Park Road leads to the visitor center and then westward through the park for 80 miles to Kantishna (see Denali Park Road Sidetrip at the end of this chapter). Only the first 15 miles are open to private vehicles; visitors who want to go farther can book a ride on a shuttle bus. The Parks Highway continues northward through the jumble of lodges, restaurants, and gift shops that make up the tourist village of Denali Park.

Leaving the buildings behind, the Parks Highway follows the Nenana River through a steep-walled canyon. Rock slides are common here; during wet weather, great slabs of loose soil and rock routinely clatter onto the roadway. The surrounding mountains are part of the Outside Range, a northern cordillera of the Alaska Range that is made up of metamorphic rock 485 million years older than the core of the range.

The worst of the slide danger is over by the time the road reaches

Lesser peaks of the Alaska Range north of Cantwell.

Iceworm Gulch at Mile 240. Ice worms are not mythical creatures but are segmented worms that live on the surface of glaciers and feed nocturnally on snow algae and wind-blown pollen. There are no glaciers in the immediate vicinity of this gulch, so this is a poor place to look for ice worms.

Meanwhile, the Nenana tracks a tumultuous course through the canyon, offering Class IV whitewater for experienced river runners. The high slopes on the opposite side of the river are home to a herd of Dall sheep that uses the area as summer range and as a late-autumn rutting ground.

At the mouth of the canyon, the highway crosses a particularly windy bridge over the river and climbs to reach two scenic overlooks. Between them is a marshy pond where moose are often sighted. The highway runs onto the high flats at the foot of the mountains, and the river flows through a narrow valley flanked by escarpments. This area is a winter range for part of the Denali moose population and is the year-round home to a handful of them. A few of these resident moose have an extremely rare trait—their coat is completely white. But these animals are not albinos. Their white color phase is the result of a rare gene, much like the one responsible for the all-white pelage, or coat, of Dall sheep. These moose are protected from hunting and are sighted on rare occasions between the foot of the mountains and the bridge over Panguingue Creek at Mile 252.5.

The road enters Healy, where coal has been mined since 1904. The original mining settlement was called Suntrana, an Athapaskan word for "burning hills." The coal seams once smoldered with underground fires that never went out. Just north of town, watch for the open-pit operation of the Usibelli Coal Mine on the bluff-top beyond the river. To the south you can see the pointed summit of Usibelli Peak and to the west the unbroken wall of the Outside Range in Denali National Park. Dry Creek winds along the north edge of town, and archaeological diggings here have linked prehistoric hunters with Pleistocene mammals as recently as 11,700 years ago.

The hay fields on the valley floor sit on well-drained outwash gravel brought here by the Nenana Glacier during the height of the ice ages. The northern limit of the most recent glaciation was just north of town, and beyond this point, permafrost underlies the valley floor. What appear to be grassy meadows are really peat bogs and swampy tussock tundra.

At Mile 256, the slopes above the road have been slowly sliding downhill, forcing relocation of the highway to the east. This slow-motion landslide began with an earthquake, which "liquefied" the clay soil by breaking the bonds between soil particles. Trees topple at crazy angles as the slide pushes them downhill.

The valley is flanked by rounded plateaus, and the bare stone summit of Jumbo Dome rises above the foothills to the east. The hills dissolve into a vast expanse of lowland as the road crosses the Nenana River at Mile 276. A spur road soon leads west for 6 miles to the village of Anderson and the DEW (Distant Early Warning) Line station at Clear. The station is closed to the public. Clear Creek runs nearby. Fed by warm springs, it supports a unique winter run of silver and chum salmon that arrives in December.

The highway continues northward across the flats. Permafrost lies just below the surface of the soil here, preventing water from filtering into it. The result is a muskeg bog of black spruce and sphagnum moss in an area that would qualify as a desert judging by the scarcity of rain and snow. Cotton grass, a marsh sedge that "blooms" with fuzzy seed heads in midsummer, grows in openings in the woods. Road-building has presented a formidable challenge here: the black asphalt absorbs heat from the sun and melts the permafrost beneath. The roadway then buckles, forming dips called "frost heaves." The highway has been reconstructed a number of times to try to prevent this major road hazard.

At Mile 286, you will reach Julius Creek. Several roadside ponds just beyond it are good spots to watch for waterfowl. There is another pond just south of Nenana where you might see buffleheads, mallards, wigeons, and common loons.

At Mile 304, the highway enters Nenana, which was originally a trading post built at a Tanana Indian fishing site where the Nenana River joins the Tanana. Saint Mark's Mission was added in 1904, and it still stands along the waterfront. The town boomed with the construction of the Alaska Railroad, and in 1923 President Warren Harding visited the town to drive in the golden spike that signified the completion of the line.

The town languished in the years that followed, but it retained a small amount of commerce by becoming a hub for barge traffic that serves the native villages along the Tanana River. The wooden-hulled tug Taku Chief stands next to the roadside visitor center, and the old railway station downtown has been converted to a historical museum. The town is best known for the Nenana Ice Classic, a unique Alaskan lottery in which participants try to guess the date and time when the ice on the Tanana River will break up in the spring. A large metal tripod is placed on the ice and attached to a tripwire that records the exact moment the ice begins to move. The prize has exceeded $300,000 in recent years.

Leaving Nenana, the highway crosses the Tanana River and climbs into the Tanana Hills. There are a number of pullouts along the way from which you can get panoramic views of the Alaska Range. The lighting is most spectacular in the evening.

During the Pleistocene, the Tanana Hills were covered with an arid steppe inhabited by mammoths, cave lions, steppe bison, saiga antelope, and a primitive form of horse. Enormous valley glaciers poured from the Alaska Range and stretched far into the lowlands. These rivers of ice left behind finely ground silt that was picked up by strong winds and deposited many miles from its source. This glacial dust formed the deep, buff-colored loess that now covers the Tanana Hills. The mineral-rich soil provides good growing conditions for white spruce, balsam poplar, and aspen. Black spruce grows atop the permafrost on north-facing slopes and in poorly drained depressions.

At Mile 348, the road begins its long descent toward the lowlands, where it will end in Fairbanks. At the bottom of the grade, a short spur road leads to the hamlet of Ester. During the turn-of-the-century gold rush in the Alaska interior, Ester was a wild boom town of 5,000, supporting placer-mining activity on Ester, Eva, and Cripple creeks. In recent years, gold miners on Ester Creek have found the stone points of prehistoric spears with the bones of mammoths, mastodons, and steppe bison.

The Ester Gold Camp is on the National Register of Historic Places. You can see the preserved bunkhouses of a large-scale dredging operation run by the Fairbanks Exploration Company, as well as several old gold dredges beside the highway. As you enter the outskirts of Fairbanks, watch for the scars of hydraulic mining operations above the road on the slopes of Gold Hill. Fairbanks is described in the Fairbanks Sidetrip at the end of Drive 18.

Denali Park Road Sidetrip

The Denali Park Road runs through the northern marches of the stunning Alaska Range. You can drive the first 15 miles to the Savage River; travel beyond this point is limited to shuttle buses.

Most development within the park is near its entrance. The road passes the visitor center and Riley Creek Campground and then crosses the railroad tracks to reach the Denali Park Hotel and the railway station, which sits beside the airstrip. As the road climbs through the forest, it passes park headquarters (and its sled-dog kennels) before entering the valley of Hines Creek. Here, a wilderness of white spruce closes in around the road. Watch for moose among the trees.

The road climbs steadily, finally topping out at the timberline at Mile 5.5. Look eastward for an excellent view of Mount Deborah, one of the dominant peaks on the eastern end of the Alaska Range. Straight ahead, a broad rift valley formed around the Hines Creek Fault stretches eastward as far as you can see. Sedimentary and igneous peaks rise to the south of this long rift valley, while much older metamorphic schists form the Outside Range to the north. The road crosses the valley of brushy tundra, which is interrupted here and there by isolated stands of white spruce. On a clear day, you can see Denali towering in snowy majesty to the southwest, more than 70 miles away.

The road passes the Savage Campground at Mile 12.8 and begins a gradual descent toward the Savage River. The wide gravel bars that flank the water are a travel corridor for grizzly bears and caribou. The jagged summit of Mount Fang rises upriver like the fossilized jawbone of some outlandish predator. There is a parking area just before the bridge, and you can often spot Dall sheep on the slopes beyond the river. In early spring, the rams graze on the succulent vegetation of the lower slopes, while the ewes and their lambs stay near the cliffs for safety. A guard station known as the "Savage Box" stands on the far side of the bridge, and private vehicles are not allowed beyond it without a special permit.

21

Hatcher Pass Road

Official Designation: Willow-Fishhook Road
Description: Improved gravel road from Palmer to Willow; 49 miles (79 kilometers)
Recommended Maximum: 35 mph/55 kph
Hazards: Narrow, winding road with potholes and washboards; not recommended for RVs or trailers
Distance Markers: Mileposts count west from Palmer
Information Sources: Independence Mine State Historical Park

 ## The Drive

This gravel road (also known as the Fishhook-Willow Road) climbs over a high tundra pass in the Talkeetna Mountains, linking the Glenn and Parks highways. It travels through the Willow Creek Mining District, site of the Independence Mine State Historical Park and other abandoned structures from the hard-rock gold-mining days of the early 1900s. One of the first roads in the original Alaska Territory ran between the town of Knik and the Grubstake Gulch placer fields on Willow Creek. Another road was later built from Palmer to the Independence Mine.

The alpine scenery along this road is fantastic, including brilliant wildflower displays and possibly some of the wildlife that lives above the timberline. The road is closed in the winter and opens when the snow has melted, usually by late June or early July. It is quite narrow and steep in sections and has no guardrails. It is not recommended for wide vehicles or trailers.

From Palmer, follow the Glenn Highway east for 2 miles to a hilltop junction with Fishhook Road. Turn north to pass through fertile farmland. You will have fine southward views of Twin Peaks and Pioneer Peak.

As the road nears the Talkeetna Mountains, a dense forest dominated by birch replaces the agricultural land. Ahead are Government Peak and Arkose Ridge, the outer portals of the Little Susitna River valley. You will follow the river upward into a narrow, steep-walled canyon. The pavement ends at a bridge over the river (Mile 8.5), and just beyond this point the road bends sharply to the left as it enters an east-west trending vale that runs perpendicular to the river. This odd geologic feature indicates the Castle

Mountain Fault, where shearing forces have crushed the rock at the contact zone between two great tectonic plates. The weakened rock around the fault eroded, leaving behind this small transverse valley.

The canyon opens onto a lush bottomland populated by stout cottonwoods and tall brush. Watch for moose and black bears as the road continues to follow the Little Susitna. After the road passes a lodge, it turns sharply to the southwest and begins to climb toward Hatcher Pass. The peaks to the north rise at the edge of the Talkeetna Mountain Batholith, formed about 55 million years ago. *Batholith* is a Latin word meaning "sea of stone;" the formation is created when a pool of molten magma rises through weaknesses in the earth's crust and cools to form a huge dome of granite within the older rock. The Talkeetna Mountain Batholith measures 150 miles from north to south and is 50 miles wide. As the granite cooled, cracks formed on the edge of the batholith, and superheated water filled the cracks with quartz and gold to form solid veins of ore.

At Mile 14.5, a rough spur road takes off to the north and leads into the Archangel Valley. This road provides access to a basin lined with incredible sawtooth crags, a wonderland for hikers and climbers alike. The main road continues to climb and soon passes above the timberline. This country looks like ideal habitat for Dall sheep, but it receives more than 25 feet of snow in the winter and there is not enough wind to clear the ridges. A Dall

Bald Mountain Ridge guards the western approach to Hatcher Pass.

Hatcher Pass Road

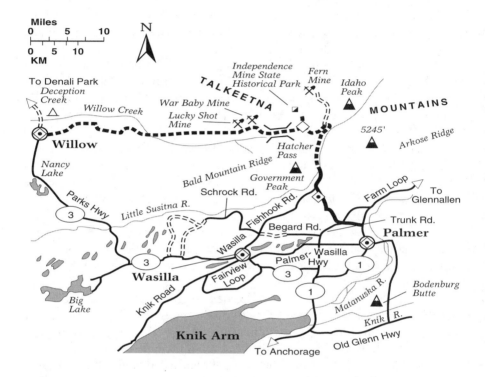

sheep that wintered here would not be able to move about or feed and would soon face starvation.

In the absence of competition from large herbivores, small mammals abound on the swards of alpine tundra. Arctic ground squirrels and hoary marmots gambol about in the meadows, and pikas inhabit the rock slides. The abundance of rodents makes this area a prime hunting ground for golden eagles, which nest among the crags.

The road soon reaches the headwaters valley of Fishhook Creek, bounded on the east by Marmot Mountain and on the west by Skyscraper Mountain. A hanging glacier carved a "cirque," or natural amphitheater, into the east face of Skyscraper during the Pleistocene epoch. This cirque is known as Eldorado Bowl, and it was there that Robert Lee Hatcher staked the Willow Mining District's first hard-rock gold claim in 1906. In the years that followed, dozens of mines appeared in the Talkeetna Mountains.

The Gold Cord Road runs a short distance northward from Mile 17.4 to reach Independence Mine State Historical Park, where one of the largest mines in the district has been preserved. Run by the Alaska-Pacific Consolidated Mining Company, this operation produced more than $1 million in gold during its peak year. Gold mining was suspended during World War II, and after the war, fixed gold prices and rampant inflation made mining unprofitable. The mine closed for good in 1951.

You can take a self-guided walking tour of the living quarters, ore-crushing mills, an assay office, and the tunnel entrance. The Gold Cord Mine on the hill above the Independence complex is privately owned and continues to produce gold. The open tundra in this area offers intriguing possibilities for day hikers.

The main road continues its ascent to Hatcher Pass. You have a good chance of seeing pikas and other rodents around the tiny tarn known as Summit Lake. This area is for day use only, and picking the wildflowers is forbidden. The restriction does not extend to the dwarf blueberries that grow in abundance on the alpine tundra.

The road zigzags down from the pass before jogging to the north into the headwaters valley of Willow Creek. There, recent exploratory shafts have been blasted into the old Independence Mine workings from the west side of Skyscraper Mountain.

The road continues around the next ridge and enters the valley of Craigie Creek (spelled "Craggy Creek" on the maps of early prospectors). It was in this valley that Chet Bartholf struck gold while hunting ptarmigans in 1906. Bartholf shot at a bird and missed, but the bullet struck an outcrop and broke it open, revealing a rich vein of quartz and gold. This find came to be known as the Lucky Shot Mine, which ultimately became the richest producer in the district, giving up $9 million in gold before closing in the 1940s.

The great mound of tailings on the east-facing slope of the valley marks the portal of the Lucky Shot, while to its right is the less obvious entrance to the War Baby Mine. Modern efforts to reopen the Lucky Shot account for the buildings south of the road. On the valley floor you can see an enormous boulder that was deposited by a retreating glacier. Placer miners have dug out the gravel beneath the boulder in their quest for gold.

As the road makes its final descent, Grubstake Gulch enters the valley of Willow Creek from the south. This tiny vale was the site of the first placer mining in the district. Prospectors were staking claims on the creekbed as early as 1897. The mountains south of Willow Creek are made of ancient metamorphic rock that contains small amounts of soapstone used by local natives for carving. The road drops into a loose growth of spruce on the valley floor. The groves of hardwoods on the neighboring slopes are black

Looking into the headwaters of Willow Creek from Hatcher Pass.

cottonwood, a rare sight near the timberline.

The road now follows Willow Creek, whose riffles indicate it might offer blue-ribbon flyfishing. In reality, the stream is almost barren. The road follows it westward as the mountains give way to rounded foothills. The trees grow more thickly on the valley floor near the mouth of the valley, and beyond this point the road runs across the broad lowland of the Susitna Valley to meet the Parks Highway in the settlement of Willow.

22

Glenn Highway

Official Designation: Alaska Highway 1
Description: Paved highway from Anchorage to Glennallen; 189 miles (304 kilometers)
Recommended Maximum: Highway speeds
Hazards: Frost heaves prevalent in Copper River basin
Distance Markers: Mileposts count eastward from Anchorage
Further Reading: *Knik, Matanuska, Susitna: A Visual History of the Valleys*
Information Sources: Anchorage Convention and Visitors Bureau, Greater Palmer Chamber of Commerce, Greater Copper Valley Chamber of Commerce

 The Drive

The Glenn Highway runs eastward from Anchorage, passing through the Matanuska Valley on its way to the Copper River basin. The highway follows a trail that was blazed in 1898 by Lieutenant Joseph Castner and his guide, mountain man H. H. Hicks. Castner's superior, Captain Edwin F. Glenn, took the lion's share of the credit for the expedition even though he was absent during most of it.

A railway line was built through the lower reaches of the Matanuska Valley in 1916, but the land to the east remained a hostile wilderness. The eastern portions of the Glenn Highway existed as a pack trail through the 1930s. It was not until World War II that it was upgraded to a highway to link Elmendorf Air Force Base with the rest of the Alaska highway system. The route follows the Border Ranges Fault, which defines the northern edge of the Chugach terrane. The modern highway is paved, and highlights include views of the glaciers that descend from the Chugach Mountains and vistas of the Wrangell volcanoes, clad eternally in snow.

The highway leaves Anchorage as a four-lane expressway and passes the Merrill Field airport for small planes on the way out of town. On the outskirts of the city, the highway passes the Fort Richardson Army Base and Elmendorf Air Force Base. Moose migrate across this section of highway between their summer range on the flats and their winter range on the slopes east of the road. This used to be a major cause of accidents, but now the

Glenn Highway

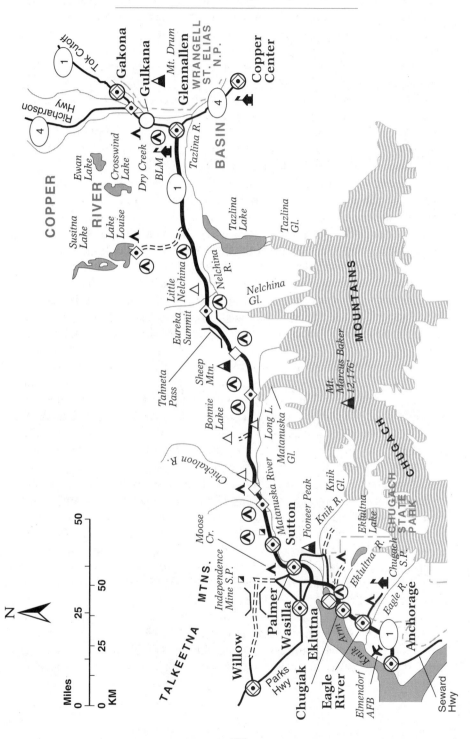

moose have been rerouted through specially modified underpasses. A tall fence keeps the animals off the highway. If a moose does manage to breach the fence, it can follow the fence line until it reaches a wing fence that funnels it through a one-way gate to the outside. The Anchorage moose fence has been a great success: the number of moose-related traffic accidents has declined markedly.

The Chugach Mountains soar east of the highway, within the boundaries of Chugach State Park. This park encompasses 775 square miles (2,000 square kilometers) of steep mountain country, making it one of the largest state parks in the nation. You can reach it from the Glenn Highway via Eagle River Road at Mile 13.4 or Eklutna Lake Road at Mile 26.3.

You can view spawning salmon at the visitor center at the end of Eagle River Road. From there, a section of the old Iditarod Trail leads backpackers deep into the mountains. Eklutna Lake offers lakeside camping and a variety of shorter trails, and there is good blueberry picking on the slopes surrounding the lake. The rolling foothills through which the highway passes are clothed in a dense forest dominated by birch.

At Mile 25.3, an exit leads to the Thunderbird Falls trailhead (southbound traffic can use the Eklutna exit). A one-mile trail leads through the woods to a viewing platform above this powerful cascade on the Eklutna River. The local Dena'ina Indians once fished for salmon at the base of the falls.

One of the centers of Dena'ina culture is located at Eklutna Village, just north of the falls. The Dena'ina are the only Athapaskan-speaking tribe to live along the coast. The more ocean-oriented Inuit and Salishan peoples had appropriated most of the coastal areas in Alaska before the Athapaskans arrived. During the fur-trading days of Russian Alaska, traders employed the Dena'ina as go-betweens with the hostile Ahtna Indians of the interior.

Prior to 1868, the Dena'ina built the Russian Orthodox mission of Saint Nicholas, under the direction of Father Igumen Nikolai. It has become a cultural heritage site, featuring a cemetery filled with colorful "spirit houses." Spirit houses are a Dena'ina tradition that was later incorporated into Russian Orthodox beliefs brought by the missionaries. A spirit house is constructed above a grave after a 40-day period of mourning (while the spirit of the dead wanders the earth) and is painted with clan colors. It is oriented eastward toward the rising sun and is adorned with the Russian Orthodox cross.

Leaving Eklutna, the highway follows the shore of the Knik Arm of Cook Inlet. The tidewater lowland of Eklutna Flats lies below the highway and is adorned in early summer with the blossoms of wild iris and shooting stars. This area is privately owned, and picking the wildflowers is strictly prohibited.

Across the inlet is the rounded mass of Mount Susitna, known locally as "The Sleeping Lady" for its resemblance to the profile of a woman lying down. Massive glaciers rounded the summit of Mount Susitna during the ice ages. The ice was more than 4,000 feet (1,220 meters) deep at this point, and it extended all the way down Cook Inlet to form an ice shelf far out in the North Pacific.

The road crosses the silty channels of the Knik River and proceeds across the Palmer Hay Flats. This brackish tideland was once the site of haying activity, but the land dropped significantly during the 1964 earthquake, and vast areas of the flats are now covered by salt water during the highest tides. The skeletons of dead trees testify to the toxicity of the salt water.

The Palmer Hay Flats are a major staging area for waterfowl during the spring and fall, featuring pintails, teal, wigeon, canvasbacks, and scaup. The birds come to eat tideland sedges that have oil-rich seeds. Moose congregate along Rabbit Slough in the winter and use the Palmer Hay Flats as a calving ground.

The Glenn Highway then returns to dry ground and swings into the fertile valley of the Matanuska River, while the Parks Highway branches off to the north. The Matanuska River valley is mantled in loess deposits up to 30 feet deep in places. Loess is the mineral-rich soil made up of finely ground rock that is deposited at the feet of glaciers, then blown inland by strong winds. This fertile soil combines with 20 hours of summer daylight to nurture the 50-pound cabbages and teacup-sized strawberries for which the valley is famous.

Homesteading began here in 1916, but progress was slow due to the difficulty of cutting the forest, clearing the brush, and pulling out the stumps. Large-scale agriculture came to the valley in 1935 with the Matanuska Colony. Franklin D. Roosevelt conceived this project during the depths of the Great Depression as a means of putting farmers back to work. Most of the 2,000 participants were recruited from the depressed farmlands of Great Lakes states. It was hoped that their Nordic heritage and expertise with cold-weather farming would help them cope with the extreme conditions in Alaska, but most of the colonists ultimately abandoned the project. Nonetheless, they first cleared much of the arable land and created a viable farming economy in the region.

The fertile Matanuska Valley is ringed by impressive summits: the ragged Talkeetna Mountains rise to the north, Matanuska Mountain stands to the southeast, and Twin Peaks and Pioneer Peak scrape the clouds to the south. The road runs eastward to the town of Palmer at Mile 42. George Palmer established a post here in 1875 to trade for furs with the Ahtna Indians of the Copper River basin. The post became a station along the

Palisades of basalt rise above Long Lake.

Matanuska Spur of the Alaska Railroad, which was built in 1916 to serve the coal mines to the east, then blossomed into the hub of Alaskan agriculture in the 1930s. It is now the location of the Agricultural Experiment Station run by the University of Alaska. The Alaska State Fair is held in Palmer each year in late August. Farm roads crisscross the countryside, permitting scenic side trips through the farmlands (see map on page 191).

As the Glenn Highway leaves Palmer, it climbs to a high overlook that commands a fine view of the braided channels of the Matanuska River. *Matanuska* is a Russian word that can be roughly translated as "Copper River Indians," in reference to the Ahtnas who ranged westward into the head of this valley. Just beyond Palmer, the Fishhook Road branches northward toward Hatcher Pass (see Drive 21).

The Glenn Highway continues eastward and enters the Matanuska Valley Moose Range. This area is specifically managed for moose, and openings are cleared in the forest to allow the growth of the shrubs that moose feed upon.

As the valley constricts, the road reaches the old coal-mining settlement of Sutton. Millions of years ago, this area was a swampy tropical forest, and the dying vegetation was transformed over time into seams of coal in the Talkeetna Mountains to the north. The coal is intermixed with shale and sandstone that bear the fossils of ginkgo leaves and other tropical plants. Inquire locally to find the best spots to hunt for fossils.

The Matanuska coal beds were first discovered in 1899 and were being mined on a small scale by 1906. A spur of the Alaska Railroad was built westward to the town of Chickaloon to obtain coal for its locomotives. Peak production in the coal fields occurred in the early 1920s, when the U.S. Navy built a coal washery to process Matanuska coal to fire the boilers of its Pacific Fleet. Two weeks after the washery was completed, the ships of the Pacific Fleet were converted to oil burners and the coal fields were all but abandoned. The foundations of the washery and associated powder magazines have been incorporated into the Alpine Historical Park at Mile 61.6.

West of Sutton, the highway follows the old railway grade of the Matanuska Spur. From Glacier Creek, Crag Peak is visible to the southwest at the edge of the Chugach Mountains. The Dena'ina called this peak *Neltsiiy Ce'e*, meaning "Big One That Is Made Like a Face." Its outline resembles a human profile facing skyward.

Farther east is the sharp spire of Pinnacle Mountain, and the symmetrical point of Kings Mountain rises upriver at the edge of vision. The latter represents an intrusion of hard granite within the weaker sedimentary rock of the Chugach Mountains. The road follows the river past this distinctive mountain to reach the mouth of the Chickaloon River. This is the put-in spot for day-long, Class III floats down the Matanuska to Palmer. Outfitters along this stretch of the highway offer whitewater trips of varying levels of difficulty.

After crossing the Chickaloon, the highway moves inland and begins to climb. At Mile 83, an unmarked spur road takes off northward to a camp-

The Matanuska Glacier is three miles wide where it exits the Chugach Mountains.

ground on Lower Bonnie Lake. Just beyond this point, the highway hugs the shoreline of Long Lake, which is guarded by a craggy escarpment of basalt.

The road continues to climb to reach the shores of Weiner Lake; both Weiner and Long lakes occupy narrow basins that were gouged out of the bedrock by a glacier that once filled the valley. The road descends to the valley floor, and rockhounds may find agates and petrified wood in the streams that drain Anthracite Ridge to the north.

After another climb, the road reaches a highway maintenance station at Mile 93.4. From here, there are excellent views of a small glacier high on the face of Monument Peak. The ice has surrounded and isolated one of the peak's rocky points. Pinnacles that rise from the midst of the ice like this are known as *nunataks*, an Inuit term meaning "lonely peaks."

The road swings southward for an excellent view of the Matanuska River, then crosses Hicks Creek and disappears into the brushy defile of Pinochle Canyon. During the ice ages, Matanuska Glacier was much larger, and it dammed Caribou Creek. The water found an outlet to the east and carved the deep canyon of Pinochle Creek into the bedrock. When the glacier retreated, Caribou Creek returned to its original course.

After climbing along the rim of the cleft, the road emerges onto high slopes that look out over the Matanuska Glacier. About 18,000 years ago, this massive river of ice stretched all the way to the modern site of Palmer. A warming trend occurred 8,000 years ago, causing the glacier to melt back into the mountains. It then surged forward to reach its present position, which it has occupied for the past 7,000 years. Matanuska State Recreation Site offers trails that overlook the glacier, but if you want want to visit its toe, you will have to pay a hefty admission fee to the privately owned Glacier Park Resort, which controls access to the glacier's terminus.

The highway continues to climb, passing behind a distinctive promontory of rock known locally as Lion Head. The resemblance can best be seen when you view it from the west. The road then makes a steep descent to cross Caribou Creek. Follow the steep spur road to find a good spot for gold-panning and rock-hounding. Across the creek, the highway begins to climb, allowing views up the Matanuska Glacier that feature the ice-capped summits at the heart of the Chugach Mountains. Road cuts in this area support wild raspberries that ripen in August.

The road tops out on a high bench below the foot of Sheep Mountain. The colorful reds of this eroded massif derive from oxidizing iron compounds within the rock. Dall sheep graze above the timberline and often can be spotted with binoculars.

The road continues across the hillsides above Tahneta Pass, which marks the drainage divide between the Matanuska and Copper rivers. The pass itself is a broad, glacier-carved trough covered in a mosaic of sedge

Lions Head.

meadows, brushy tundra, spruce stands, and shining wetlands. The largest lakes are Leila Lake (closest to the road) and Tahneta Lake (in the distance).

As the road heads onto the rolling upland, you can look west and see Gunsight Mountain, the easternmost summit of the Sheep Mountain massif. During clear weather, you can see the snowy tops of the Wrangell volcanoes rising far to the east. The loose forest of spruce and willow found in this area makes excellent summer range for moose.

A collection of buildings at Mile 128 marks the location of Eureka Summit, which at 3,322 feet (1,013 meters) is the highest point on the Glenn Highway. Beside the newer Eureka Lodge is a log structure built in 1937 that was the first roadhouse in the area. Watch for caribou in this upland of brushy tundra; parts of the Nelchina herd are sometimes spotted here in early autumn.

For eastbound travelers, Eureka Summit offers the first views of the Nelchina Glacier. This glacier flows from the Chugach Mountains to the south and is striped with ridges of rock debris known as medial moraines. The glacier remains in view as far east as Mile 131. At this point, you will see a new glacier within the folds of the mountains. This narrower, steeper river of ice is called the Sylvester Glacier, and it descends from the flanks of Mount Thor (12,251 feet/3,734 meters). This eye-catching view can be seen as far as the Little Nelchina River, which you cross at Mile 137.5.

Soon after crossing Mendeltna Creek at Mile 153, the highway returns to the upland, and a spectacular panorama of Tazlina Lake unfolds to the south. The Tazlina Glacier pours down from the heights of the Chugach chain and calves icebergs directly into the lake. Views are intermittent because a ragged growth of black spruce rises on both sides of the road. This tree specializes in growing on sites with poorly drained permafrost.

The highway now enters a region of enormous kettle lakes, left behind by melting glaciers. The lakes are known the world over for their outstanding rainbow trout fishing, but are accessible only by air. Trumpeter swans often stop here during their annual migration. A spur road runs northward from Mile 160 on a 19-mile journey to Lake Louise in the heart of this lake district.

The road passes through the heart of the Copper River basin, which was once submerged beneath Glacial Lake Atna. The lake filled and drained repeatedly during the ice ages, as glaciers in the Chugach Mountains alternately dammed the Copper River and retreated to unleash the waters. Silt deposits covered the basin, and when at last the lake drained for good, the water-saturated sediments froze to form the permafrost layer that underlies most of the basin today.

The road crosses Tolsona Creek at Mile 173, and the hilltop above its east bank is the site of several "mud volcanoes." These are really thermal springs that discharge silty sediments and methane gas from heated magma deep in the earth's crust. They are located on private land just north of the road and are hidden from view by the trees.

The next hilltop beyond Tolsona Creek has a pullout that boasts a superb view of the high peaks of the Wrangell Mountains. The farthest to the right is Mount Blackburn, the tallest of the Wrangells. Mount Wrangell, to its left, is the youngest of the group. It retains the classic form of a shield volcano, unscarred by explosive eruptions and glacial erosion. Next in line and slightly in front is Mount Drum, while farthest north is Mount Sanford, with the spectacular Nadina Glacier descending its steep south face. The buildings of Glennallen soon begin to crop up along the roadside, and at Mile 187 the highway reaches the center of town. Two miles beyond this point, the Glenn Highway ends at a junction with the Richardson Highway.

Anchorage Sidetrip

Anchorage is Alaska's largest city, with a population of more than 250,000. It was founded relatively recently—in 1913—as a tent camp for construction workers of the Alaska Railroad, which was to link Seward with the interior town of Fairbanks. Initially called Ship Creek Anchorage, the settlement quickly grew to become the hub for construction on the railway. The name was shortened to Anchorage in 1915, and by 1917 the population had ballooned to 4,000. The town almost died when the railroad was completed, and in 1920 there were fewer than 2,000 residents. The establishment of military bases there prior to World War II breathed new life into the budding metropolis, and it grew to be the chief city in Alaska.

Anchorage sits on a broad peninsula between Knik Arm and Turnagain Arm, an area rife with swamps and peat bogs. Before anyone can build there, they must remove the peat and replace it with gravel fill. On Good Friday 1964, an earthquake measuring 9.2 on the Richter scale wreaked havoc on the city. The Bootlegger Cove clay formation, which underlies the city, liquified and slid toward the sea, toppling buildings and opening gaping rents in the ground. Rather than learn from past mistakes, developers have rebuilt atop the Bootlegger clay despite the continued high risk of earthquakes. In the absence of unified zoning codes, skyscrapers have sprung up beside log cabins in a crazy hodgepodge that has become a defining characteristic of the city. Today, Anchorage has all the trappings of a modern metroplex: museums and theaters, shopping malls and downtown business districts, expressways and traffic jams.

Anchorage offers tourists an array of activities and attractions. You can get information at the downtown visitor center at 4th Avenue and F Street or at the Alaska Public Lands Information Center, also located downtown. The Alaska Museum of History and Art, at 121 West 7th Avenue, has an outstanding collection of Alaskan paintings, as well as displays on the cultural heritage of the state. The Alaska Aviation Heritage Museum is on the south shore of Lake Hood, near the float-plane base. You can view migrating salmon at the Ship Creek spillway and at Potters Marsh, just east of town on the Seward Highway (bird watching is also good there).

Chugach State Park encompasses the mountains that rise above town and offers trails for hikers of all abilities. From Anchorage, you can take day trips to Portage Glacier (see Portage Highway Sidetrip toward the end of Drive 26), the gold-mining ghost town of Hope (see Hope Highway Sidetrip at the end of Drive 26), and the agricultural lands of the Matanuska Valley (see the Glenn Highway section, Drive 22).

23

Tok Cutoff

Official Designation: Alaska Route I
Description: Paved highway from Gakona Junction to Tok; 125 miles (201 kilometers)
Recommended Maximum: Highway speeds
Hazards: Frost heaves prevalent in Copper River basin
Distance Markers: Mileposts count northward from Gakona Junction
Information Sources: Greater Copper Valley Chamber of Commerce, Wrangell-Saint Elias National Park, Tok Chamber of Commerce

 The Drive

This highway has the same route number as the Glenn Highway. It connects the Copper River basin with the town of Tok on the Alaska Highway and offers outstanding mountain scenery, including the Wrangell and Mentasta ranges. The Nabesna Road (see Drive 24) splits away from the highway to penetrate the northern end of Wrangell-Saint Elias National Park. The Tok Cutoff follows the old Eagle-Valdez Trail, blazed in 1902 to service a military telegraph line that stretched from the coast to the Alaskan interior.

The road begins in the heart of the Copper River basin, at a small cluster of businesses called Gakona Junction. This junction lies 14 miles (23 kilometers) north of Glennallen on the Richardson Highway. The Tok Cutoff bears northeast from the junction, descending to the tiny community of Gakona. Located where the Gakona River pours into the much larger Copper River, the site was a traditional summer gathering place for the Ahtna Indians.

A settler named Jim Doyle built his homestead here in 1902, and when the Eagle-Valdez Trail was constructed through his back yard, he erected a roadhouse. The inn came to be known as Doyle's Ranch, and the two-story log structure still stands on the property of the Gakona Lodge. Doyle ultimately sold his business to a family of Norwegian immigrants named the Sundts, and this industrious family built the current roadhouse, carriage house, and other outbuildings in the 1920s. In the early days, it cost a dollar to stay for the night and another dollar for a hot meal. You can see traces of the old Eagle-Valdez Trail along the riverbank behind the lodge.

The highway passes a small Ahtna community and climbs to the bluffs above the Copper River. Openings in the trees reveal the snowy volcanoes of the Wrangell Mountains. Mount Sanford is close at hand, while its smaller neighbor, Mount Drum, rises to the south. These peaks will dominate the scenery for the remainder of your journey through the Copper River basin.

At Mile 35.5, the road descends to cross the many channels of the Chistochina River. Most of the Klondike-bound stampeders who crossed the Valdez Glacier in 1898 had lost their appetites for traveling by the time they reached the Copper River. Many of them prospected in the nearby waterways, and they found the largest deposits of placer gold here, in the gravels of the Chistochina.

The northern rim of the Copper River basin is crowded by the rugged outriders of the Alaska Range, and the highway soon climbs onto their shoulders. From these heights, you can see a vast plain of forests and lakes stretching below, as well as the snowbound peaks of the Wrangell Mountains. Mount Sanford continues to dominate the scene, while the much smaller Tanada Peak rises to the northeast. Grizzly and Cobb lakes are the large meres that lie just below the highway.

At the head of the basin, the Mentasta Mountains march eastward in orderly ranks, an extension of the Alaska Range. The Nabesna Road runs

Wet Meadows along the Slana River.

Tok Cutoff and Nabesna Road

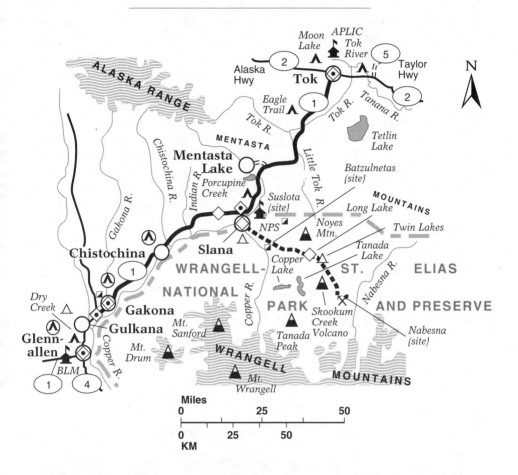

eastward from Mile 60, passing the small settlement of Slana and penetrating deep into the northern quadrant of Wrangell-Saint Elias National Park (see Drive 24).

The Tok Cutoff bears northward, climbing over a hill and then dropping to the banks of the Slana River. This sluggish tributary of the Copper River flows through a wetland of marshes and ponds, and you can see signs of beaver everywhere. The road follows the river into the heart of the Mentasta Mountains, and the steep-sided peaks soon press in from all sides. The valley eventually opens into a broad, flooded plain that trends northwest toward the glacial source of the river, high in the Alaska Range.

The road soon leaves this valley through a narrow gap in the mountains known as Mentasta Pass (Mile 79.5). The pass was a traditional travel corridor for Ahtna Indians, linking summer fishing camps on the Copper River with autumn hunting grounds in the mountains. The native village of Mentasta Lake lies on a short spur road just north of the pass.

The highway descends into the watershed of the Little Tok River, which is framed by blade-shaped peaks. The river meanders through a picturesque valley until it reaches a confluence with the Tok River. The forest is still in the early stages of regeneration after a fire burned near the confluence.

The road crosses the Tok River at Mile 104. Glance up its broad valley for fine views of the Mentasta Mountains. The peaks dwindle to rounded domes as the road follows the river northward, reaching the Eagle Trail State Recreation Site at Mile 109. Here, you can stroll along a section of the original Eagle-Valdez Trail, a route first blazed by Lieutenant Henry Allen during his 1885 expedition up the Copper River and through the Alaskan interior. In 1902, it was upgraded to a pack trail under the direction of Lieutenant Billy Mitchell. From this point northward, the hills give way to the wooded lowland of the Tanana River, and the highway runs arrow-straight to its terminus at Tok.

24

Nabesna Road

Official Designation: Nabesna Road
Description: Improved gravel road from Tok Cutoff to end in Wrangell-Saint Elias National Park; 42 miles (68 kilometers)
Recommended Maximum: 35 mph/55 kph
Hazards: The road fords streams that can rise and become impassable during wet weather
Distance Markers: Mileposts count eastward from Tok Cutoff
Information Sources: Wrangell-Saint Elias National Park

 The Drive

This gravel road begins at the Tok Cutoff and runs through the wild northern reaches of Wrangell-Saint Elias National Park. Sport hunting is allowed within the national preserve north of the road, subject to state and federal regulations. All-terrain-vehicle use requires a permit from the National Park Service. The road is passable to all types of vehicles as far as Trail Creek, at Mile 29.4.

Beyond this point, the road fords several substantial streams, and you shouldn't attempt to cross unless your vehicle has high clearance. The streams may rise and become completely impassable in early spring and after rainstorms. Check at the Park Service ranger station at Slana for current conditions. The last three miles of the road into the privately-owned gold-mining settlement of Nabesna require four-wheel drive and may not be passable.

After passing the ranger station, the road crosses a bridge over the Slana River. A major Ahtna village once stood on the north bank of the river. Today, a few dwellings and limited services are scattered on both sides of the river. A spur road leads from Mile 1.7 to an undeveloped camping area on the riverbank.

The road then passes through a loose forest of white spruce that occupies the well-drained lowland along the river. Both grizzly and black bears migrate down this waterway in April and May, leaving their dens in the mountains for the moose calving grounds in the Copper River lowlands.

After you leave the settlement of Slana, you will have excellent views of the surrounding country through a dwarfed forest of black spruce. The Mentasta Mountains form a rugged wall north of the valley, while the snowy peaks of the Wrangell Mountains rise beyond the Copper River to the south. Mount Sanford is the most prominent of these extinct volcanos; the rugged crest of Capital Mountain is silhouetted against its lower slopes.

The road crosses Caribou Creek at Mile 19.5. The former site of the Ahtna village of Batzulnetas lies a few miles to the south, on the banks of the Copper River. This spot is the high-water mark of Russian exploration during the early fur-trading years. In 1794, the Lebedev-Lastochkin Company sent a party of traders under a man named Samailov into the Copper River basin. Russian fur traders had a reputation for committing atrocities, and one of the best-known incidents occurred after this party arrived at Batzultnetas in the winter. The Russians seized the Ahtnas' weapons, abducted the women, and turned the warriors out into the cold without any clothing. Unbeknownst to the Russians, the Ahtna village of Suslota lay just seven miles away, and the warriors from Batzultnetas were able to travel through the extreme cold to find safety there. Later, a party of Ahtnas returned to Batzulnetas to exact their revenge. The Russians had a Dena'ina guide, who secretly passed spears to the waiting warriors. The women inside the village plugged the invaders' rifles with sticks. The war party then descended on the Russians, killing them all in a blood bath.

More than 50 years later, the competing Shelikhov Company sent a party into the Copper River area to explore and establish trade relations with the Ahtnas. Ruf Serebrennikov led this peaceful party, which arrived at the village of Slana in 1848. The Ahtnas, who had not seen a Russian since the massacre at Batzulnetas, feared that the fur traders in their military-style uniforms had come to avenge their fallen countrymen. The chief of the Mentasta village had been sired by a member of the ill-fated Lebedev-Lastochkin party during their brief occupation of Batzulnetas, and he advised the Ahtnas to wipe out this group of Russians. So the Ahtnas massacred the members of Serebrennikov's expedition. One of the Russians escaped into the willows only to be tracked down and killed near present-day Chitina. The Ahtnas sent Serebrennikov's diary back to his Russian superiors, who never again attempted to send traders into Ahtna territory.

At Mile 22, the road enters a series of low gravel ridges left behind by retreating glaciers. Kettle lakes such as Rock Lake (Mile 22.2) and Twin Lakes (Mile 28) were formed by chunks of glacial ice that were buried in the gravel and later melted to form depressions. Trumpeter swans are regularly spotted on these lakes. From Mile 26, there is an excellent view of Tanada Peak, a dormant volcano that last erupted almost a million years ago. Just beyond Twin Lakes, the road makes tricky fords of Trail and Lost creeks. Keep up your momentum during the crossings and avoid shifting gears, as this causes the engine to suck up water.

The road enters a narrow valley where you might see bands of Dall sheep above the timberline. The Boyden Hills stand to the north, while to

An eroded remnant of the Skookum Creek volcano stands sentinel over the Nabesna Road.

the south are the many domes of the ancient Skookum Creek Volcano. These eroded domes and exposed dikes of hardened magma are spaced in a circle 9 miles in diameter around the central vent of the extinct volcano. Geologists believe they may have been extruded through cracks along the rim of a collapsed caldera. Hike into the high country for a better view of this interesting geological phenomenon.

The road now crosses a major but almost imperceptible drainage divide, and the hills soon open onto the broad valley of the Nabesna River. The Nabesna flows northward through the mountains and joins the Chisana to form the Tanana River, whose waters flow westward into the Yukon River and then to the Bering Sea. The state no longer maintains the road past Devil's Mountain Hunting Lodge, at Mile 42. Four miles to the east lies the old Nabesna Mine, where veins in the bedrock once yielded vast quantities of gold. The first gold strike in the area was made along Jacksina Creek in 1899. According to legend, Carl Whitham tracked a wounded bear into a cave in 1930 and discovered a vein of quartz and gold that is now known as the Bear Claims.

25

Edgerton Highway - McCarthy Road

Official Designation: Alaska Route 10/McCarthy Road
Description: Paved road from Richardson Highway to Chitina; 35 miles (56 kilometers). Narrow gravel road from Chitina to McCarthy; 61 miles (98 kilometers)
Recommended Maximum: 25 mph/40 kph on gravel sections
Hazards: Road between Chitina and McCarthy narrow and not recommended for RVs and trailers. Railroad spikes often surface on road after grading and during rainstorms
Distance Markers: Mileposts count eastward from Richardson Highway, reset at zero at Copper River Bridge, and count eastward for remaining distance to McCarthy
Further Reading: *Historic McCarthy* by M. J. Kirchhoff
Information Sources: Wrangell-Saint Elias National Park, Kennicott-McCarthy Chamber of Commerce

 The Drive

This route is the primary road into Wrangell-Saint Elias National Park, the largest park in the United States (six times as big as Yellowstone). The first 33 miles to Chitina are paved. Beyond this point, the McCarthy Road follows the abandoned grade of the Copper River and Northwestern Railway.

This route is extremely narrow, so pass oncoming vehicles with caution. Even if you are driving a passenger car, you may have to find a wide spot to pull over to allow another vehicle to pass. This part of the route runs through Wrangell-Saint Elias National Park, but most of the roadway is flanked by privately owned land. The road dead-ends on the banks of the Kennicott River. The town of McCarthy and the abandoned Kennecott Copper Mine lie across the river, and at the time this book was written, they could only be reached via a hand-powered cable tram above the water.

The Edgerton Highway leaves the Richardson Highway 32 miles south of Glennallen. It begins as an arrow-straight ribbon of asphalt that descends a long grade to the floor of the Copper River basin. Views along the way are spectacular, featuring the lofty volcanoes of the Wrangell Mountains: Mounts

Drum, Sanford, Wrangell, and Blackburn. Closer at hand, the northern marches of the Chugach Mountains form a wall south of the highway.

At the bottom of the grade, the road enters the settlement of Kenny Lake. Here, homesteaders have cleared pastures and hay fields from the endless forest. A small herd of bison was introduced on the far side of the Copper River, and the animals have occasionally wandered as far south as the outskirts of Kenny Lake.

At Mile 19.5, the road drops steeply to cross the Tonsina River. The road cuts reveal deep beds of gravel deposited during great mud slides that originated on Mount Drum to the north. Later, during the Pleistocene, ice sheets covered the southern half of the Copper River basin, damming the river and creating an immense lake that filled the remainder of the basin. The settlement of Lower Tonsina once stood here on the west bank of the Tonsina River, with a roadhouse that served travelers along the Copper River.

Your first view of the Copper River comes just beyond the crossing of the Tonsina. The road climbs a steep and winding course that was blasted into the bedrock above the river. Pause at the pullout at Mile 21 to look for bison, which were introduced in 1950. You can sometimes spot them on the bluffs beyond the Copper River. At Mile 23.5, there is a campground beside scenic Liberty Falls, which pours through a cleft in the bedrock just out of sight of the road.

As you continue on, the highway seeks a narrow pocket valley that parallels the Copper River. Geologists believe that this steep-walled vale was carved into the bedrock by a stream flowing along the edge of the glacier that once filled the current river course. When the ice melted, the Copper River sought the lower channel that the ice had carved, and this small valley became isolated. The Ahtna Indians knew this steep-walled pocket as the Cheenan Lakes. *Cheenan* means "thank you" in the Ahtna tongue and was conferred out of gratitude for the lakes' abundant grayling. The lakes are now known as Three Mile, Two Mile, and One Mile, in reference to their distance from the town of Chitina.

Chitina was established in 1910 at the terminus of the Copper River and Northwest Railway, which served the Kennecott copper mines. Dubious sourdoughs jokingly called the CR & NW the Can't Run & Never Will, but run it did from 1911 to 1938, transporting more than 200 million dollars worth of copper ore to the port of Cordova on Prince William Sound. During this period, the town of Chitina became the supply hub for the Copper River basin, complete with false-fronted buildings and log cabin residences. After the railroad was abandoned, Chitina became a ghost town, and beavers moved in to flood parts of the already swampy area. Today, a few of the old buildings have been restored, but most are sagging into ruin. There is a ranger station in town that provides information about Wrangell-

Edgerton Highway - McCarthy Road

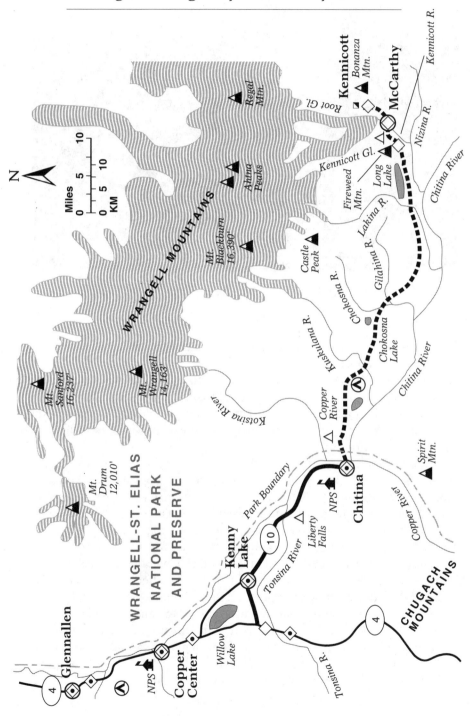

An old train trestle from the CR&NW railway spans the Gilahina River.

Saint Elias National Park and Preserve, which the McCarthy Road enters as it crosses the Copper River.

The route follows the McCarthy Road through a narrow cut blasted through the hills to accommodate the railroad. From there, it follows the river westward for a brief stretch to a bridge that crosses the Copper's silty channels. Subsistence fishermen set up fishwheels in this area to harvest salmon during June and July.

If you look southward down the river, you can see the snow-capped crags surrounding Spirit Mountain, portals to a steep-walled canyon that bears the river through the Chugach Mountains. Once you cross the bridge, you are on a rocky finger of land between the Kotsina and Chitina rivers, which join the Copper River from the east. Spur roads lead to primitive campgrounds on the gravel bars along the Copper River.

As it turns eastward, the road initially offers views of the Kotsina River. It then crosses the heights, and a pullout at Mile 3.9 offers an excellent view of the Chitina River. These rivers have all the hallmarks of geological youth. Their channels move enormous quantities of gravel, and as it piles up, the rivers reroute themselves to lower paths. In this way, the river channels constantly split and shift across broad plains of gravel. Periodic floods keep the bottomland scoured free of vegetation.

As the road moves inland, it passes through an open forest of white spruce and willow that limits your view but makes excellent moose habitat. Ahtna Incorporated, a regional native corporation, has clearcut extensive tracts of this forest on land it owns near the road, citing the danger of a beetle infestation that has destroyed the forests far to the south.

The terrain soon gets boggier, and the road passes among a series of lakes that were gouged out by passing glaciers. The larger ones have been stocked with trout and salmon, and there are several privately run campgrounds in the area. Rugged foothills rise a short distance to the north, obscuring the taller summits that rise beyond them. These foothills are excellent habitat for Dall sheep. A spur road beginning at Mile 13.5 runs north along Strelna Creek to provide access to hiking trails into the mountains.

At Mile 17, a lofty bridge spans the spectacular gorge of the Kuskulana River. The bridge is the original railway span built in 1910, and it stands a dizzying 238 feet above the churning waters. The bridge had no guardrails until 1988 and was regarded by many as the journey's biggest thrill.

The road passes through a series of broad sedge bogs—shallow lakes that have filled with sediment over time. Eventually, dead vegetation will build up to form a well-drained soil, and the forest will take over here. At Mile 22.5, the road leaves the national park and enters the national preserve lands. Sport hunting is allowed within the preserve but is prohibited within the park. Chokosna Lake lies north of the road a short distance beyond the boundary, reflecting the snowy heights of Mount Blackburn. This peak is the oldest and tallest of the extinct Wrangell volcanoes.

After wandering across the flats, the road dips to cross the Chokosna and Gilahina rivers. These clear-flowing streams originate in the foothills, which lack the glaciers that make so many of the local waterways silty. An elevated railway trestle still stands at the crossing of the Gilahina. The two-fanged peak that rises ahead marks the western end of the Crystalline Hills, a craggy chain that will flank the road for the next 20 miles.

The road climbs back onto the flats, where you will have views of the Chugach Mountains and several lakes to the south. The road crosses the Lakina River at Mile 44 and reaches the shoreline of Long Lake. There are several homes along its shores, and the residents have pooled their land to establish a privately owned wildlife sanctuary around the lake. As the road leaves Long Lake, Fireweed Mountain rises ahead, and the snowy crest of Mount Blackburn is briefly visible to the north.

The road rounds Fireweed Mountain and then runs onto the gravel outwash plain of the Kennicott River. At Mile 60.5, a primitive road heads northward toward the terminal moraine of the Kennicott Glacier. The McCarthy Road ends half a mile later at the west bank of the Kennicott River. You can park or camp on private land here for a fee. Do not camp on the lower terrace near the river; a glacier-dammed lake floods each summer and inundates the land along the river.

From the riverbank, you can look upstream to view the snowy summit of Regal Mountain and the Root Glacier. A cable tram provides access across the raging river; it is much easier to have someone at one end pull the tram across than to try propelling yourself. At the time of this writing, there was talk of building a footbridge over the river, but many locals dislike the idea.

The quaint town of McCarthy still has many of its original structures, which date from the boom years of copper mining. However, its authentic ghost-town character is fast disappearing before the inexorable tide of commercialism. Its airstrip is a jumping-off point for "flight-seeing" tours and air-taxi services that drop hikers at remote points within Wrangell-Saint Elias National Park. A small museum is located in the old railway station, and it features a fine collection of photographs from the copper-mining era. A pamphlet for a self-guided walking tour of the Kennecott Copper Mine is available here. The old mine structures are accessible via a 4-mile road that runs north along the river. You can travel the road on a shuttle van, by mountain bike, or on foot. A pamphlet describing a self-guided walking tour of McCarthy and Kennicott is available at several locations in town.

The copper deposits along the Kennicott River were originally the property of an Ahtna chief named Nicolai. Lieutenant Henry Allen heard about the deposits during his exploration of the Copper River in 1885, but the

Tramming across the Kennicott River.

lode remained a rumor until 1899. That year, overfishing by coastal canneries depleted the salmon runs and left the Ahtnas starving. Chief Nicolai gave directions to the deposit to prospectors in exchange for a cache full of food. The prospectors explored the Chitina River area and found a lode of high-grade copper ore near Dan Creek. Even richer lodes were found on the upper slopes of Bonanza Mountain a few years later. These claims changed hands several times before they were acquired and developed in 1915 by a syndicate backed by mining tycoons J.P. Morgan and the Guggenheim brothers.

The Kennicott River and town were named for an American explorer, but the Kennecott Copper Corporation misspelled the name when adopting it. The Copper River and Northwest Railway was built to haul ore to the seaport of Cordova. From there, the ore was carried south by the Alaska Steamship Company, which was owned by the same cartel.

At the mine, a self-sufficient company town sprang up, featuring its own hospital, dairy operation, general store, and school. Aerial tramways brought the ore down from mine shafts high on the mountainside to be processed. The mine operated until 1938, when the high-grade veins of copper played out. The town was quickly abandoned, and the empty, red buildings stand today much as they did when the miners left. A walking tour of this rustic ghost town features an ore-processing mill, ammonia-leaching plant, power plant, company store, and miners' quarters. The Ahtna Peaks can be seen clearly from Kennicott, and hikers can reach the Kennicott and Root glaciers from the old mine site.

26

Seward Highway

Official Designation: Alaska Routes 1 and 9
Description: Paved highway from Anchorage to Seward; 127 miles (204 kilometers)
Recommended Maximum: Highway speeds
Distance Markers: Mileposts count northward from Seward
Further Reading: *Wilderness* by Rockwell Kent, *A Naturalist's Guide to Chugach State Park* by Jenny Zimmerman
Information Sources: Chugach State Park, Chugach National Forest, Kenai Fjords National Park, Seward Chamber of Commerce

 ## The Drive

The Seward Highway begins as a six-lane expressway that runs through the suburbs and shopping malls east of Anchorage. As the buildings and telephone poles fall away, the mighty inner peaks of the Chugach Mountains reveal themselves through glacier-carved gaps in the foothills. At the edge of town is Potter Marsh, a productive wetland ecosystem that offers habitat for wading birds and waterfowl. It was created when the railroad embankment dammed several sluggish streams at the edge of Turnagain Arm. A wooden causeway runs over the brackish marshland, and viewing platforms allow close observation of the silver, pink, and king salmon that spawn here.

The highway soon seeks the shoreline of Turnagain Arm and becomes a two-lane road. Turnagain Arm is a long, fjordlike bay crowded by the Chugach Mountains on the north and the Kenai Mountains on the far shore. Captain James Cook explored this area during his quest for a Northwest Passage in 1778 and named the inlet the River Turnagain. It seems curious today to call this estuary a river, but before the 1964 Good Friday earthquake, it was 8 feet shallower. It emptied completely at low tide to expose the tangled channels of the rivers that feed it. Looking east across the waters of Cook Inlet, you can see Mount Spurr, an extinct volcano.

The highway enters Chugach State Park at Mile 115. The park headquarters occupies the Potter Section House by the roadside. Stations such as this one were built at regular intervals along the Alaska Railroad to house section gangs, which maintained the track. This one has been converted to a visitor center, and it features a collection of historic photographs as well as an old rotary snowplow mounted on a locomotive that was used to clear avalanches from the railroad tracks.

Beyond the section house, the highway clings to the base of steep slopes at the edge of the water, following the tracks of the Alaska Railroad. Numerous hiking trails begin at the roadside and climb steeply into the Chugach Mountains, and a number of small waterfalls tumble from the inaccessible heights.

At Mile 110, the road rounds a rocky headland known as Beluga Point. There are a number of interpretive plaques beside a large pullout here. This promontory has attracted people for more than 8,000 years. The first wayfarers to stop here were probably the predecessors of the Sugpiaq, or Chugach Eskimos, a maritime people who traveled the seas in kayaks and open baidarkas, another type of skin boat. Dwarfed spruce trees, blasted by winter gales and sculpted by salt spray, grow among the rocks that jut into the sea. Coin-operated telescopes aid the search for beluga whales, which can sometimes be seen from this point. These small, white whales are quite sociable, traveling in pods that follow migratory schools of salmon and eulachon. They are relatively safe in Turnagain Arm, which is too shallow for their major predator, the orca, or killer whale. If you turn your binoculars upward, you might spot Dall sheep or even mountain goats on the slopes above the highway between Beluga Point and Indian Creek.

This stretch of highway is also a good place to watch the bore tide, a wall of water that races up the inlet with advancing tides. The bore tide forms because the changing of the tides is exactly synchronized with the

Peaks of Kenai Mountains rise beyond Turnagain Arm.

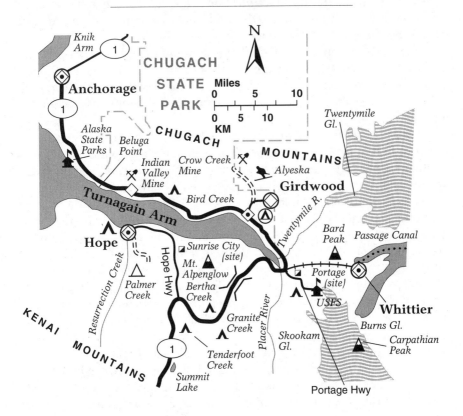

12-hour journey that the tide makes up the inlet. As a result, a slug of water travels down the inlet with each receding tide, reaching the sea in time to meet the incoming tide, which shoves the water back up the inlet in a tidal bore. Turnagain Arm has one of the greatest tidal fluxes in the world, second only to the Bay of Fundy in Nova Scotia. The tidal bore travels at 10 knots and can reach a height of six feet during a "spring tide," when the sun, moon, and earth align. If you want to see the bore tide, you will have to do some advance planning with a tide table: the tidal bore arrives along this stretch of highway about 2 hours and 15 minutes after low tide in Anchorage.

The highway reaches the Indian Valley Mine at Mile 104, just before reaching a small settlement along Indian Creek. Following the 1896 gold strike at Hope, prospectors combed the shores of Turnagain Arm for other lodes of the precious metal. In 1910, a grizzled miner named Peter Strong discovered and staked a vein of quartz and gold that ran through the bedrock on the north shore of Turnagain Arm. He dug an "adit," or horizontal shaft, into the mountainside and began excavation. He worked the claims on and off until 1949, when at the age of 95 he moved to the Pioneer Home in Sitka. He died a short time later. His cabin and mine have become a National Historic Site, with a small museum and gold-panning opportunities.

The highway continues eastward along the shoreline, crossing Indian and Bird creeks, both of which have strong runs of pink salmon. Across the water, Alpenglow Mountain is the most distinctive peak in the Kenai Mountains. The major valley west of this peak bears Sixmile Creek, where the gold-rush boom town of Sunrise City once stood at the edge of the water. The road climbs around a major headland, and avalanche chutes mark the places where periodic snowslides tumble from the peaks above the road. The slides clear away the stiff-trunked conifers, but flexible shrubs such as

Seward Highway

the Sitka alder bend under the weight of the snow and flourish in the open sunlight of these steep clearings. You soon can see the spectacular peaks at the head of Turnagain Arm, clad in glaciers and eternal snow fields.

The road leaves Chugach State Park at the next bay, which contains the town of Girdwood, at Mile 90. This town was a rough-and-tumble center for prospecting activity on the north shore of Turnagain Arm during the late 1800s. As you look inland, the craggy peaks of Summit and Goat mountains wall off the head of the valley, bearing three visible glaciers on their slopes. The flats along the shoreline subsided during the 1964 earthquake, and the salt-water tides moved in and killed the trees near the water's edge, forming a "ghost forest." A spur road leads north to the center of Girdwood, which was moved to higher ground following the quake.

Today, Girdwood is a year-round destination for tourists. Winter visitors flock to the Alyeska Resort, the only major ski resort in Alaska. Summer tourists visit the Crow Creek Mine, located on Crow Creek Road, 5 miles inland. The mine was established in 1897 to work the placer gravel along Crow Creek. It was originally run by a small outfit known locally as "The Crow Creek Boys." The gold-bearing gravels occurred in two distinct formations. The surface gravel was easy to mine and was removed quickly, but a much larger pay streak lay in the ancient stream gravels, buried beneath a thick layer of glacial overburden laid down during the ice ages. Miners built an elevated flume to direct Crow Creek away from the gravels so that they could excavate the deep placer bed with hydraulic cannons. The mine was worked commercially until 1957 and yielded an average of 700 ounces of gold a month during its heyday. It is now managed as a historic site, offering a collection of picturesque log buildings and the opportunity to pan for gold.

From Girdwood, the Seward Highway rounds the base of the next mountain and enters a similar valley, where the Twentymile River flows to the sea. Look southeast for a view of the Skookum Glacier, which descends from a fold in Carpathian Peak. The toe of this glacier is buried in rocky debris, a testimony to the frequent rock slides that hurtle down from the surrounding slopes.

As the highway rounds the end of Turnagain Arm, a train depot at Mile 80 marks the spot where vehicles can be loaded onto flatcars for the overland trip to Whittier, a port on the Prince William Sound ferry route. The Seward Highway bends southward, crossing the wandering channels of Portage Creek. The small town of Portage once stood here, but it was flooded repeatedly by tides in the wake of the 1964 earthquake and had to be abandoned. The Portage Highway runs eastward from this point, providing access to the spectacular glaciers of the Whittier Icefield (see Portage Highway Sidetrip toward the end of this chapter).

The Seward Highway continues around the head of Turnagain Arm and crosses the Placer River. The wetlands in this area sometimes harbor harlequin ducks, and you can occasionally spot bald eagles in the dead snags along the shore. At Ingram Creek, the highway turns inland, climbing steadily through a lush forest of Sitka spruce. This coastal tree has no means of controlling its water loss, so its range is restricted to seacoasts where frequent fog and high humidity keep it moist.

At Mile 68, the road crests the top of a tundra-clad divide known as Turnagain Pass. Meadows spangled with wildflowers mark the swales where snow fields linger into the summer months. Rocky peaks rise all around, dappled with small snow fields or drifts that never melt. The peaks originated as seafloor sediments deposited on the continental shelf 65 million years ago.

Next, the road drops into the Bertha Creek drainage. Here, a drier climate suits the white spruce, which dominates the forests of the Alaskan interior. Substantial tributaries join the creek to create the small river known as Sixmile Creek. An intricate bridge spans Canyon Creek at Mile 57. Just beyond it, the Hope Highway heads east on its way to a picturesque gold-rush town on the shores of Turnagain Arm (see Hope Highway Sidetrip at the end of this chapter).

The Seward Highway begins to climb again and reaches the long pass that contains Summit Lake and its neighbor to the south, Upper Summit Lake. Only the valley floors are forested here: the lower slopes of the mountains are choked with impenetrable brush, and alpine tundra covers the

Upper Trail Lake.

blunted points of the outer peaks. Beyond this first rank of summits lie stark, barren crags.

The Seward Highway drops through a small valley to a junction with the Sterling Highway at Mile 37. Tern Lake lies just south of this junction; its weedy margins and floating mats of vegetation are used by Arctic terns as nesting platforms. Barrow's goldeneyes and common loons are also spotted here with some regularity. Salmon spawn in the outlet of the lake, and you can view them from a Forest Service campground on the western shore.

Steep mountains rise to impressive heights around the valley as the Seward Highway continues southward. The road reaches the Trail Lakes at Mile 32.5, and a lakeshore hatchery raises salmon fingerlings that are planted in lakes and streams throughout the Kenai Peninsula. There is a camping area along Upper Trail Lake at Mile 30.

After passing Upper Trail Lake, the road enters the settlement of Moose Pass. A water wheel at the Estes Grocery turns a grindstone, and a sign proclaims that "Moose Pass is a peaceful little town. If you have an ax to grind, do it here." The road then passes Lower Trail Lake and follows the Trail River down to the heavily timbered shore of Kenai Lake. The road follows the shoreline to the head of the lake, where you will cross the many channels of the Snow River.

To the east, the sedge meadows and spruce copses of the Paradise Valley are flanked by stunning crags. The most impressive of these is Paradise Peak, which rises south of the valley and is graced with several glaciers. A narrow, forested valley leads down to the head of Resurrection Bay, where the highway ends in the town of Seward.

The first European settlement in this area was a ship-building camp built by Russian fur traders under the direction of Alexei Baranoff in 1793. Local spruce was used for lumber, and tar to seal the vessels was made from spruce pitch, sulphur, whale oil, and ocher. A number of small three-masted merchantmen were launched from this shipyard, substantiating Baranoff's boast that his Shelikhov Company was the leader in the Alaskan fur trade.

Bolstered by political approval in the court of the czar, Baranoff's company was subsequently granted a monopoly on the Alaskan trade, and the competing Lebedev-Lastochkin Company was forced to merge with it to form the Russian American Company. When the territory was purchased by the United States, this powerful trading house became the Alaska Commercial Company, which was to become the dominant mercantile force in frontier Alaska.

Seward is headquarters for Kenai Fjords National Park, which encompasses a vast stretch of the Kenai coastline. Glaciers descend from the 950-square-mile Harding Icefield and pour through steep valleys to meet the sea in narrow fjords. Off the coast, the Pacific Plate is actively subducting beneath the continental margin. As it does, it causes frequent earthquakes

Seward has one of the busier boat harbors in Alaska.

during which the coastline sinks into the sea. The long fjords and circular bays were carved by glaciers well above the high-tide mark, but as the coastline subsided, salt water inundated these glacial valleys and cirques.

Tour boats ply the waters of the park, visiting tidewater glaciers that calve icebergs into the sea. Offshore seabird rookeries feature puffins, murres, and kittiwakes, while marine mammals that are commonly sighted include humpback and killer whales, sea otters, and the endangered Steller's sea lion. Shorebound travelers can hike along the spectacular Exit Glacier, which is riddled with deep crevasses that emit a distinctive bluish glow. The Exit Glacier Road departs the Seward Highway north of town at Mile 3.7.

The town itself offers a number of tourist activities. Hiking possibilities in the Seward area include the Mount Marathon Trail, a strenuous climb to the summit of the peak that rises above the townsite. Each year, a no-holds-barred footrace is held along this trail; contestants race to the top of the mountain, then career down the slopes at breakneck speeds to reach the finish line. A longer, gentler trail follows the coastline southward to Caines Head State Park, where old naval gun emplacements were built during World War II to defend the port against Japanese attack. The Seward Museum features artifacts from the city's pioneer days, as well as displays about the 1964 earthquake. The waterfront and boat harbor always bustle with fishing boats, making a colorful and interesting sight. A silver-salmon derby held in mid-August attracts salt-water anglers from around the state.

Portage Highway Sidetrip

This paved road runs eastward for 5.5 miles to reach a Forest Service visitor center at Portage Glacier. The road begins by following Portage Creek up a marshy valley pocked with ponds. Some of these ponds are old gravel pits that were intentionally flooded to create spawning habitat for salmon. Canada geese and whistling swans visit the ponds during the spring and autumn, while harlequin ducks are summer residents along the creek. Both grizzly and black bears visit the lowland when the salmon are in; watch for them on the valley floor. The Explorer Glacier is the first of two hanging glaciers that cling to the mountain crags east of the road. The second is Middle Glacier, which can be seen from the Willawaw Ponds.

After 5.2 miles, the highway reaches the foot of Portage Lake and splits. The road to the right follows the lakeshore for 1.5 miles to a tour-boat dock. Near its end, you will have a fine view of the Byron Glacier. A one-mile hiking trail leads to its snout. Turn left at the foot of the lake for the visitor center, which features interpretive exhibits, an award-winning film presentation, and an indoor platform built over the lake for iceberg viewing. The ice floes calve away from the foot of the Portage Glacier, which lies beyond a rocky shoulder and cannot be seen from the visitor center.

As recently as 1893, the toe of the Portage Glacier rested at the current location of the visitor center, but it has since retreated. It left behind a basin carved 825 feet deep into the bedrock. The basin has filled with meltwater to form Portage Lake.

Bard Peak dominates the head of the lake, with the Bard Glacier perched atop its eastern face. To the left of the peak is the Shakespeare Glacier, which is still advancing. To the right of the peaks is the Burns Glacier, once used as a portage route by Chugach Eskimos and Russian fur traders carrying small boats between Turnagain Arm and Prince William Sound.

Hope Highway Sidetrip

This paved byway runs west for 17 miles (27 kilometers) to reach the former gold-mining town of Hope. The road begins by following the valley of Sixmile Creek to the shore of Turnagain Arm. This stream was heavily worked by prospectors in the late 1800s, and today its raging Class V rapids draw a rush of serious whitewater enthusiasts. The stream pours into the sea at the former site of Sunrise City (Mile 10), which boasted a population of more than 5,000 miners during the height of the gold rush. The townsite has disappeared over time.

From here, the road runs westward along the coast, offering sporadic views of the Chugach Mountains on the far side of Turnagain Arm. The brooding Kenai Mountains loom over a succession of tiny coves and rocky headlands.

The mountains part as the road enters the valley of Resurrection Creek, where the town of Hope harks back to the glory days of the gold rush. Alexander King headed up Turnagain Arm in 1888 to prospect for gold. He never staked a claim, but two years later he showed up in Kenai with four "pokes," or sacks, filled with gold. Charles Miller staked the first claim on Resurrection Creek. He leased his claim to latecomers for a share of the profits, and by his own admission "made a good living for ten years and never hit a lick."

The town of Hope was soon established at the mouth of Resurrection Creek. It was named in honor of Percy Hope, the youngest of a party of prospectors who arrived at the gold fields by schooner. Later, big mining corporations poured into the area, buying exhausted claims with the vain hope of working them using more efficient methods. Geologist F. H. Moffit made the following caustic comment about their futile efforts: "It is doubtful if there is any other part of Alaska where time and money has been wasted in a more enthusiastically ignorant manner or concerning which stockholders in mining companies have been more utterly misled than some places on the Kenai Peninsula."

In 1911, a prospector named John Hirshey located the Lucky Strike vein on Palmer Creek, and his hard-rock mine became a steady producer of gold through the 1930s, accounting for most of the district's production during that time. Today, you will find rustic cabins, clapboard buildings, and a small museum that highlights Hope's gold-rush roots. From town, the Palmer Creek Road climbs into the mountains, providing access to a primitive campground and the head of the Resurrection Trail, a popular backpacking route that travels the length of the Kenai Peninsula through the wildest and most remote mountains.

27
Sterling Highway

Official Designation: Alaska Route I
Description: Paved highway from junction with Seward Highway to Homer; 142 miles (228 kilometers)
Recommended Maximum: Highway speeds
Hazards: Watch out for moose crossing the road, especially at twilight
Distance Markers: Mileposts count distance from Seward
Further Reading: *K'tlegh'i Sukdu: A Dena'ina Legacy* by Peter Kalifornsky, *Kenai*, edited by Angela Tripp
Information Sources: Chugach National Forest, Kenai National Wildlife Refuge, Kenai Chamber of Commerce, Homer Chamber of Commerce

 ## The Drive

This highway emerges from the Kenai Mountains and follows the lowlands along Cook Inlet southward to reach a spectacular end at the tip of the Homer Spit, which juts into Kachemak Bay. Along the way, it passes through one of the cradles of Russian America, visits the Kenai Peninsula's legendary salmon streams, and offers access to numerous beaches along the coast. Much of the lowlands fall within the Kenai National Wildlife Refuge, which was set aside as a moose range in 1941. Give these enormous herbivores the right-of-way when they cross the road.

From its junction with the Seward Highway at Tern Lake, the Sterling runs west and descends through a pretty valley flanked by the tall peaks of the Kenai Mountains. Watch the slopes to the south for signs of controlled burns that were set by the Forest Service to improve moose habitat. Moose browse upon the shrubs that spring up in the wake of forest fires. In the early 1900s, residents set extensive fires on the Kenai Peninsula in a misguided effort to reduce mosquito populations, and the moose population erupted to record levels as brush grew over the burned areas. In recent times, forest succession has replaced these massive brush fields with young stands of conifers, which offer little forage for moose. The controlled burning program is an effort to provide an additional supply of forage shrubs so that the moose population can be maintained at a stable level.

Sterling Highway

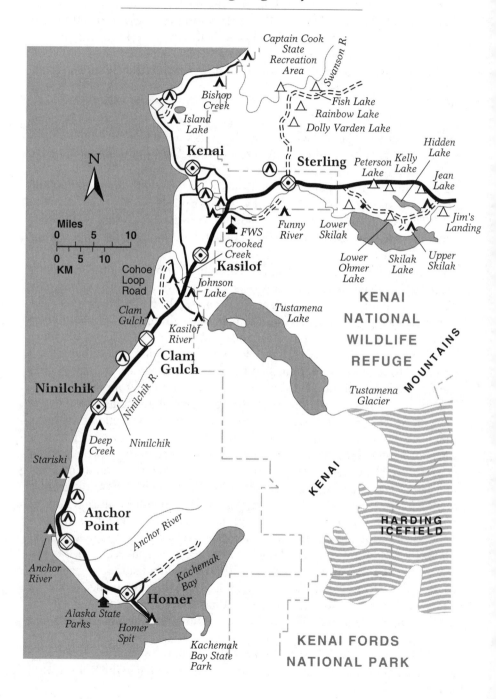

At Mile 45, the road strikes the shoreline of Kenai Lake, an important rearing habitat for juvenile red salmon. The lake occupies a glacial trough that has been dammed by an old terminal moraine. You will travel beside water for the next 3 miles. It derives its distinctive hue from the fine silt carried into it by glacier-fed streams. Scan the slopes to the north for bands of Dall sheep, which use this area as a lambing ground in early spring. Look for mountain goats on Cecil Rhode Mountain, which rises above the south shore of the lake.

At the foot of the lake, the highway crosses the Kenai River, and the Snug Harbor Road splits away to the left on its way to Cooper Lake and the Upper Russian Lake trailhead. As the highway follows the Kenai River, it passes among the scattered businesses of Cooper Landing. In 1848, a Russian mining engineer named Peter Doroshin discovered small amounts of placer gold in the river, but the find was never pursued.

The Kenai River is one of Alaska's most important salmon spawning streams with impressive runs of reds and silvers as well as the largest king salmon in the world. These abundant salmon runs attract coastal brown bears and bald eagles, which fish for live salmon and feed on the spawned-out hulks of dead ones. This area was also a seasonal focal point for the Kenaitze Indians, who built dugout houses along the banks of the river. The Kenaitze, a subgroup of the Dena'ina Athapaskans, lived a traditional lifestyle heavily oriented toward the sea. Linguist James Carrie termed the Kenaitze "a mountain people on salt water," because they are the only Athapaskan-speaking tribe on the continent that inhabits a coastal area. It is likely that the Kenaitze gained much of their maritime technology from the Chugach Eskimos, who lived along the neighboring shores of Kachemak Bay.

At Mile 53.8, there is a self-guiding interpretive trail along the river that visits house pits that are more than 500 years old. They were part of a summer fishing encampment. The Kenaitze returned parts of their catch to the river to release the guiding spirit for returning salmon. A new interpretive center is being constructed across from the Russian River Campground at Mile 52. It is scheduled to open in August 1996. It will feature a replica of a Kenaitze fish camp, complete with pit houses and live demonstrations.

The confluence of the Kenai and Russian rivers is one of the focal points for freshwater salmon fishing in southcentral Alaska. When the salmon are in, Anchorage residents pour into the Kenai Peninsula to engage in a traditional rite known as "combat fishing." They line the banks, elbow to elbow, and when a lucky angler hooks a salmon, he shouts "Fish On!" Neighboring anglers haul in their lines to avoid entangling the fighting fish—in theory, at least. Even when the fish has been subdued, the game is not over: brown bears occasionally sidle in to steal the catch. In such an event, wise anglers will cut their lines, surrender their catch, and give the bears a wide berth.

There is a boat launch and angler's ferry here, which provide access to the south bank of the Kenai River and to the mouth of the Russian River. Fishing regulations in this area are quite complicated, so you should familiarize yourself in advance with the seasons and limits that apply to each stream.

The highway now enters the vast expanse of the Kenai National Wildlife Refuge. Search the tributary streams for mergansers and water ouzels. The refuge encompasses the western fringes of the Kenai Mountains and much of the lowlands that extend to Cook Inlet. At the turn of the century, wildlife populations in the area were decimated by the market hunters who supplied meat to the gold-mining boom towns of Hope and Sunrise City. At the same time, residents set forest fires in the boggy lowland west of the mountains, part of their anti-mosquito crusade. In the ensuing years, the burned area became a vast brushland, where moose thrived on a diet of shrubbery and reached record populations by the 1930s.

It was during this period that the Kenai Peninsula gained recognition as one of the world's great wildlife sanctuaries, and in 1941 it was set aside as the Kenai National Moose Range. The refuge has since been renamed and expanded to include almost 2 million acres. It provides outstanding canoeing, fishing, and hiking opportunities. You are most likely to see moose by the Skilak Lake and Swanson River roads.

The mountains dissolve into isolated knobs as the highway continues westward. At Mile 58, the Skilak Lake Road departs to the south opposite a Fish and Wildlife Service visitor information station. The Skilak Lake Road loops away from the Sterling Highway to pass among a number of large lakes at the foot of the mountains. Then it rejoins the highway at Mile 75.

Meanwhile, the Sterling Highway wanders past Jean Lake on its way out of the mountains. A broad and rumpled lowland stretches westward for 40 miles to Cook Inlet. Glacially carved lakes are scattered across the plain like so many shining mirrors. They provide opportunities to catch rainbow trout, arctic char, and salmon. Sticklebacks share the waters with other young fish, and this bounty of small fish sustains nesting populations of red-necked grebes, common and Arctic loons, and trumpeter swans.

The land between the lakes is often boggy, due in large part to the hardpan that underlies the surface soil and prevents water from percolating downward. The only tree that thrives in these swampy acidic soils is the black spruce. In the Alaskan interior, this tree is an indicator of permafrost. In the relatively balmy climate of southeast Alaska, it is found on poorly drained fens underlain by layers of impermeable clay. Beneath this surface mantle, the lowlands rest upon beds of gravel outwash deposited by the glacial ice that once covered the region. In some places, these gravel beds are more than 20,000 feet deep.

At Mile 68.3, a gravel road departs southward to primitive campsites on Kelly and Peterson lakes. These small lakes fringed in water lilies are typical of the lowlands. From them, you will have good views of the Kenai Mountains to the south and east. Ten miles beyond this point, the highway crests a rise above the town of Sterling. From the heights, you will have a clear view of the snow-mantled summits of the Chigmit Mountains beyond the waters of Cook Inlet. From north to south, you can see Mounts Spurr, Redoubt, and Iliamna. They are just the northern tip of a vast arc of volcanoes that stretches a thousand miles into the North Pacific to form the Aleutian Islands. Each of these volcanoes has erupted in recent times. In 1992, Mount Spurr sent an explosive plume of ash aloft, wreaking havoc with commercial airliners bound for the Anchorage airport.

At the bottom of the grade lies the town of Sterling, a hub of freshwater sport-fishing on the Kenai Peninsula. The Swanson River Road runs northward from town through extensive natural-gas drilling fields. It provides access to two popular canoe trails that link the many lakes and streams of the Kenai lowlands. The Swan Lake complex is the easier of the two, offering the possibility of loop trips of varying lengths. The Swanson River Canoe Trail is more challenging, with steeper portages, frequent logjams, and dense aquatic vegetation in places. Check at the Kenai National Wildlife Refuge visitor center in Soldotna for more information on canoeing on the Kenai Peninsula.

The highway continues westward for 14 miles through increasingly populated country to reach the town of Soldotna. There is a wildlife and historical museum on Centennial Park Road, and the Kenai National Wildlife Refuge operates a visitor center off Funny River Road that houses interpretive displays and offers free wildlife films. This is a modern community of suburbs, shopping malls, and fast-food outlets. A spur road runs northwest to the town of Kenai, a colorful coastal settlement steeped in the history of the Russian fur trade (see Kenai Spur Highway Sidetrip at the end of this chapter). The Sterling Highway bends southward here, on its way down the length of the Kenai Peninsula.

The Sterling Highway now heads inland, following a crest of low ridges that offers frequent views to the east, where the Kenai Mountains form a wall along the horizon. The first settlement along this southern leg of the highway—and one of the first in Russian Alaska—is Kasilof, established by the Lebedev-Lastochkin Trading Company in 1786 as Saint George. Very little evidence remains of the trading post and the Indian village that grew up around it, and the "town" now exists only as a rural community. The Kasilof River runs through it, bearing the water of Tustamena Lake to the sea. You can reach the lake by boat. Follow a 6.4-mile road that has a sign for Johnson Lake State Recreation Area. This immense lake receives the meltwater of the vast Tustamena Glacier. Boaters should be aware that dangerous gales blow up without warning on this lake.

The highway strikes the coastline at Clam Gulch and follows the blufftops overlooking Cook Inlet for the remaining 50 miles to Homer. The tidal flats that stretch from Clam Gulch to Stariski Creek hide rich beds of razor clams. If you plan to dig for clams, be sure to check clamming regulations and ask locally about the danger of shellfish poisoning.

Blufftop overlooks along this stretch of highway offer views of the mighty Chigmit volcanoes beyond the inlet. Mounts Redoubt and Iliamna are closest. Mount Spurr is to the north and the island volcano of Mount Saint Augustine becomes visible as you approach Anchor Point. State recreation areas provide access to the beach at Clam Gulch (Mile 177), Ninilchik (Mile 135), Deep Creek (Mile 138), and Anchor River (Mile 157).

On the north bank of the Ninilchik River sits the historic village of Ninilchik. It was first settled in 1820 by Russian fur traders who had married native wives and wished to remain in Alaska after their retirement. The Russian American Company encouraged intermarriage as a means to solidify trade ties with local tribes and offered a small pension to employees who wished to remain here.

Early Ninilchik was a self-sufficient farming community, where raising farm stock and vegetables was supplemented by fishing and hunting. Several old cabins, of dovetail construction, remain from the early days, and a beautiful Russian Orthodox Church stands on the blufftop overlooking the old village. A group of Russian Old Believers settled to the east of Anchor Point in the 1960s, forming a small agricultural colony called Nikolaevsk. These people are primarily commercial fishermen and small farmers, and dress in the traditional outfits of the Russian countryfolk. They do not consider themselves a tourist attraction: Respect their privacy.

The vegetation on the seaside bluffs is quite different from that found in the black-spruce bogs farther inland. Here, elegant Sitka spruce rise from a parkland of tallgrass meadows and great rounded hedges of alder. Fireweed is the dominant wildflower along this stretch of highway. Captain Cook sailed along this reach of coastline as he sought a Northwest Passage around the top of the continent. He dropped anchor and went ashore at the Kenaitze village of Laida, which has since been renamed Anchor Point.

A small settlement here serves this thriving sport-fishing area. This is the westernmost point on the continent that can be reached by automobile, and it is a good area for bird watching. You can see mergansers and belted kingfishers along the river, ducks and sea gulls on the marshy river estuary, and pelagic birds such as cormorants, murres, and puffins along the shore of Cook Inlet.

The highway continues southward, crosses the Anchor River, and runs inland for a time. It emerges on the oceanside bluffs just north of Homer and passes the headquarters of Kachemak Bay State Park at Mile 168.5. The park itself lies beyond Kachemak Bay and is accessible by boat.

The road soon arrives at two pullouts that command a spectacular view of Kachemak Bay and the mountains beyond. Looking from south to north, you can see the Doroshin, Wosnesenski, and Grewingk glaciers among the southern Kenai Mountains. Long ago, an immense glacier scooped out Kachemak Bay and created the great wall of gravel debris that became Homer Spit. You can see it jutting 5 miles into the water. Some geologists believe that the whirling currents of Cook Inlet have added to the spit by depositing cobbles. The spit was once much wider, but as the entire landscape subsided during the Good Friday earthquake of 1964, about two-thirds of the old spit slipped beneath the sea.

Kachemak Bay was once a cultural center for the Sugpiaq (or Chugach Eskimos), who arrived here by sea some 2,500 years ago. *Kachemak* is an Eskimo word meaning "Smoking Bay," and it refers to the smoldering seams of coal that line its coastal bluffs. Russian fur traders established a small coal mine near Port Graham on the far shore of the bay in 1853.

Homer enjoyed a brief coal boom between 1899 and 1907, and a short railway ran from the mines to the end of the spit, where the coal was loaded onto ocean-going freighters. After the coal industry petered out, the area dwindled (or, some would say, progressed) into a rural district of small homesteads. Today, residents still gather coal on the tidal flats to fuel their furnaces in the winter. Homer remained a backwater until the 1950s when the highway linked it to the rest of Alaska and allowed an influx of artists who came to enjoy the spectacular scenery and unhurried lifestyle. When the 1964 earthquake destroyed the Seldovia waterfront, most of the canneries on Kachemak Bay moved to Homer. The move boosted the Homer economy by making the town the home port of a large commercial fishing fleet.

The highway descends from the hilltops and enters the outskirts of Homer. The center of town lies uphill from the highway on Pioneer Avenue, where you will find the Pratt Museum. It houses a collection of wildlife displays and a haunting exhibit on the *Exxon Valdez* oil spill. Another cluster of businesses lines the Homer Spit, which is also where you will find the boat harbor. The highway traverses the spit all the way to a barricade at its spectacular tip, surrounded by the deep waters of Kachemak Bay. Camping is allowed on city land along the spit for a small fee.

If you wish to explore farther by car, you can take a drive along Diamond Ridge Road and Skyline Drive, which run atop the high bluffs above town and yield spectacular views of Kachemak Bay. The East End Road runs eastward along the shoreline for 20 miles, ultimately offering views of the Portlock and Dixon glaciers at the head of Kachemak Bay.

The spit attracts fishermen, both professionals and amateurs. The busy boat harbor is home to a large fishing fleet, most of which is at sea during the fishing season, supported by huge factory trawlers that process the catch on the fishing grounds. Kachemak Bay and Cook Inlet are famous for their halibut fishing, and each year the city puts on a Halibut Derby with cash prizes for the largest fish and for tagged halibut. The Alaska Department of Fish and Game rears young king and silver salmon in a lagoon known as the "Fishing Hole." After the fish have been released and have grown to adulthood, their uncanny migration instinct leads them back to this spot. However, these fish cannot spawn: there is no spawning gravel. Most of them are caught by waiting anglers.

Wildlife-viewing opportunities abound in Homer and the greater Kachemak Bay area. Mud Flat, near the base of the Homer Spit, supports the largest concentration of shorebirds on the Alaska highway system each spring. A Shorebird Festival is held in early May, celebrating the passage of thousands of dunlins, dowitchers, surfbirds, sandpipers, and turnstones. In the winter, the spit is home to bald eagles, eider ducks, and loons. You can take a boat tour of Kachemak Bay to visit the seabird rookeries at Gull Island, where guillemots, kittiwakes, murres, cormorants, and puffins nest on the steep cliffs. You also are likely to see sea otters and perhaps even minke and killer whales.

Homer is the gateway to some of the more inaccessible spots along the Alaskan coastline. There is regular ferry service from Homer to nearby Seldovia, as well as to distant ports such as Kodiak Island and Dutch Harbor. Seldovia is a quiet fishing village nestled on a neck of land between saltwater arms, across the mouth of the bay from Homer. It is known for its

Murres and kittiwakes crowd a rookery island in Katchemak Bay.

historic boardwalk district. Halibut Cove lies directly across the bay from Homer, east-southeast, and is accessible by a smaller ferry. The community is laid out along sinuous salt-water channels and on tiny islands, and residents use small boats to get around "town." Nearby is Kachemak Bay State Park, which offers hiking trails to alpine tundra, enormous valley glaciers, and the forested lowland along its sheltered coves. To the east is a more primitive wilderness area where there are no trails.

Kenai Spur Highway Sidetrip

This paved spur road runs 11 miles to the northwest to reach the town of Kenai and then continues up the coast to Captain Cook State Recreation Area at the mouth of the Swanson River. Kenai is situated at the point where the meandering Kenai River pours into Cook Inlet. The site was originally inhabited by the Kenaitze Indians, and in 1791, Russian fur traders built a redoubt and trading post here and called it Saint Nicholas. In the centuries that followed, Kenai has seen the coming of missionaries, a fishing fleet, and finally the oil industry. Each has left its own characteristic mark upon the town.

The visitor center in the midst of town is one of the most advanced of its kind. It features mounts of local wildlife as well as cultural exhibits featuring the Kenaitze and Sugpiaq peoples and life in Russian America. Just down the street, the Russian Orthodox Church of the Holy Assumption is topped by three onion-shaped domes. The original church was founded by Father Egumen Nikolai, who became famous as a traveling missionary to the Dena'ina people throughout the Cook Inlet region. The modern church was built 50 years later and is considered by architects to be one of the finest examples of this architectural style in the world.

Across the street from the church is a replica of the barracks building from Fort Kenay, a short-lived outpost constructed in 1869 to consolidate America's newly purchased claim on the territory of Alaska. The Kenaitze Indians have an office in this building, and they conduct interpretive walking tours of the former native village site within the modern town of Kenai. The commercial fishing fleet has its harbor near the mouth of the river. If you arrive just before one of the season openings, you can watch the parade of boats queuing up in the estuary to set sail the moment the season opens.

At Forest Park, you can look for beluga whales in the Kenai River estuary. Pods of these small, white mammals swim into the river in pursuit of migrating schools of salmon. The Kenai Flats, just south of town along the river, are a spring stopover for Canada geese, as well as for snow geese bound for their nesting grounds in Siberia. Viewing platforms have been outfitted with telescopes, and you can also get a good view of Mounts Spurr, Redoubt and Iliamna. A small population of caribou was introduced here in 1965, and you occasionally can spot these animals on the Kenai Flats or along Marathon Road, which leads to the first natural-gas wells in the region. They are closed to the public. Look for sandhill cranes in these same places.

After leaving town, the highway runs north along the coastline for ten miles to the town of Nikiski. This settlement has boomed with the discovery of offshore oil fields in Cook Inlet. Several major oil companies have operations in this town, and you can sometimes spot oil tankers at the dock. Offshore drilling rigs are visible to the west.

The road continues northward, passing several lakes and entering Captain Cook State Recreation Area at Mile 36. This park has lakes for fishing and swimming, campgrounds and picnic areas, and access to the beach along Cook Inlet. The Swanson River pours into the sea here, marking the end of the Swanson River Canoe Trail. The road ends within the park, on a bluff overlooking Cook Inlet and the Chigmit Mountains beyond.

28

Steese Highway

Official Designation: Alaska Routes 2 and 6
Description: Paved highway from Fairbanks to Chatanika, gravel road for remaining distance to Circle; 162 miles (261 kilometers) overall
Recommended Maximum: 45 mph/80 kph on gravel sections; 35 mph/55 kph beyond Central
Hazards: Frost heaves near Chatanika; gravel sections prone to potholes and washboards after wet weather
Distance Markers: Mileposts count distance from Fairbanks
Further Reading: *The Blue Parka Man* by H.C. Landru
Information Sources: Bureau of Land Management (Northern District)

 ## The Drive

The Steese Highway is the oldest established travel route in the Alaskan interior. It was originally blazed in 1894 as a freight trail from Circle to the placer mines along Birch Creek and was extended to Fairbanks when gold was discovered there in 1902. It was upgraded to a road in 1927 to provide access to the Davidson Ditch, an aqueduct system that brought water from the Chatanika River to the gold fields around Fairbanks.

The highway is paved as far as the lower reaches of the Chatanika and is a wide gravel highway from there to Central. The final distance to Circle is narrow and winding. Popular attractions along the way include several high alpine passes in the White Mountains and hot-springs resorts near Central and at the end of the Chena Hot Springs Road.

The highway leaves Fairbanks as the Steese Expressway and rns north through the settled outskirts of town. At Mile 5, the Chena Hot Springs Road runs eastward up the valley of the Chena River (see Chena Hot Springs Road Sidetrip at the end of this chapter). A short distance beyond this junction is an exit for Hagelbarger Road, which is Alaska's answer to Mulholland Drive in Los Angeles. Locals come to a hilltop overlook on this road for nighttime views of the lights of Fairbanks.

The highway continues northward, following the Trans-Alaska Pipeline. There is a pipeline viewpoint with interpretive displays at Mile 8.5. A mile past it, the Goldstream Road departs to the west, leading to Gold Dredge Number 8. Tis dredge has been restored and is operated as a private conces-

Steese Highway

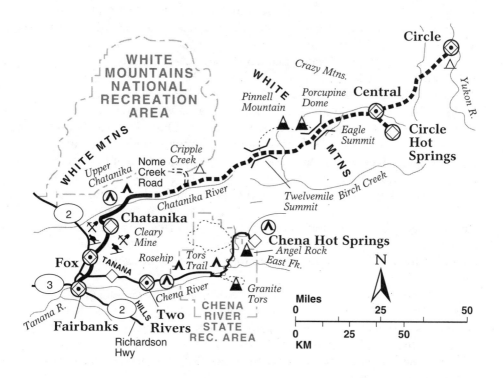

sion with guided tours, a small museum, and gold-panning opportunities.

The valley of Goldstream Creek lies at the heart of the Fairbanks gold fields, which stretch from Ester Dome to Cleary Summit. They have produced more than 8 million ounces of gold during their long and colorful history. The first prospectors used drift-mining methods, digging tunnels into the frozen ground in the winter. Once they reached the gold-bearing gravel, the miners "drifted" along the paystreak, using timbers to stabilize their tunnels. They processed the gravel they extracted with either sluice boxes or rockers, which used moving water to separate the heavy gold from lighter rock deposits.

These primitive methods were only suited to rich deposits, and when these played out, the big mining corporations moved in with water cannons and floating dredges. There was not enough water in the Goldstream Valley to sustain these enormous operations, so an aqueduct called the Davidson Ditch was built to bring water from the Chatanika River watershed. The large-scale dredging operations shut down in the 1950s, but mining on a smaller scale has continued in the area.

In the 1960s, the University of Alaska-Fairbanks, in cooperation with the U.S. Army, dug a tunnel into the permafrost. Researchers found that some wedges of ice within the permafrost were more than 30,000 years old, dating from the middle of the ice ages. Numerous fossils were found during the excavation, providing insight into the mammals that roamed central Alaska during the Pleistocene. The bones of steppe bison dominated the remains that were found. Nearby placer-mining operations also unearthed a number of fossils. The most famous of these was "Blue Babe," a steppe bison that was killed by a cave lion and later mummified almost intact in the frozen soil. It is on display at the University of Alaska Museum in Fairbanks.

The expressway ends at the crossroads town of Fox. Travelers bound for the Elliott and Dalton highways should continue straight ahead here, while motorists heading up the Steese should turn right at the intersection.

The Steese Highway runs east up the valley of Pedro Creek. The stream is named for prospector Felice Pedroni (known to the local miners as "Felix Pedro"), who discovered gold here in 1902 and started the rush to the Fairbanks gold fields. The town of Golden City soon grew up at the head of the valley. Ironically, this was one of the first communities to be plowed under by the massive gold dredges that followed on the heels of the small-time drift miners.

Upon reaching the head of the valley, the road climbs a long grade to Cleary Summit. Denali stands out from the snowy crags of the Alaska Range far to the south, and on a clear day you can see it from here. There are two small ski areas at Cleary Summit, and the enormous Fort Knox Mine lies just over the hilltop to the east. When it begins operation, it will be the largest open-pit gold mine in the world.

The road descends into the valley of Cleary Creek. As it approaches the bottom of the grade, watch for an unmarked spur road at Mile 24.2 that leads to the old Cleary Mine on the far wall of the valley. This hard-rock mine is on private property, but its stamp mill and other buildings are still largely intact.

The town of Cleary once occupied the upper part of this basin, and at its peak from 1904 to 1906, it was the largest gold producer in the region. The gold played out by 1908, and shopkeepers relocated downstream to the town of Chatanika. This rollicking mining settlement boasted a dance hall, a hospital, three hotels, and even a baseball team. Prospectors who staked their claims here were drift-mining the widest placer streak in the world.

After prospectors removed all the easy gold, the Fairbanks Exploration Company (known locally as the F. E. Company) moved in with enormous bucket-line dredges. The company's gold camp, built in 1921, has been refurbished as a full-service lodge. A dredge in excellent condition still floats in its pond amid the gravel at Mile 28.5. The dredge was a floating processing mill, with a conveyor belt of buckets that scooped out gravel and carried it into the bowels of the dredge. Here, the gravel was processed to remove the gold, and the waste gravel was discharged from the rear of the dredge to form great, sinuous gravel piles called "tailings heaps." Most of the bottomland along Cleary Creek was dredged at one time or another, and tailings heaps fill the valley floor. From this dredge, trails run west across Cleary Creek to visit the ruins of some old prospectors' shacks that predate the dredging era.

The highway soon strikes the Chatanika River and turns east to follow it upward through a valley filled with spruce-peat bogs. Permafrost lies just beneath the bottomland soil, and the warmth of the highway has caused this frozen layer to melt in places. This causes the pavement to buckle and forms dips and rises known as frost heaves.

The Poker Flats Rocket Range lies south of the road, but it is not open to the public. The facility is operated by the Geophysical Institute at the University of Alaska and is used to fire unmanned rockets into the aurora borealis to gather scientific data.

The aurora, also known as the northern lights, are vast curtains of colored light in the night sky. The phenomenon is most intense near the Arctic Circle and is best seen in autumn or spring when the midnight sun does not overwhelm the display. The northern lights are formed when storms on the surface of the sun emit great quantities of charged particles known as "solar winds." As a result of forces caused by the earth's rotation, these charged particles funnel down to the earth near the poles. They glow as they fall through the atmosphere, forming the bands of colored light that are a defining feature of the Far North.

The highway continues up the valley of the Chatanika. A number of gravel pits have been converted to ponds between Miles 36 and 40. They have been stocked with grayling and may harbor waterfowl during the autumn migrations. The road crosses the Chatanika at Mile 39, and a state campground on its north bank is a popular take-out point for floaters on the Chatanika Canoe Trail. Most canoeists put in at Cripple Creek (Mile 60) for a one-day float. The trip features relaxing Class II water with a few "sweepers," trees leaning into the water from the riverbanks, posing a serious danger to paddlers. Give these as wide a berth as possible. The Chatanika may be too shallow to float during late summer. The pavement ends at Mile 44, and beyond this point, the road becomes a broad gravel thoroughfare.

Signs of civilization fall away as the road continues up the valley, and forested domes crowd in around the river. There are a number of fine overlooks of the water as the road sticks mainly to the slopes above it. Stands of tall white spruce line the insides of the river bends, where the water has thawed the underlying permafrost. On the outsides of the curves, the frozen ground lies just beneath the surface, and so the streambank vegetation is mostly spindly black spruce and peat bogs. As the river flows around the outside of the curves, it melts the permafrost and thus accelerates its carving action in this direction. Sediments are deposited in the eddies along the inside of the curve, and these will ultimately form dry, frost-free gravel bars where young white spruce can take root. As the river channel moves farther away, permafrost will creep into the sediments and black spruce will take over. In this manner, the river channels are continually shifting across the bottomland, rearranging the distribution of permafrost in the soil and influencing the plant communities of the riverbanks.

The slopes that line the valley also show the influence of permafrost on the forest community. North-facing slopes receive less sunlight, so permafrost lies just below the surface. Black spruce, the permafrost specialist, grows here. On the south-facing slopes, white spruce is the climax tree, while balsam poplar grows on old burn sites. The poplar provides spectacular displays of autumn color that peak in mid-September.

At Mile 57.3, a narrow spur road leads north over a divide to Nome Creek, a popular gold-panning spot. Dredges worked this creek in the early 1900s, but its gravel still contains small quantities of gold.

You can see the Davidson Ditch here; other sections are visible from the road at Miles 63.6 and 65.6. This system of ditches, flumes, and inverted siphons formed an aqueduct to carry water from the upper Chatanika watershed to the placer fields of Goldstream Creek. In the gold fields, the water was used to power hydraulic cannons that washed the gold-bearing gravel down from the hillsides and to float the dredges that worked the valley bottoms. The ditch was 83 miles long and was Alaska's first pipeline, completed in 1929. After the last gold dredges shut down, water from the ditch was used to generate electricity. The Chena River flood of 1967 destroyed part of the pipe and finally put an end to its usefulness.

The Chatanika soon shrinks to a trickle, and tundra-capped mountains rise on either side of the valley. The road makes a long ascent to Twelvemile Summit, where it breaks into the open tundra at Mile 85.5. Spectacular wildflower displays peak here in late June, featuring arctic bell heather, anemone, mountain avens, oxytrope, and the arctic forget-me-not. Autumns are equally brilliant, as the arctic willow, dwarf birch, and alpine bearberry of the tundra burst into shades of gold and crimson before dropping their leaves.

The Pinnell Mountain Trail runs north from Twelvemile Summit, looping 27 miles across the tundra ridgetops before returning to the highway at Eagle Summit. A short spur road running south from the pass visits an old section of the Circle-Fairbanks wagon trail. The pack trail that preceded the wagon road was renowned for its steep grades. Josiah Spurr led a Geological Survey expedition over this trail in 1897 and proclaimed it "tougher than the dreaded Chilkoot Pass."

The road drops into the headwaters of Birch Creek's North Fork, which flows from the heart of the White Mountains. The valley bottoms

Rainbow along the Chatanika River.

The old Circle-Fairbanks wagon road runs south from Twelvemile Summit.

retain an alpine quality here, with broad swards of tundra interspersed with stands of miniature black spruce. Just beyond the North Fork bridge is a side road that leads to a canoe launch for the Birch Creek National Wild and Scenic River. From here, you can take a one-week float over Class III water past boulder fields, sweepers, and small drop-offs. Birch Creek returns to the Steese Highway at Mile 147.

The road soon strikes a course up the valley of Ptarmigan Creek, which has seen a great deal of placer-mining activity in recent years. This is the beginning of the Circle Mining District, which has been a steady producer of placer gold for more than a century. Watch for mining camps along the valley floor as the highway begins its ascent to Eagle Summit.

At 3,624 feet (1,105 meters), Eagle Summit is the loftiest point on the Steese Highway. Tundra-clad mountaintops stretch away on all sides, a botanical wonderland for wildflower fanciers. Although the summit is well south of the Arctic Circle, its high elevation makes it possible to view the midnight sun on June 21 if you make a short trek to the mountaintop to the north. The Pinnell Mountain Trail joins the highway here, after traversing the high country along the watershed divide of the North Fork of Birch Creek. Splinter groups of the Fortymile caribou herd sometimes wander through this area during the autumn.

Mastodon Dome rises south of Eagle Summit, and the streams that radiate from it contain much of the district's placer gold. Pat Kinnally and John Gregor staked the first claims on Mastodon Creek in 1893. They named the stream for the large number of fossilized bones they uncovered during their excavations for gold. Warm springs keep the ground thawed in this area, so miners did not have to cope with permafrost as they did in Fairbanks and the Klondike.

The highway descends into the valley of Mammoth Creek. Watch for diggings on the valley floor. At the bottom of the grade, the highway crosses the stream and runs onto the flats that stretch eastward from the base of the mountains. As the hills fall away, the Crazy Mountains become visible to the north, beyond a broad stretch of black-spruce bog.

The highway crosses the flats to reach the town of Central at Mile 127. This small settlement sprang up around Central House, a roadhouse that still stands in ruins on the north bank of Crooked Creek. The roadhouse got its name from its position in the heart of the Circle Mining District, and the name carried over to the town. Crooked Creek was also a gold producer, and placer miners have found several diamonds in its waters over the course of a century. Diamonds are typically found in volcanic intrusions (or "pipes") of a mineral called kimberlite. No kimberlite has ever been found in this area, and the source of the diamonds remains a mystery. You will find a small historical museum and most visitor services in Central.

A wide, 8-mile spur road leads southeast from Central to reach the Circle Hot Springs Resort. The hot springs bubble up through fractures in the earth's crust that are associated with the Tintina Fault, which runs through the valley to the northeast. Athapaskan Indians knew about the springs long ago, but they were not discovered by white people until 1893. That year, a prospector named Bill Great stumbled upon them while tracking a moose he had wounded. Ever the entrepreneur, Great built a cabin here and charged prospectors for the pleasure of bathing in the 136-degree Fahrenheit (58-degree Celsius) water.

A businessman named Frank Leach bought the springs from Great in 1905 and developed the European-style spa resort that still stands today. The waters were touted for their curative powers and were supposedly "effective in all forms of arthritis, rheumatism, congested and torpid liver, digestive disorders, etc." The springs are now siphoned into an outdoor swimming pool that has a year-round temperature of 103 degrees Fahrenheit (39 degrees Celsius).

The Steese Highway charts a narrow, winding course through the undulating lowland that lies to the northeast of Central. Tall stands of white spruce line the road, which reaches the banks of Birch Creek at Mile 146.3 and crosses it a mile later. As the road climbs into a series of small hills, it is lined by a tall shrub called Bebb's willow. This shrub has a curious diamond pattern in its wood and is prized by furniture craftsmen. The hills ultimately give way to the broad Yukon River flood plain, and the highway ends in the town of Circle at Mile 162.

Circle was founded by Jack McQuesten, an enterprising trader whose reputation for fair dealing had spread up and down the Yukon River, among Athapaskans and whites alike. McQuesten had heard rumors that, in the 1860s, an Anglican missionary named Robert McDonald had found a place where gold could be scooped from the sand bars with a kitchen spoon. McQuesten grubstaked prospectors to search for the "preacher's gold," in return for a share of the profits. Among these prospectors were two men of mixed Russian and Athapaskan descent, Pitka Pavaloff and Serge Cherosky. They struck gold on Birch Creek in 1893, but they were unfamiliar with the mining laws and their claims were usurped by white prospectors.

The rush was on, and McQuesten built a trading post at a good steamboat landing on the Yukon River. He named the post Circle, on the mistaken assumption that the Arctic Circle ran through the center of town. It is actually 60 miles to the north.

During the years that followed the gold rush, a bustling city of log buildings chinked with moss grew up on the site. In its heyday, Circle City was the largest metropolis north of Seattle, with 2 theaters, 8 dance halls, and 28 saloons. Initially, law was dispensed by popular vote at the miners' meetings, a grass-roots justice system in which theft was sometimes punished by hanging. As the city became a major population center, the territorial government established a jail. During the winter, a placard above its door read, "Notice: all prisoners must report by 9:00 pm or they will be locked out for the night. By order of U.S. Marshal." Few prisoners even dreamed of escape when temperatures hovered below minus 30 degrees Fahrenheit (minus 34 degrees Celsius).

In 1896, the gold strike on the Klondike ended Circle's days as a thriving city. Most of the prospectors packed their meager belongings and raced for the new gold fields. Harry Ash heard the news at the roadhouse he owned and reportedly told his patrons, "Boys, help yourselves to the whole shooting match. I'm off for the Klondike."

Some of the miners stayed on to work the gravel of the Birch Creek watershed, and Circle was never quite abandoned. In 1901, Axinia Cherosky (daughter of the man who discovered gold here) married a Danish settler named Nels Rasmusson, and their two-story homestead still stands in the center of town. The old school and the telegraph building stand a few blocks east of it, and a short trail leads east from town to a pioneer-era cemetery.

The muddy waters of the Yukon roll purposefully past Circle, 3 miles (5 kilometers) wide. Only the southernmost channel can be seen from town; the others are hidden behind a wooded island. Downstream lies the Yukon

Flats National Wildlife Refuge. More than two million ducks and thousands of geese are fledged here each year. Some of them winter as far away as Venezuela.

Chena Hot Springs Road Sidetrip

This paved road runs 56.5 miles east from the Steese Highway to reach Circle Hot Springs, deep in the Tanana Hills. It provides access to Chena State Recreation Area, a large wilderness park where you can hike to impressive granite towers, or "tors;" fish for grayling; or canoe on the Chena River. The road offers a pleasant day trip from Fairbanks.

The first 25 miles cross gently rolling country, much of which has been cleared to provide pasture for horses. In the low-lying areas, sphagnum bogs sit atop permafrost, and frost heaves provide annoying obstacles. At Mile 19, the road passes the community of Two Rivers, a center for rural residents who live in the upper Chena Valley. A spur road runs north to Two Rivers Recreation Area, which has hiking and cross-country ski trails through the rolling woodlands.

Just beyond Two Rivers, the main road passes a major research facility for plasma physics. Beyond the observatory, it enters Chena State Recreation Area. The forested Tanana Hills close in around the road, which follows the Chena River upward through a narrow valley. The bottomland is pocked with sloughs, ponds, and oxbow lakes. This is excellent summer range for moose, beavers, and muskrats. The river is choked with sweepers and logjams; the easiest stretch for canoeing is from the third bridge at Mile 44 to the first bridge at Mile 37.5.

This area is known for its granite tors, which are pillars of resistant stone that have been exposed as the older and weaker rock that surrounds them weathers away. You will first see tors at Mile 36; this cluster of pinnacles belongs to the Plain of Monuments group. You will have more views of these tors from a different angle on the return trip. The Granite Tors Trail leaves the road at Mile 39.6 for an 8-mile climb into the midst of these pinnacles.

A forest of tall spruce soon surrounds the highway. The Angel Rock Trail departs from Mile 48.9 for a 3.6-mile loop through another impressive tor formation. Just across the road, the 29-mile Chena Dome Trail loops away from the road on its trek across the alpine tundra along the Angel Creek divide. If you take this trail, you will find that the south-facing slopes are covered in sage, arnica, and dogbane, relics of the mammoth-steppe ecosystem that dominated the Alaskan interior during the ice ages.

Hikers on all of the trails in this area should beware of grizzly bears. Make plenty of noise while traveling and, if you are camping, secure your food beyond the bears' reach.

At Mile 56.5, the road ends at Chena Hot Springs Resort. The thermal springs bubble up through the Hot Springs Fault, emerging in the headwaters of Monument Creek. Credit for discovering the springs goes to Robert Swan, a rheumatic prospector who followed vague Geological Survey reports to find the springs in 1905. He built a cabin here and soaked his bones in the mineral springs, finding relief from his ailment. Swan opened the springs to public use. A number of local residents heard about the healing powers of the water and built cabins nearby.

In 1908, a Canadian named George Wilson staked a homestead around the springs (which were then within the public domain) and tore down all of the cabins. A ten-year legal battle ensued, but Wilson's patent on the land ultimately held, and the resort was developed by a succession of private owners in the years that followed. The modern resort boasts a luxuriously appointed lodge, and the springs have been directed into indoor hot tubs and a swimming pool, which are open year-round.

29

Elliott Highway

Official Designation: Alaska Route 2
Description: Paved highway from Fox to Mile 28, gravel road for remaining distance to Manley Hot Springs; 152 miles (245 kilometers) overall
Recommended Maximum: 50 mph/80 kph on gravel sections as far as Livengood; 40 mph/65 kph beyond
Hazards: Road between Livengood and Manley Hot Springs has narrow and winding sections with potholes and washboards
Distance Markers: Mileposts count northwest from Fox
Further Reading: *Minto* by Peter John
Information Sources: Bureau of Land Management (Kobuk District)

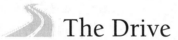 The Drive

This gravel road runs northward through the forested high country of the Yukon-Tanana uplands and then jogs westward to reach Manley Hot Springs. The road is paved as far as Wickersham Dome, is broad and graveled as far as Livengood, and becomes narrower with some twists and turns in the final stretch. It provides access to the Dalton Highway at Livengood and parallels the Trans-Alaskan Pipeline to this point.

The Elliott traverses an empty quarter of the state that retains much of its primeval wilderness character. Service stations are a rarity; you can get gas at Mile 5.5, at Minto, and at Manley Hot Springs. The road is passable in all weather, but the final stretch between Livengood and Manley Hot Springs may become potholed following rainstorms.

From the town of Fox, the Elliott Highway climbs into the forested domes that rise between the Tanana and Yukon rivers. These ancient mountain stumps are made of Precambrian schist, a brittle metamorphic rock that has been worn away by millions of years of frost shattering. The bedrock is no longer visible because it is buried beneath a thin mantle of soil. The forest that cloaks the hills is a mixture of white spruce and paper birch, with extensive stands of balsam poplar on the warm, dry exposures. On the north-facing slopes, permafrost lies just below the surface and it supports only a ragged growth of black spruce. Sphagnum bogs occupy the poorly drained folds in the hills, bearing deep accumulations of peat that have built up over the centuries.

The highway climbs a divide that, during the gold rush, carried a narrow-gauge railway to the boom towns of Olnes, Dome City, and Eldorado Camp. It then descends to cross the Chatanika River at Mile 16. Whitefish swim up this river to spawn each October. The whitefish is a coarse relative of the trout, with large scales and bony flesh. It has a very small mouth, and consequently it is difficult to catch with a hook and line.

Watch for signs of forest fires as the highway leaves the Chatanika Valley and climbs back into the hills. Fire strips away the insulating mat of moss and dead vegetation that covers the soil. As a result, the underlying permafrost may begin to melt after a burn. The soil above becomes warmer and more productive, allowing a brief bloom of growth. Ultimately, enough dead vegetation builds up on the soil to insulate it again, and the permafrost returns.

The muskeg valley of Washington Creek interrupts the hills at Mile 18. You can sometimes spot beavers in this lowland. Note that the oil pipeline has been buried on many of the south-facing slopes, where permafrost is not a major problem. On the north-facing slopes, the pipeline has been elevated on stilts, each of which is refrigerated by a specially designed system of cooling fins so that the permafrost below does not melt and cause the pipeline to shift. Each of the stilts is hollow and filled with ammonia that boils at the freezing point of water. When the stilts warm, the ammonia vaporizes and rises to the cooling fins where it condenses and releases its heat into the air.

The road begins to climb once more and finally tops out high on the

Sawtooth Mountain is the most prominent landmark to the north of the Elliott Highway.

Elliott Highway

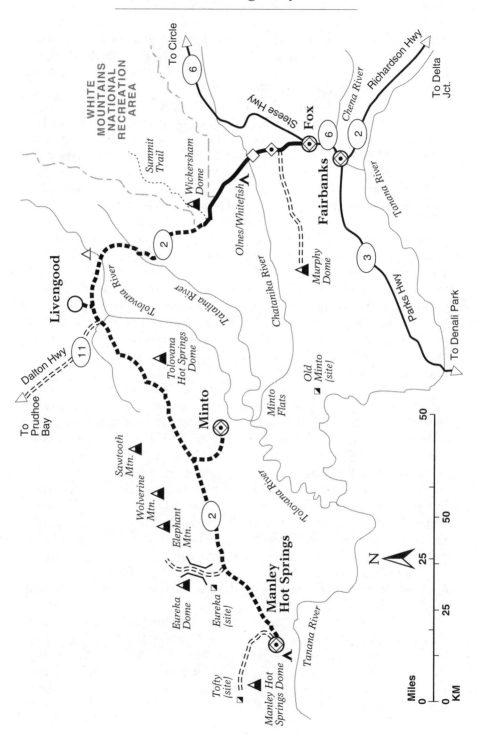

shoulder of Wickersham Dome, at Mile 28. Sawtooth Mountain rises far to the northwest. Watch for "tors," erosional remnants atop Wickersham Dome. These stone pillars were exposed as the less-resistant rock around them weathered away. This divide is known as Snowshoe Pass, and a hiking trail departs to the east, following the ridgetops for 20 miles to reach the Borealis-LeFevre cabin in the White Mountains National Recreation Area.

The pavement ends at this point and the road becomes a broad gravel haul road that winds down a long grade into the lowland. Globe Creek runs through a broad valley that begins at Mile 37.5, and a series of large tors known to climbers as the "Grapefruit Rocks" rises from the hillside just north of the stream. These tors are evidence that this area was never glaciated, even during the height of the ice ages. Glacial ice would have scoured away these pillars, leaving behind slopes unbroken by outcrops.

The road climbs through another chain of hills and then descends toward the Tatalina River, passing Pump Station Number 7 on the way. The mountains in this area are low whalebacks that rise amid broad valleys that are filled with spruce muskeg. After crossing the Tatalina, the highway climbs to the ridgetops. At Mile 51.9 there is an overlook that offers sweeping views of the White Mountains, ragged peaks of limestone that crowd the eastern horizon like a jumble of sharp teeth. The road soon returns to the lowland, and 5 miles beyond the overlook it crosses the Tolovana River. This river is popular with recreational gold-panners, and there are a few undeveloped campsites along its banks.

The road now approaches the gold-mining district of Livengood. Watch for piles of tailings along the streams that indicate placer-mining activity. A short spur road runs east from Mile 71 to the former townsite of Livengood, with its old miners' cabins and modern heavy machinery. Jay Livengood and N.R. Hudson discovered gold here in 1914.

The initial placer gravel was disappointing, but a miner named Casaden, relying on his experience in the Klondike, sensed that the pay streak would be found in the terraces above town. He discovered the rich Livengood Bench deposit in 1914 and, within two years, the population of the town swelled to 1,500. It was said that a man could walk 4 miles through the interconnected tunnels of the drift mines that honeycombed the Livengood Bench. The boom died out by 1922, but the deposit has been mined sporadically by a succession of corporations during the past 70 years. There are no visitor services here.

Just beyond Livengood, the wide, gravel Dalton Highway swings north on its way to the North Slope, while the narrower Elliott Highway turns west to follow the valley of the Tolovana River. It crosses the West Fork of the Tolovana and runs across a forested lowland. Tolovana Hot Springs Dome lies south of the road, but the springs themselves cannot be reached by road.

Soon the road reaches a rounded dome and climbs all the way above the timberline. It follows the rounded ridgetops across a tundra of tussock heath. A broad panorama stretches to the west, where the Tolovana River winds onto Minto Flats to join the much larger flow of the Tanana. The flats are speckled with lakes, ponds, and sloughs that shine like mirrors in the slanting light of afternoon. This wetland is an important breeding area for waterfowl. Canada geese, trumpeter swans, and sandhill cranes nest here, in addition to more than 12 million ducks.

The road rounds a tundra-clad hilltop, revealing the rugged crags of the Sawtooth and Wolverine mountains to the north. For the next 20 miles, the road follows the alpine ridgetops to its junction with the spur road to Minto. A 10-mile side trip leads to this Athapaskan village on the edge of the Minto Flats wetland. The original village of Minto was sited far to the south, on the shores of Minto Lake. Its residents fished for whitefish in the lowland waterways and trapped the muskrats that once thrived there.

With the coming of placer mining to the Fairbanks area, enormous quantities of silt poured into Minto Flats, burying the whitefish spawning gravels. At the same time, lakes and ponds filled with sand and became too shallow to sustain muskrats through the winter. The village was finally moved to its current site following a flood in 1971.

The main road continues westward, descending into the broad valley of Hutlitakwa Creek. The upper reaches of this valley burned in 1983, and the Elliott Highway was used as a fire break by the crews that fought the blaze. Hardwoods such as aspen and balsam poplar thrive in the wake of wildfires; their seedlings need direct sunlight to survive. Here, they contrast visibly with the white spruces that cover the unburned areas.

After a brief sojourn through the lowland, the road climbs back to the ridgetops to traverse some steep country. It follows the crest of a narrow finger of ridges that projects westward between the valleys of the Tanana and Yukon rivers. At Mile 128, it drops into the lowland on the south side of the divide and crosses Hutlinana Creek. The Eureka Road (see sidetrip next page) soon departs to the north, traveling through an old placer-mining district. The Elliott Highway continues westward through the Tanana River valley. This flood plain was repeatedly cleared by fire and logging in the early 1900s, when placer mining was at its height. As a result of these disturbances, fast-growing colonizers such as aspen and balsam poplar have replaced the spruce woodland.

The Elliott Highway reaches Manley Hot Springs at Mile 152, marking the end of the journey. The hot springs themselves emerge at the base of Manley Hot Springs Dome and were first "discovered" in 1901 by a miner named John Karshner. Karshner staked a homestead around the springs with the idea of developing a health spa. He soon teamed up with Frank Manley, a horse thief from Beaumont, Texas, who had escaped the law and then made a fortune in the Cleary Creek gold fields near Fairbanks. With Manley's financial backing, the pair built a three-story hotel, and Manley Hot Springs became a supply center for the nearby Tofty and Eureka mining districts. Steamboats brought supplies down the Tanana River, unloading them at the townsite along Manley Hot Springs Slough. The town boomed, and swaths of farmland were cleared from the forest to grow vegetables for the local miners and steamboat-company employees. At one point, the town was large enough to support two competing newspapers.

Today, Manley Hot Springs exudes a quiet charm that harks back to bygone days. Although the boom is a distant memory, gardening continues to be a popular local pastime. Manley's hotel burned in 1913 under suspicious circumstances (a nephew left in charge sold all the furnishings just before the fire), but a roadhouse dating from 1903 is still actively serving travelers on the south bank of Manley Hot Springs Slough. The hot springs themselves are located north of the slough. The sulphur-free water fills an indoor hot tub and swimming pool, and a small lodge has been developed around them.

Eureka Road Sidetrip

This narrow road (not suitable for RVs or trailers) runs through the placer fields along Eureka Creek and climbs over a high pass in the mountains to reach a valley that drains northward into the Yukon River. The road was built by miners in the early 1900s and is privately maintained to this day. It is steep and winding in places and fords a number of small creeks, but it is passable to most passenger vehicles in dry weather.

The road begins by passing through the gold fields of Eureka Creek, where great mounds of waste gravel and heavy brush testify to a century of mining activity. After 5 miles, the road makes a steep climb to the divide between the Tanana and Yukon river watersheds, reaching a pass just east of Eureka Dome. Local miners report that grizzly bears are common north of this divide, while black bears are prevalent to the south. The prominent peak that rises north of the pass is Elephant Mountain (3,661 feet/1,116 meters).

The road makes a series of steep hairpin turns to reach the valley floor, which it follows northward toward the Yukon River. Watch for an old prospector's cabin along the way. After 11 miles (18 kilometers), the road reaches the Lost Creek Guest Ranch. There are many boggy spots beyond this point, and the road often becomes impassable even to four-wheel-drive vehicles.

30

Dalton Highway

Official Designation: Alaska Route 11
Description: Wide gravel highway from junction with Elliott Highway to Deadhorse on the North Slope; 414 miles (666 kilometers)
Recommended Maximum: 50 mph/80 kph
Hazards: Rocks thrown up by oncoming vehicles are a frequent cause of windshield cracks
Distance Markers: Mileposts count northward from junction with Elliott Highway
Further Reading: *Arctic Village* and *Alaska Wilderness: Exploring the Central Brooks Range* by Robert Marshall, *Make Prayers to the Raven* by Richard Nelson
Information Sources: Bureau of Land Management (Northern District), Gates of the Arctic National Park, Arctic National Wildlife Refuge

 The Drive

The Dalton Highway, known to many Alaskans as "The Haul Road," is a truly wild and remote stretch of gravel highway that connects Fairbanks with the North Slope oil fields at Prudhoe Bay. It was originally constructed to support the building of the Trans-Alaska Pipeline, which follows the highway along its entire length. The road was initially closed to public traffic, but it is now open as far as the oil-drilling center of Deadhorse. The roads through the oil fields and to the shores of the Arctic Ocean remain closed to travelers, but several Deadhorse companies offer bus tours of these attractions.

The road begins in the rolling uplands of the Alaskan interior, traverses the remote and rugged Brooks Range, and runs onto the tundra-clad lowland of the Arctic coastal plain. Services are available at the Yukon River, Coldfoot, and Deadhorse. Bring extra gas and two spare tires along for the trip, and be sure that your vehicle is in top running condition before attempting this road.

The Dalton begins by climbing and diving over rollercoaster grades in the foothills of the White Mountains. The sparse forest is dominated by white spruce on the sunny slopes and by stunted black spruce on north-

The Dalton Highway and Alyeska Pipeline run in tandem across Hess Creek.

facing slopes and in boggy hollows. The pipeline follows the highway, snaking across the taiga like some shining serpent. The zigzags in the pipeline were constructed so that the structure can expand and shrink without breaking as temperatures rise to highs of 90 degrees Fahrenheit (32 degrees Celsius) in the summer and dive to lows of minus 80 degrees Fahrenheit (minus 62 degrees Celsius) in the winter. The oil is pumped through the pipeline at a temperature that ranges from 90 to 120 degrees Fahrenheit (32 to 49 degrees Celsius), so the stilts that support the pipe must be cooled by a specially designed system so that the permafrost beneath the soil does not thaw and buckle.

Early views feature the Ray Mountains, a rugged massif that rises far to the northwest. After 10 miles, the highway finds itself on the mountaintops, with expansive views stretching in all directions. The road descends to cross the valley of Hess Creek at Mile 23.7 and then continues through wooded hills for 22 miles to reach the Yukon River. Just before the river, the highway passes Pump Station Number 6, which helps to keep the oil moving through the pipeline.

In the early years, trucks were ferried across the Yukon River by hovercraft. The modern bridge that now spans the river was built in Seward and hauled to this location piece by piece. On the far end of the bridge, there is a service station, lodge, and Bureau of Land Management information station. A few miles upstream, the Athapaskan settlement of Stevens

Dalton Highway

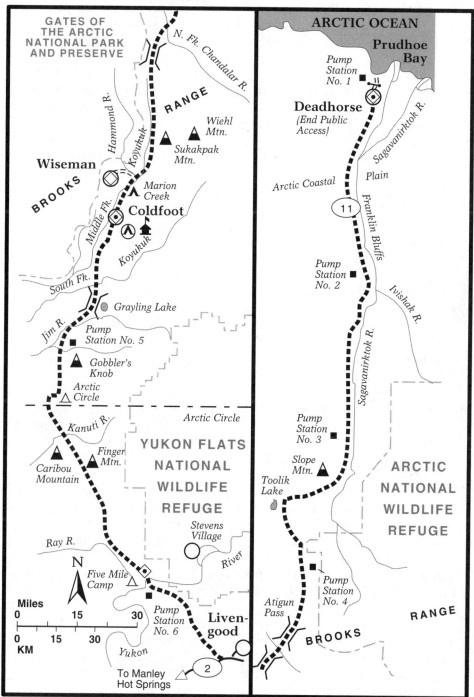

GATES OF
THE ARCTIC
NATIONAL PARK
AND PRESERVE

ARCTIC OCEAN

Prudhoe
Bay

N. Fk. Chandalar R.

RANGE

Pump
Station
No. 1

Deadhorse
*(End Public
Access)*

Hammond R.

Wiehl
Mtn.

Koyukuk

Sukakpak
Mtn.

Arctic Coastal

Plain

Sagavanirktok R.

Wiseman

BROOKS

Marion
Creek

Middle Fk.

Coldfoot

11

Franklin Bluffs

Koyukuk

Pump
Station
No. 2

Ivishak R.

South Fk.

Grayling Lake

Jim R.

Pump
Station No. 5

Gobbler's
Knob

Sagavanirktok R.

Arctic
Circle

Arctic Circle

Kanuti R.

Pump
Station
No. 3

YUKON FLATS

Finger
Mtn.

Slope
Mtn.

ARCTIC

Caribou
Mountain

NATIONAL

Toolik
Lake

NATIONAL

WILDLIFE

WILDLIFE

Ray R.

REFUGE

REFUGE

Stevens
Village

River

N

Five Mile
Camp

Pump
Station
No. 4

Miles

0   15   30

Atigun
Pass

RANGE

0   15   30
KM

Pump
Station
No. 6

Liven-
good

BROOKS

Yukon

2

To Manley
Hot Springs

Village marks the location of a traditional fishing camp, where a summer bounty of king and chum salmon is harvested and dried for winter use.

Leaving the river, the highway climbs again into the wooded hills. A short spur road leads to Five Mile Camp from Mile 60.5, just before the highway reaches an airstrip. Five Mile Camp is an old pipeline construction camp that now serves as a primitive camping area for travelers. Long grades carry you up and down the hills that rise to the north of the Yukon River. Around Mile 70, watch to the west for views of the Ray River with its many oxbow lakes. One of the loftiest domes in the area is Sand Hill, which you cross at Mile 74. This hill is formed by a "laccolith," or mass of molten igneous rock, that was intruded into the older bedrock of the surrounding hills. Frost action at the surface of the bedrock has been eroding the granite into fine sand, creating a landform known to geologists as a "sandy dome."

The highway climbs to the top of the Caribou Mountain massif and breaks into the open tundra at Mile 95. Caribou Mountain itself stands west of the highway. You cannot see it clearly above the intervening mountaintops After 3 miles, Finger Rock rises from the hillside east of the road. This granite pillar, or "tor," is the remnant of a larger body of granite that has been whittled away by frost cracking. It was used as a navigational landmark by early bush pilots. Other tors stand at the summit of Finger Mountain, where an interpretive trail provides a window onto life on the high tundra. You can also find "stone nets" on these cold mountaintops. These networks of loose boulders have been sorted and pushed to the surface by expanding ice within the soil.

The road drops into the lake-dotted basin that bears the headwaters of the Kanuti River. *Kanuti* is a Koyukon Indian word that means "Old Man's River," and a pipeline construction camp called Old Man Camp lies just beyond the bridge. Grayling swim in the Kanuti, and beavers build their dams across the water, stained by the tannin that leaches from decaying vegetation.

From this high basin, the Kanuti flows westward onto a broad lowland pocked with lakes and ponds. This wetland has been set aside as Kanuti National Wildlife Refuge, and it is a major nesting area for scaups, wigeons, and pintails, as well as for white-fronted and Canada geese. The lakes in this basin are thermokarst lakes, formed when a disturbance of the surface vegetation causes the permafrost beneath it to thaw. The water in these lakes continually melts the permafrost along the margins, and so these lakes tend to expand slowly over time.

The tundra continues for another 4 miles and the road descends Beaver Slide Hill into the valley of Fish Creek. The old "Hickel Highway" departs the modern route here, following the north bank of the stream. This ill-conceived roadway was packed into the snow to carry the first drilling equipment northward. But the passage of heavy equipment killed the un-

Mt. Sukakpak is one of the more spectacular summits in the Brooks Range.

derlying vegetation, and the following summer the permafrost beneath it melted and turned the route into an impassable quagmire.

Just after crossing Fish Creek, the Dalton crosses the Arctic Circle. The hill to the north prevents you from watching the sun circle the horizon on the summer solstice (June 21), but you can view this phenomenon farther north at Gobblers Knob. A short spur road leads uphill to an undeveloped camping area.

The highway soon climbs over another hill, and as you descend you get your first view of the Brooks Range to the north. The road then crosses the forks of Bonanza Creek and climbs onto the massif that bears Gobblers Knob. This north-facing overlook offers fine views of the southern marches of the Brooks Range, and if you make the short hike to the top of the hill you will be able to see the midnight sun on the solstice.

The road descends to the valley floor and passes Prospect Camp on the banks of Prospect Creek. After crossing the various channels of the Jim River, the route follows the valley upward, passing the buildings of Pump Station Number 5 (which is erroneously labeled "Prospect Camp" on a road sign). At the head of the valley, the road climbs through a low pass flanked by tundra-topped peaks. Grayling Lake is nestled among the folds of the hills at the top of the divide. Its basin was gouged into the mountains by a glacier some 1.5 million years ago. Scientists have analyzed the fossil pollen that blew into the lake and was preserved in the lakebed sediments. Their findings indicate that a Pleistocene shrub-tussock tundra gave way to the first spruce woodlands in this area about 7,500 years ago.

The road descends to cross the South Fork of the Koyukuk River, which the Bureau of Land Management rates as the best potential gold-panning stream along the route. The river flows through a narrow gap in the hills, but instead of following it, the highway climbs over another pass and descends into the broad trench beyond. This valley formed around the Malemute Fault, which is a westward extension of the great Tintina Fault complex that stretches across the center of the Yukon Territory. A handful of kettle lakes is scattered across the floor of the basin, and the main phalanx of the Brooks Range rises beyond it. The road soon strikes the Middle Fork of the Koyukuk and follows it upward toward the town of Coldfoot.

Coldfoot was initially the center of the Koyukuk Mining District. It got its name from the fact that many of the miners got "cold feet" and left during their first winter above the Arctic Circle. Horse teams once drew barges up the shallow Koyukuk River from Bettles, bringing supplies for the outlying mining settlements. In the winter, supplies were brought by dog sled.

The boom years of the district lasted from 1900 to 1909, when more than $2 million in placer gold was removed from the streams that flow south out of the Brooks Range. Bob Marshall, a conservationist who was to become the father of the American wilderness system, visited Coldfoot during the height of placer-mining activity. He reported that the town had "one gambling hole, two roadhouses, two stores, and seven saloons." The gold in nearby Slate Creek played out by 1908, and shortly thereafter the town was abandoned.

Coldfoot revived during the pipeline construction years, and the current town occupies the site of an old construction camp at Mile 175. The historic mining town was located on the banks of the river, just west of the airfield. It is being excavated by archaeologists; little remains of the log shanties that once stood huddled along the river. The visitor center in Coldfoot is jointly staffed by Gates of the Arctic National Park, the Arctic National Wildlife Refuge, and the Bureau of Land Management. It offers information on hiking, canoeing, and wildlife viewing along the northern stretches of the Dalton Highway.

After leaving Coldfoot, the highway follows the Middle Fork of the Koyukuk into the mountains. Despite the latitude, there are still plenty of trees in the lowlands. After the road passes the Marion Creek Campground, scan the opposite bank of the river for the old mining settlement of Wiseman. A spur road departs from Mile 189 to reach this village, which boasts historic log cabins and a two-story mercantile store that was constructed of logs and chinked with moss.

Wiseman was settled in 1911 when prospectors abandoned the depleted gold fields near Coldfoot to try their luck on the newly discovered deposits along Wiseman and Nolan creeks. The town and stream were named for Peter Wiseman, the prospector who discovered gold here. None of the trees in this area was large enough to use for building cabins, so the miners hauled in logs from far to the south. They also dismantled cabins in Coldfoot and moved them piece by piece to the new town.

The gold fields around Wiseman have remained productive, and a handful of miners still work the placer gravels here, supplementing their income by trapping wolves, foxes, and wolverines during the winter. One of the luckiest gold strikes in Wiseman occurred in the 1950s, when a miner from Chatanika bought a cabin near town. The floorboards were rotting, and the miner was removing them when he discovered a number of canning jars caked with dust. Each jar contained a moosehide sack filled with gold dust— a small fortune altogether. A minister was standing in the doorway at the time of the discovery and was rewarded for his presence at the lucky moment with a gift of several thousand dollars.

Just beyond the spur road to Wiseman, the highway crosses a bridge over the Hammond River. The Hammond and Dietrich rivers join just downstream to form the Middle Fork of the Koyukuk. At Mile 197, an old prospector's cabin stands west of the road on the banks of Gold Creek. A massive peak of marble and dolomite soon towers ahead with sheer cliffs and fantastic towers of brilliant white. This is Mount Sukakpak, and its twin to the east is Wiehl Mountain. *Sukakpak* is an Inuit word meaning "marten deadfall." Look for ice-cored mounds at the base of the mountain. The peak marked an ancient boundary between the Inuit people to the north and the Athapaskan tribes of the interior.

The Inuit who inhabited the Brooks Range were a mountain tribe of caribou hunters known as the Nunamiut. They often trekked more than 50 miles a day through mountain passes they knew by heart. Their hunters were legendary shots with their rifles; in the early days, shells were hard to come by, and each bullet had to find its target so that the hunter's family would have food to eat. Today, the center of Nunamiut culture is at Anaktuvuk Pass in the heart of Gates of the Arctic National Park.

As the highway nears the head of the valley, it leaves the last of the trees behind and climbs over a low grade into the watershed of the Chandalar River. Chandalar is a corruption of the French *gens de large*, which means "nomadic people." French-speaking voyageurs who visited the lower reaches of this river applied this name to the Gwitch'in people who lived along its banks.

The highway traverses the headwaters of the Chandalar's north fork. The country is robed in rich tundra and inhabited by collared lemmings and arctic ground squirrels. An endemic species of rodent called the Alaska marmot lives among the loose rocks of the steep talus slopes; its closest

Tundra country in the upper Chandalar watershed.

relative lives in Siberia. The valley owes its characteristic U shape to glaciers that scoured the mountains 12,000 years ago. Today, only a few small glaciers remain in the loftiest and most remote pockets of the Brooks Range.

After only a short distance, rugged peaks wall off the head of the valley, and the highway begins its ascent to Atigun Pass. Because of the severe avalanche danger in this area, the pipeline was buried in the permafrost with a thick buffer of refrigerated insulation. The top of the pass is at Mile 245, and a perfectly formed glacial cirque adorns the peak to the east. This natural amphitheater was scooped out of the bedrock by a small hanging glacier that once graced the mountainside.

The descent from Atigun Pass is even more impressive than the climb to reach it: the road plunges almost 1,000 feet (305 meters) down steep mountainsides, losing most of the elevation that it gradually gained after crossing Prospect Creek. Dall sheep are commonly spotted grazing across the high slopes that surround the road.

The highway bottoms out at the headwaters of the Atigun River and follows it through a broad, glacier-carved valley flanked by rugged peaks of sedimentary rock. Steep side valleys unload their waste rock in rounded alluvial fans along the fringes of the main basin. This is prime habitat for grizzly bears, and the higher slopes are home to bands of Dall sheep. The Arctic National Wildlife Refuge lies just east of the highway, stretching across mountains and tundra plains to the Canadian border. The refuge was set aside to preserve the calving grounds of the Porcupine caribou herd. The area has been likened to an American Serengeti. In the words of the great naturalist Olaus Murie, "The idea, not yet understood by all, was to protect permanently another portion of our planet for sensitive people to go and get acquainted with themselves, to enjoy untouched nature, and to leave the lovely, unmarked country as they found it."

In 1967, muskoxen were reintroduced along the Sadlerochit River in the heart of the Arctic National Wildlife Refuge. The herd has since been expanding westward, and groups of muskoxen have even been seen as far south as the Atigun River valley. More commonly, they are sighted along the Sagwon and Franklin bluffs. A wild population once flourished on the Arctic coastal plain, but it was completely wiped out by market hunters who supplied meat to the whalers plying the Arctic Ocean in the mid-1800s. When confronted by predators, muskoxen form a defensive circle, horns outward, and stand their ground. This is not a very viable strategy when the predators carry high-powered rifles.

There are a number of lakes at the mouth of the Atigun Valley, the largest of which is Galbraith Lake. A spur road leads around the lake from Mile 274.7, passing an airstrip on its way to a streamside camping area. This spot is a jumping-off point for backpackers bound through the low passes to the west and into the great tundra-clad valleys of Gates of the Arctic National Park. Old terminal moraines north of Galbraith Lake once impounded water that filled the entire valley and formed a giant lake.

The highway soon leaves the mountains behind and climbs onto an upland. A spur road descends to Toolik Lake from Mile 284, providing access to one of North America's premier research facilities for the study of arctic ecosystems. Ongoing projects include research into aquatic ecology, nutrient cycling in tundra soils, and hibernation in arctic ground squirrels. The research facility is not open to the public. *Toolik* is an Inuit term for the red-throated loon, which is sometimes spotted on lakes in this area. Camping is strictly prohibited on the lakeshore.

As it leaves Toolik Lake, the highway crests a rise that is crisscrossed with stone nets. The ranges along the Atigun River disappear from view, and the road runs eastward across rolling uplands where the long-tailed jaeger hovers above the tundra hunting for voles, lemmings, and the eggs of ground-nesting birds. New ranges of craggy peaks soon appear on the eastern horizon, beyond a broad reach of open country.

Slope Mountain presents its massive, rounded profile directly to the north. Its tilted bands of sandstone were laid down as a river delta at the edge of the Arctic Ocean. A small land mass collided with the continent from the north and uplifted these fossilized sediments to their present height. A mineral lick at the base of the mountain attracts Dall sheep. Prehistoric hunters paused on the terraces below this peak some 10,550 years ago, leaving behind flakes of stone at a site known to archaeologists as the Gallagher Flint Station. The Mesa Site, 170 miles to the west, has yielded artifacts dating back 11,700 years.

About 30 miles north of Galbraith Lake, the highway descends into the valley of the Sagavanirktok River. *Sagavanirktok* is an Inuit word meaning "strong current." Many white people who came later had a hard time pronouncing this word, so the river's name has been shortened to "the Sag" in the local argot. Some of the most enthralling mountain vistas of the entire route extend eastward from its banks.

The river swings away from the mountains at Pump Station Number 3 (Mile 311.9), although southbound travelers will have distant views of the peaks as far north as the Franklin Bluffs. Rolling uplands extend from both sides of the river, providing a transitional range for the central Arctic herd of caribou during its migrations between wintering grounds in the mountains and summer calving grounds along the Arctic Ocean. There are fewer predators on the Arctic coastal plain, making this a better place for caribou to give birth to vulnerable calves. You can also see muskoxen in these uplands on occasion. Damp swales shelter thickets of low-growing willows, which turn bright shades of orange and yellow when the Arctic autumn arrives in late August.

At Mile 356, the uplands end and the road drops onto the vast lowland of the Arctic coastal plain. Permafrost lies only 2 feet (60 centimeters) be-

The highway leaves the mountains near Pump Station No. 3.

Barren ground caribou are commonly sighted along the Dalton.

low the surface and extends downward for 2,000 feet (610 meters). The resulting lack of drainage holds water at the surface. The region only receives 5 to 7 inches (13 to 18 centimeters) of precipitation each year, which would qualify it as a desert in other parts of the world. However, because of the poor drainage and slow rates of evaporation, the Arctic coastal plain is a vast wetland of tussocks, cotton grass, and open ponds.

You may notice that most of the ponds are oriented along a northwest-southeast axis. Prevailing summer winds blow from the northwest, pushing the warm surface water to the southeastern edge of the ponds. The warm water melts the permafrost at the lake margin, eating away at the lakeshore and lengthening the ponds in that direction.

At Mile 380, the Franklin Bluffs rise from the otherwise featureless flatland on the far side of the Sagavanirktok. They are composed of beds of clay and silt that have hardened into a loose form of rock. Erosion has carved the bluffs into convoluted ribs, exposing the pink and buff bands of the bedrock. You can sometimes see muskoxen on the blufftops, and gyrfalcons, rough-legged hawks, and peregrine falcons nest on the low cliffs.

The Toolik River pingo fields stretch away west of the highway at this point. These miniature, tundra-covered domes occur when conical cores of ice form in the water-saturated sediments of ponds that have filled with vegetation. The ice pushes the tundra upward, sometimes to heights of 50 feet or more. These pingos are the favorite denning sites of the arctic fox, which has a coat of fur that changes from black in the summer to white in the winter. After 15 miles, the bluffs give way to a lowland, and the highway crosses the final 20 miles of billiard-table-flat tundra to reach the oil fields of Prudhoe Bay.

A welter of prefabricated buildings announces your arrival at Deadhorse, the administrative and supply center for the Prudhoe Bay oil fields. You can drive no farther, but tour companies will take you on an interpretive tour of the oil fields, with a stop along the shore of the Arctic Ocean. The drilling rigs have been assembled atop thick pads of gravel to insulate the permafrost beneath and thus prevent slumping. The pads were placed miles apart to minimize their impact on the tundra environment, and from each pad, four wells are drilled diagonally in different directions to maximize the subsurface coverage while minimizing the surface disturbance. When the drilling companies leased the Prudhoe Bay oil fields from the state, they agreed to remove all the gravel pads and roadways and restore the area to its natural state when they leave.

Excellent examples of patterned ground are visible on the oil fields tour, with pingos and frost polygons the most captivating of the permafrost features. Frost polygons form where air temperatures drop quickly in the winter, causing fine sediments in the soil to contract, forming geometrical cracks in the soil. Water fills the interstices and ultimately freezes to form frost wedges around the edges of the polygon.

Wetlands among the drilling pads offer nesting habitat for oldsquaw ducks, spectacled and king eiders, snow geese, and tundra swans. Caribou are often spotted among the rigs, their numbers peaking along with insect populations in mid-July. These animals are part of the central Arctic herd, a group that winters in the central Brooks Range. Their numbers have increased markedly since the oil fields were developed, a fact that the oil companies ballyhoo in an effort to show that drilling is good for caribou populations. However, calving females no longer use this former calving ground, and population increases are most likely due to emigration from the splintering western Arctic herd rather than to calving success.

On the return to Deadhorse, the oil-field tour passes millions of dollars' worth of drilling equipment that is standing idle. This exploratory equipment is earmarked for the calving grounds in the Arctic National Wildlife Refuge. Oil companies are pressuring the U.S. Congress to open this area to full-scale drilling. The refuge is underlain by the same oil-bearing strata as Prudhoe Bay, but even the rosiest industry forecasts indicate that the refuge would yield only a small fraction of the Prudhoe Bay oil. Because of a current political trend to weaken or eliminate environmental laws in the United States, oil corporations expect the refuge to be opened to heavy industry within a few years.

Appendix A
Public Campgrounds

Campground	Agency	Campsites	Camping Fee	Water	Boat Launch	Fishing	Location
ALASKA							
Anchor River SRA	State Parks	213	•	•		•	Mi. 157 Sterling Hwy
Anchor River SRS	State Parks	9	•	•		•	Mi. 162 Sterling Hwy
Arctic Circle	BLM	und.					Mi 115 Dalton Hwy
Bertha Creek	USFS	12	•	•			Mi. 65.3 Seward Hwy
Big Delta	State Parks	25	•	•			Mi. 274.5 Richardson Hwy
Big Lake	State Parks	80	•	•	•	•	Mi. 51 Parks Hwy (Big L, Rd)
Bings Landing	State Parks	37	•	•	•	•	Mi 79 Sterling Hwy
Birch Lake	State Parks	10	•		•	•	Mi. 305.5 Richardson Hwy
Bird Creek	State Parks	27	•	•		•	Mi. 101.2 Seward Hwy
Black Bear	USFS	12	•	•			Mi. 3.7 Portage Hwy
Blueberry Lake	State Parks	15	•			•	Mi. 23 Richardson Hwy
Bonnie Lake	State Parks	8			•	•	Mi. 83.3 Glenn Hwy
Brushkana River	BLM	18		•		•	Mi. 104 Denali Hwy
Byers Lake	State Parks	73	•	•	•	•	Mi. 147 Parks Hwy
Capt. Cook (Bishop Cr.)	State Parks	12	•	•		•	Mi. 36 Kenai Spur Hwy
Capt. Cook (Discovery)	State Parks	53	•	•			Mi. 39 Kenai Spur Hwy
Chena River	State Parks	63	•	•	•	•	University Ave., Fairbanks
Chilkat	State Parks	35	•	•	•	•	Mi. 7 Mud Bay Rd.
Chilkoot Lake	State Parks	32	•	•	•	•	Mi. 10 Lutak Rd.
Clam Gulch	State Parks	116	•	•		•	Mi. 117 Sterling Hwy
Clearwater	State Parks	18	•	•	•	•	9.7 mi on Clearwater & Remington Rds.
Cooper Creek	USFS	26	•	•		•	Mi. 505 Sterling Hwy
Crescent Creek	USFS	9	•	•		•	Mi. 8 Quartz Creek Rd.
Cripple Creek	BLM	21	•	•		•	Mi. 60 Steese Hwy
Crooked Creek	State Parks	75	•	•		•	Mi. 1.8 Cohoe Loop Rd.
Deception Creek	State Parks	7				•	Mi. 48 Hatcher Pass Rd.
Delta	State Parks	22	•	•			Mi. 267 Richardson Hwy
Deep Creek	State Parks	300	•	•	•	•	Mi. 138 Sterling Hwy
Dolly Varden Lake	Kenai NWR	12		•	•	•	Mi. 14.2 Swanson River Rd.
Donnelly Creek	State Parks	12	•	•			Mi. 233 Richardson Hwy
Dry Creek	State Parks	58	•	•		•	Mi. 117.5 Richardson Hwy
Eagle	BLM	15	•	•	•	•	Just west of Eagle, Alaska
Eagle River	State Parks	50	•	•		•	Mi. 1.4 Eagle River Rd.
Eagle Trail	State Parks	45	•	•			Mi. 109.5 Tok Cutoff
Eklutna Lake	State Parks	50	•	•		•	Mi. 26.5 Glenn Hwy
Fielding Lake	State Parks	7			•	•	Mi. 200.5 Richardson Hwy

Campground	Agency	Campsites	Camping Fee	Water	Boat Launch	Fishing	Location
Finger Lake	State Parks	41	•	•	•	•	Bogard Rd., Palmer
Five Mile Camp	BLM	und.		•			Mi. 60.5 Dalton Hwy
Funny River	State Parks	5	•	•		•	Mi. 10 Funny River Rd.
Galbraith Lake	BLM	und.					Mi. 275 Dalton Hwy
Gerstle River	Alaska DOT	15					Mi. 1393 Alaska Hwy
Granite Creek	USFS	19	•	•		•	Mi. 63 Seward Hwy
Harding Lake	State Parks	125	•	•	•	•	Mi. 321.4 Richardson Hwy
Hidden Lake	Kenai NWR	44	•	•	•	•	Mi. 3.6 Skilak Lake Rd.
Izaak Walton	State Parks	38	•	•	•	•	Mi. 81 Sterling Hwy
Jim River	BLM	und.				•	Mi. 136 Dalton Hwy
Johnson Lake	State Parks	50	•	•	•	•	Mi. 110 Sterling Hwy
Kasilof River	State Parks	16	•	•	•	•	Mi. 109.5 Sterling Hwy
Kelly Lake	Kenai NWR	3		•	•	•	Mi. 68.3 Sterling Hwy
King Mountain	State Parks	22	•	•			Mi. 76 Glenn Hwy
Lake Louise	State Parks	60	•	•	•	•	Mi. 19 Lake Louise Rd.
Liberty Falls	State Parks	10					Mi. 23.5 Edgerton Hwy
Little Nelchina	State Parks	11			•	•	Mi. 137.4 Glenn Hwy
Little Tonsina	State Parks	8	•	•		•	Mi. 65 Richardson Hwy
Long Lake	State Parks	9			•	•	Mi. 85.3 Glenn Hwy
Lost Lake	State Parks	8	•		•		Mi. 277.8 Richardson Hwy
Lower Ohmer Lake	Kenai NWR	4			•	•	Mi. 8.5 Skilak Lake Rd.
Lower Skilak Lake	Kenai NWR	14		•	•	•	Mi. 13.8 Skilak Lake Rd.
Marion Creek	BLM	27	•	•		•	Mi. 180 Dalton Hwy
Matanuska Glacier	State Parks	12	•	•			Mi. 101 Glenn Hwy
Moon Lake	State Parks	15	•	•	•		Mi. 1332 Alaska Hwy
Moose Creek	State Parks	12	•	•		•	Mi. 54.4 Glenn Hwy
Morgans Landing	State Parks	50	•	•		•	Mi. 85 Sterling Hwy
Mosquito Lake	State Parks	10	•	•	•	•	Mi. 27.2 Haines Hwy
Nancy Lake (S. Rolly L.)	State Parks	98	•	•	•	•	Mi. 67.2 Parks Hwy
Ninilchik	State Parks	165	•	•		•	Mi. 135 Sterling Hwy
Olnes Pond	State Parks	55	•	•		•	Mi. 10.5 Elliott Hwy
Couer D'Alene	USFS	und.					Mi. 5 Palmer Creek Rd. near Hope
Paxson Lake	BLM	50	•		•	•	Mi. 175 Richardson Hwy
Peterson Lake	Kenai NWR	3		•		•	Mi. 68.3 Sterling Hwy
Porcupine	USFS	24	•	•		•	Mi. 18 Hope Hwy
Porcupine Creek	State Parks	12	•	•		•	Mi. 64 Tok Cutoff
Portage Cove	State Parks	9		•		•	Mi. 1 Beach Rd. (Haines)
Primrose	USFS	10	•	•	•	•	Mi. 17 Seward Hwy
Ptarmigan Creek	USFS	16	•	•		•	Mi. 23.1 Seward Hwy
Quartz Creek	USFS	31	•	•	•	•	Mi. 45 Sterling Hwy
Quartz Lake	State Parks	80	•	•	•	•	Mi. 277.8 Richardson Hwy
Rainbow Lake	Kenai NWR	3		•	•	•	Mi. 15.7 Swanson River Rd.
Riley Creek	Denali NP	100	•	•			Mi. 0.3 Denali Park Rd.
Rocky Lake	State Parks	10	•	•	•	•	Mi. 51 Parks Hwy (Big L Rd.)
Rosehip	State Parks	38	•	•		•	Mi. 27 Chena Hot Sprs. Rd.

Campground	Agency	Campsites	Camping Fee	Water	Boat Launch	Fishing	Location
Russian River	Kenai NWR	180	•	•	•	•	Mi. 52.6 Sterling Hwy
Tern Lake	USFS	25	•	•		•	Jct. of Seward and Sterling Hwys
Trail River	USFS	64	•			•	Mi. 24.2 Seward Hwy
Salcha River	State Parks	95	•	•	•	•	Mi. 323.3 Richardson Hwy
Savage River	Denali NP	33	•	•		•	Mi. 13 Denali Park Rd.
Scout Lake	State Parks	8	•	•		•	Mi. 85 Sterling Hwy
Sourdough	BLM	43	•		•	•	Mi. 147.5 Richardson Hwy
Squirrel Creek	State Parks	23	•	•		•	Mi. 79.5 Richardson Hwy
Stariski	State Parks	13	•	•			Mi. 151 Sterling Hwy
Swanson River	Kenai NWR	4			•	•	Mi. 17.2 Swanson River Rd.
Tangle Lakes	BLM	25	•	•	•	•	Mi. 21.5 Denali Hwy
Tangle River	BLM	8	•		•	•	Mi. 21.7 Denali Hwy
Teklanika River	Denali NP	53	•	•			Mi. 29 Denali Park Rd.
Tenderfoot Creek	USFS	28	•	•	•	•	Mi. 46 Seward Hwy
Tok River	State Parks	43	•	•			Mi. 1309 Alaska Hwy
Tors Trail	State Parks	23	•	•		•	Mi. 39 Chena Hot Sprs. Rd.
Troublesome Creek	State Parks	20	•	•		•	Mi. 137.2 Parks Hwy
Upper Chatanika	State Parks	35	•	•		•	Mi. 39 Steese Hwy
Upper Skilak Lake	Kenai NWR	26	•	•	•	•	Mi. 8.5 Skilak Lake Rd.
Walker Fork	BLM	16	•	•	•	•	Mi. 82.1 Taylor Hwy
West Fork	BLM	25	•		•	•	Mi. 49 Taylor Hwy
Whitefish	State Parks	25	•		•	•	Mi. 11 Elliott Hwy
Williwaw	USFS	38	•	•			Mi. 4.1 Portage Hwy
Willow Creek	State Parks	145	•	•		•	Mi. 70.8 Parks Hwy
Wolf Lake	State Parks	4				•	Mi. 2.5 Engstrom Dr., Palmer

YUKON TERRITORY

Campground	Agency	Campsites	Camping Fee	Water	Boat Launch	Fishing	Location
Aishihik Lake	Territorial	13	•		•	•	km 42 Aishihik Lake Rd.
Carcross	Territorial	12	•	•			km 106 White Pass route
Carmacks	First Nations	20	•				km 358 Klondike Hwy
Congdon Creek	Territorial	78	•	•			km 1722 Alaska Hwy
Dezadeash Lake	Territorial	20	•		•	•	km 205 Haines Hwy
Drury Creek	Territorial	18	•	•	•	•	km 483 Campbell Hwy
Engineer Creek	Territorial	23	•				km 194 Dempster Hwy
Ethel Lake	Territorial	14	•		•	•	km 24 Ethel Lake Rd.
Five Mile Lake	Territorial	20	•			•	km 60 Silver Trail
Fox Lake	Territorial	33	•	•	•	•	km 248 Klondike Hwy
Frances Lake	Territorial	19	•		•	•	km 175 Campbell Hwy
Frenchman Lake	Territorial	10	•		•	•	km 41.7 Tatchun Lake Rd.
Johnson Lake	Territorial	15	•		•	•	km 432 Campbell Hwy
Kathleen Lake	Kluane N.P.	41	•	•	•	•	km 220 Haines Hwy
Klondike River	Territorial	38	•	•			km 698 Klondike Hwy
Kusawa Lake	Territorial	25	•	•	•	•	km 22.5 Kusawa Lake Rd.
Lake Creek	Territorial	28	•	•		•	km 1854 Alaska Hwy

Campground	Agency	Campsites	Camping Fee	Water	Boat Launch	Fishing	Location
Lake LaBerge	Territorial	22	•	•	•	•	km 226 Klondike Hwy
Lapie Lakes	primitive	und.			•	•	km 164 South Canol Rd.
Lapie Canyon	Territorial	19	•		•		km 376 Campbell Hwy
Little Salmon Lake	Territorial	12	•	•	•	•	km 517 Campbell Hwy
Marsh Lake	Territorial	41	•	•			km 1430 Alaska Hwy
Minto Landing	First Nations	10	•	•			km 432 Klondike Hwy
Million Dollar Falls	Territorial	27	•	•		•	km 167 Haines Hwy
Moose Creek	Territorial	36	•	•			km 562 Klondike Hwy
Morley Lake	BC Forestry	und.			•	•	km 1249 Alaska Hwy
Nunatak	Territorial	10	•		•	•	km 33.3 Tatchun Lake Rd.
Pine Lake	Territorial	40	•	•	•	•	km 1628 Alaska Hwy
Quiet Lake	Territorial	20	•		•	•	km 77 South Canol Rd.
Rock River	Territorial	20	•			•	km 447 Dempster Hwy
Silver Centre	Municipal	und.				•	km 8 S. McQuesten R. Rd.
Simpson Lake	Territorial	19	•		•	•	km 83.4 Campbell Hwy
Snafu Lake	Territorial	4	•		•	•	km 26 Atlin Rd.
Snag Junction	Territorial	15	•				km 1913 Alaska Hwy
Squanga Lake	Territorial	12	•	•		•	km 1368 Alaska Hwy
Sulphur Lake	Territorial	und.				•	km 1671 Alaska Hwy
Tarfu Lake	Territorial	4	•		•	•	km 33 Atlin Rd.
Takhini River	Territorial	8				•	km 14.5 Kusawa Lake Rd.
Tatchun Creek	Territorial	13	•			•	km 383 Klondike Hwy
Tatchun Lake	Territorial	20	•		•	•	km 8.4 Tatchun Lake Rd.
Teslin Lake	Territorial	19	•	•	•	•	km 1309 Alaska Hwy
Tombstone	Territorial	22	•			•	km 71 Dempster Hwy
Twin Lakes	Territorial	8	•	•	•	•	km 308 Klondike Hwy
Watson Lake	Territorial	55	•	•	•	•	km 1025 Alaska Hwy
Wolf Creek	Territorial	40	•	•			km 1458 Alaska Hwy
Yukon River	Territorial	98	•	•			km 1 Top of the World Hwy

BRITISH COLUMBIA

Campground	Agency	Campsites	Camping Fee	Water	Boat Launch	Fishing	Location
Allen Lake	BC Forestry	und.					just W of Dease Lake townsite
Andy Bailey Lake	BC Parks	12	•	•		•	km 427 Alaska Hwy
Atlin Lake	Crown	6			•	•	km 53 Atlin Rd.
Beatton	BC Parks	37	•	•	•	•	8 km east of km 82 Alaska Hwy
Bob Quinn Lake	BC Forestry	und.		•	•	•	km 142 N of Meziadin Jct., Cassiar Hwy
Boya Lake	BC Parks	44	•	•	•	•	km 150 N of Dease Lake, Cassiar Hwy
Buckinghorse River	BC Parks	30	•	•		•	km 281 Alaska Hwy
Charlie Lake	BC Parks	58	•	•	•	•	km 82 Alaska Hwy
Clements Lake	BC Forestry	und.					km 49 Glacier Hwy
Dodjatin Creek	BC Forestry	und.			•	•	11 km beyond Telegraph Creek townsite
Dragon Lake	BC Forestry	und.			•	•	km 46 Nass Forest Service Road
Duhu Lake	BC Forestry	und.			•		On spur road 8 km S of Sikanni Chief
French River	BC Forestry	und.			•	•	km 178 N of Dease Lake, Cassiar Hwy

Campground	Agency	Campsites	Camping Fee	Water	Boat Launch	Fishing	Location
Grotto	BC Forestry	4					km 26.2 Warm Bay Rd.
Halfway River	BC Forestry	und.			•		60 km of FR 117, 10 km S of Wonowon
Inga Lake	BC forestry	und.			•		3 km of FR 116, 15 km S of Wonowon
Kinaskan Lake	BC Parks	50	•	•	•	•	km 210 N of Meziadin Jct., Cassiar Hwy
Kiskatinaw	BC Parks	28	•	•		•	km 29 Alaska Hwy
Liard River Hot Springs	BC Parks	52	•	•			km 798 Alaska Hwy
Mc Donald Lakes	BC Forestry	und.			•	•	km 3.2 Ruffner Mine Rd., off Atlin Rd.
Meziadin Lake	BC Parks	42	•		•	•	km 156 Cassiar Hwy
Moberly Lake	BC Parks	109	•	•	•	•	BC 29 between Hudson Hope & Chetwyn
Morchuea Lake	BC Forestry	und.			•		km 270 N of Meziadin Jct., Cassiar Hwy
Muncho Lake	BC Parks	30	•	•	•	•	km 734 Alaska Hwy
One Fifteen Creek	BC Parks	8	•	•			km 647 Alaska Hwy
Pine Creek	Municipal	14	•	•		•	km 2.6 Warm Bay Rd.
Prophet River	BC Parks	56	•	•		•	km 360 Alaska Hwy
Sikanni Chief Falls	BC Forestry	4					on spur road, km 271 Alaska Hwy
Summit Lake	BC Parks	28	•	•	•	•	km 631 Alaska Hwy
Surprise Lake	BC Forestry	7			•	•	km 19 Discovery Rd.
Tetsa River	BC Parks	25	•	•		•	km 586 Alaska Hwy
Tutshi Lake	BC Forestry	und.			•	•	km 64.5 White Pass route
Warm Bay	BC Forestry	4			•	•	km 14 Warm Bay Rd.
Winter Creek	BC Forestry	und.			•	•	14 km beyond Telegraph Creek townsite

Appendix B
Selected Fishing Streams and Lakes

KEY TO GAMEFISH SPECIES

GRY .... Arctic Grayling

CHR .... Arctic Char

DVT .... Dolly Varden

LKT .... Lake Trout (or Char)

RBT .... Rainbow Trout

STL .... Steelhead

WF .... Whitefish

INC .... Inconnu (or Sheefish)

RSM .... Red (Sockeye) Salmon

KSM .... King (Chinook) Salmon

SSM .... Silver (Coho) Salmon

PSM .... Pink (Humpy) Salmon

DSM .... Chum (Dog) Salmon

KOK .... Kokanee (landlocked sockeye salmon)

WLL .... Walleye

PKE .... Northern PIke

BBT .... Burbot (freshwater lingcod)

PCH .... Yellow Perch

Body of Water	Species	Location
CASSIAR HIGHWAY		
Cranberry River	RSM	km 63.1
Meziadin Lake	RBT, WF, DVT	km 157
Hanna Creek	RSM	km 165
Hodder Lake	RBT	km 89 from Meziadin Jct.
Ningunsaw River	WF, DVT	km 121-125 from Meziadin Jct.
Bob Quinn Lake	RBT, DVT	km 141 from Meziadin Jct.
Kinaskan Lake	RBT	km 210 from Meziadin Jct.
Eddontenajon Lake	RBT	km 243 from Meziadin Jct.
Gnat Lakes	RBT	km 309 from Meziadin Jct.
Tanzilla River	GRY	km 325 from Meziadin Jct.
ALASKA HIGHWAY		
Charlie Lake	PKE, WLL, PCH	km 79.6; on 8 km spur road to E
Sikanni Chief River	PKE, GRY, WF	km 159
Buckinghorse River	GRY	km 279
Beaver Creek	GRY	km 328
Andy Bailey Lake	PKE	km 426.5; on 11 km spur road to E
Muskwa River	PKE	km 451.4
Summit Lake	LKT, RBT, WF	km 598
MacDonald Creek	GRY, DVT	km 615, 628
Racing River	DVT	km 641
Toad River	GRY, DVT	km 647-657
Muncho Lake	DVT, GRY, WF, LKT, RBT	km 699-711
Trout River	GRY, WF	km 733
Liard River	DVT, GRY, WF, PKE	km 763-958

Body of Water	Species	Location
Smith River	GRY	km 792
Hyland River	RBT, DVT, GRY	km 937
Lucky Lake	RBT	km 1012
Watson Lake	GRY, RBT, PKE	km 1021
Rancheria River	DVT, GRY	km 1106-1156
Swan Lake	DVT, WF	km 1196
Morley River	GRY	km 1251
Teslin Lake	LKT, GRY, PKE, WF, KSM	km 1292-1308
Teslin River	GRY, KSM	km 1345
Squanga Lake	PKE, GRY, WF, RBT, BBT	km 1366
Marsh Lake	PKE, GRY	km 1413-1434
Yukon River	GRY, LKT, WF, PKE	km 1442
Kusawa Lake	LKT, GRY, PKE	km 1453; on 24 km spur road to S
Aishihik Lake	LKT, GRY	km 1602; on 42 km spur road to N
Pine Lake	LKT, GRY, PKE	km 1628
Jarvis River	GRY, DVT	km 1665.5
Kluane Lake	LKT, PKE, GRY	km 1693-1759
Edith Lake	GRY	km 1844
Pickhandle Lake	PKE, GRY, WF, BBT	km 1865
Scottie Creek	GRY, BBT	mile 1229
Hidden Lake	RBT	mile 1240; 0.8 mi. trail to S
Deadman Lake	PKE, BBT	mile 1249.3
Berry Creek	GRY, DVT	mile 1371.5
Lisa Lake	RBT	mile 1381.1; 0.7 mi. trail to S

TAGISH ROAD

Six Mile River	LKT, GRY, WF, PKE	km 21
Tagish Lake	LKT, PKE, WF, GRY	km 26.2; on 2-km spur road to S
Crag Lake	LKT, GRY, PKE	km 40

CAMPBELL HIGHWAY

Frances River	GRY	km 58.1
Simpson Lake	LKT, GRY, PKE	km 83.4; on 3-km spur road to W
Frances Lake	LKT, GRY, PKE	km 175; on 1-km spur road to E
Little Salmon Lake	PKE, LKT, WF, GRY	km 483-517.3
Frenchman Lake	LKT, PKE, GRY	km 559; 8 km to N on spur road

NAHANNI RANGE ROAD

Frances River	GRY	km 8.2
Long Lake	GRY	km 32.7
Spruce Creek	GRY	km 65.3
Conglomerate Creek	GRY	km 73.7
Hyland River	GRY, DVT, RBT	km 84-110

Body of Water	Species	Location

CANOL ROAD

Sidney Lake	LKT, GRY, PKE	km 49.2; on spur road to E
Quiet Lake	LKT, GRY, PKE	km 77-99
Lapie Lakes	LKT, GRY	km 163
Lapie River	GRY	km 173-213
Marjorie Lake	LKT, GRY	km 263; on spur road to W
Dragon Lake	LKT, GRY, WF	km 333.7

ATLIN ROAD

Little Atlin Lake	LKT, GRY, PKE, WF	km 1.8-12
Lubbock River	GRY	km 13.8; on 4-km spur road to W
Snafu Lake	LKT, GRY, PKE	km 26; on 1-km spur road to E
Tarfu Lake	LKT, GRY, PKE	km 33; on 4-km spur road to E
Hitchcock Creek	GRY	km 52.6
Atlin Lake	LKT, GRY, PKE	km 53-94
MacDonald Lake	LKT	km 83; on 3-km spur road to E
Como Lake	RBT	km 89
Surprise Lake	GRY	km 19 Discovery Road
Palmer Lake	RBT	km 19 Warm Bay Road

WHITE PASS ROUTE

Annie Lake	GRY	km 139.4; on 18-km spur road to W
Lewes Lake	LKT, GRY, PKE	km 136.3; on 2-km spur road to W
Lake Bennett	LKT, GRY, PKE	km 106.5; west of Carcross townsite
Tagish Lake (Windy Arm)	LKT, PKE, WF, GRY	km 78-96
Tutshi Lake	LKT, GRY	km 50-70.5

HAINES HIGHWAY

Kathleen River	RBT, LKT, GRY	km 220.5
Kathleen Lake	LKT, GRY, RBT, KOK	km 219; on spur road to W
Dezadeash Lake	LKT, GRY, PKE	km 193-196
Klukshu Creek	spawn for SSM, KSM, RSM, STL	km 181.6
Klukshu Lake	LKT, RBT, RSM	km 183; on 2-km spur road to E
Tatsenshini River	STL, DVT, KSM, SSM, RSM	km 164.5; on 8-km spur road to W
Takhanne River	GRY, DVT, RBT	km 159.4

KLONDIKE HIGHWAY

Lake LaBerge	LKT, GRY, PKE, INC, BBT	km 225; on 3 km spur road to E
Fox Creek	GRY	km 228.5
Fox Lake	LKT, GRY, PKE	km 238-256
Little Fox Lake	LKT, GRY, PKE	km 259.4
Braeburn Lake	LKT, GRY, PKE	km 281.5
Twin Lakes	LKT, GRY, PKE	km 308.2
Nordenskiold River	GRY	km 355

Body of Water	Species	Location
Tatchun Creek	GRY; KSM spawning Sept.	km 381
Tachun Lake	PKE	km 381.8; 7 km E on spur road
Von Wilczek Lake	PKE	km 450.5; on spur road to E
Crooked Creek	GRY	km 524.6
Ethel Lake	LKT, GRY, PKE, WF	km 526.7; on 27 spur road to E
Moose Creek	GRY	km 562
McQuesten River	GRY	km 584
Klondike River	GRY; KSM spawn Jul.-Aug.	km 669-720
Yukon River	GRY, KSM	km 720

SILVER TRAIL

Mayo River	GRY	km 50.3
Minto Lake	LKT, GRY, PKE	km 69; on 19 km spur road to W
Halfway Lakes	PKE	km 77.2
Mayo Lake	LKT, GRY, PKE	10-km spur leaves km 22 Duncan Cr. Rd.

DEMPSTER HIGHWAY

Klondike River	GRY	km 0.3
Blackstone River	GRY	km 115
Chapman Lake	GRY	km 116; lake is to W of road
Ogilvie River	GRY	km 196-244
Eagle River	GRY	km 378
James Creek	GRY	km 14 from NWT border
Peel River	INC, WF	km 74 from NWT border
Rengling River	GRY	km 178 from NWT border
Campbell Lake	PKE, WF, INC	km 247 from NWT border

TAYLOR HIGHWAY

Four Mile Lake	RBY, LKT, INC	mile 4.5; 0.5 mile trail to E
Logging Cabin Creek	GRY	mile 43
Fortymile River (all forks)	GRY	
O'Brien Creek	GRY	mile 113.5
Columbia Creek	GRY	mile 124..5
King Solomon Creek	GRY	mile 134
American Creek	GRY	mile 153-160

RICHARDSON HIGHWAY

Robe River	SSM, RSM, DSM, PSM, DVT	mile 4.7
Lowe River	DVT	mile 7.3-16
Blueberry Lake	RBT	mile 24.1
Tiekel RIver	DVT	mile 47-59
Little Tonsina River	SSM, DVT, RBT	mile 65.1
Squirrel Creek	GRY	mile 79.6
Klutina River	KSM, RSM, LKT, DVT, GRY, BBT	mile 100.7

Body of Water	Species	Location
Dry Creek	GRY	mile 118
Gulkana River	KSM, RSM, GRY, BBT	mile 128-148
Sourdough Creek	GRY	mile 147.7
June and Nita Lakes	WF, GRY	mile 166.5; 0.25-mile trail to W
Meiers Lake	GRY	mile 170
Dick Lake	GRY	mile 173.2
Paxson Lake	RSM, LKT, GRY, WF, BBT	mile 175
Summit Lake	RSM, LKT, GRY, WRF, BBT	mile 192.2
Fielding Lake	LKT, GRY, BBT	mile 200.4; on 2-mile spur road to S
Clearwater Lake	GRY, PKE, LWF, BBT	mile 431.7; take Jack Warren Rd. to E
Quartz Lake	RBT, SSM, CHR	mile 277.7; 2.7 mi. spur rd.
Shaw Creek	GRY, BBT	mile 286.7
Birch Lake	RBT, SSM, GRY, CHR	mile 307
Harding Lake	CHR, PKE, LKT, BBT	mile 321.5
Salcha River	GRY, KSM, DSM, WF	mile 323.3
Little Salcha River	GRY	mile 327.7
Chena Lake	RBT, SSM, CHR, GRY	mile 346.7
Lower Chena River	GRY, SSM, KSM, BBT, PKE, WF, INC	mile 364

DENALI HIGHWAY

Body of Water	Species	Location
Sevenmile Lake	LKT	mile 6.8 on 0.75-mile spur rd. to N
Tenmile Lake	LKT, GRY, WF, BBT	mile 10.1
Seventeen Mile Lake	LKT, GRY	mile 17
Tangle Lakes	LKT, GRY, WF, BBT	mile 22
Rock Creek	GRY	mile 25
Clearwater Creek	GRY	mile 56
Brushkana Creek	GRY, DVT	mile 104.6
Jerry Lake	GRY	mile 125.7; 0.8 mi. N of road
Joe Lake	GRY	mile 125.7; S of road

PARKS HIGHWAY

Body of Water	Species	Location
Wasilla Creek	DVT. SSM	mile 34
Wasilla Lake	RBT	mile 41.5
Big Lake	RBT, CHR, BBT	mile 51; 5 mi. W on Big Lake Rd.
Little Susitna River	RBT, DVT, KSM, SSM, DSM, PSM, RSM, WF	mile 58
Nancy Lakes	RBT, DVT, BBT, PKE	mile 67.2
Willow Creek	RBT, GRY, DVT, KSM, SSM, DSM, PSM	mile 71.4
Deception Creek	RBT, GRY, DVT	mile 71.2; 2 mi. on Hatcher Pass Rd.
Little Willow Creek	RBT, GRY, KSM, SSM, DSM, PSM	mile 74.7
Kashwitna Lake	RBT	mile 76.5
Kashwitna River	RBT, GRY, KSM, SSM	mile 83.2
Caswell Creek	RBT, GRY, KSM, SSM, BBT	mile 84.9
Sheep Creek	RBT, GRY, KSM, SSM, DSM, PSM	mile 86
Goose Creek	RBT, GRY, KSM, SSM, DSM, PSM	mile 93.5
Montana Creek	RBT, GRY, KSM, SSM, DSM, PSM	mile 96.5

Body of Water	Species	Location
Talkeetna River	RBT, GRY, KSM, SSM, DSM, RSM, BBT	mile 98.7; 12 mi. N on Talkeetna Spur
Rabideaux Creek	RBT, GRY, KSM, SSM, DSM, BBT	mile 105.9
Troublesome Creek	GRY	mile 137.3
Byers Lake	LKT, BBT, WF	mile 147
Honolulu Creek	GRY	mile 178.1
Mile 180 Lake	GRY	mile 180
Upper Chulitna River	KSM, SSM, RBT, GRY, WF	mile 185.1, 194.5
Lakes at Broad Pass	GRY, WF, LKT, BBT	mile 195
Panguinque Creek	GRY	mile 252.5
Bear Creek	GRY	mile 269.3
Julius Creek	GRY	mile 294.2

GLENN HIGHWAY

Body of Water	Species	Location
Eagle River	KSM, SSM, RBT, DVT	mile 12.8
Eklutna Lake	RBT, DVT	mile 26.3; follow road to state park
Matanuska Lake	RBT, SSM, GRY	mile 36.4; N of highway
Echo Lake	RBT, SSM	mile 37; N of highway
Moose Creek	DVT, SSM	mile 54.8
Eska Lake	RBT	mile 70; 2 mi. N on Jonesville Rd.
Chicaloon River	DVT	mile 77.7
Lower Bonnie Lake	RBT, GRY	mile 83.2; on 2 mile spur road to N
Long Lake	GRY, BBT, LKT	mile 85.3
Wiener Lake	RBT, GRY	mile 88.5
Liela Lake	GRY, BBT, WF	mile 122
Tahneta Lake	GRY	mile 122.9
Cache Creek	GRY	mile 147.3
Mirror Lake	RBT, GRY	mile 149; 200 yds. S of highway
Mendeltna Creek	GRY	mile 152.8
Lake Louise	LKT, GRY, WF	mile 160; 19 mi N on L. Louise Rd.
Buffalo Lake	RBT	mile 156; N of highway
Tex Smith Lake	RBT	mile 162; trail to N
Tolsona Lake	GRY, BBT, RBT, KSM	mile 170.5; on spur road to N
Tolsona Creek	GRY	mile 173
Moose Creek	GRY	mile 186

TOK CUTOFF

Body of Water	Species	Location
Tulsona Creek	GRY	mile 104.1
Sinona Creek	GRY, DVT	mile 90.4
Ahtell Creek	GRY	mile 64.2
Menatasta Lake	GRY, WF	mile 44
Little Tok River	GRY	mile 20.5

Body of Water	Species	Location

NABESNA ROAD

Kettle Lake	SSM, RBT, GRY	mile 19
Long Lake	GRY, BBT	mile 22.9
Little Twin Lake	GRY, LKT, BBT	mile 28.2
Big Twin Lake	GRY, BBT	mile 29

EDGERTON HIGHWAY-MCCARTHY ROAD

Liberty Falls Creek	GRY	mile 23.7
3-Mile Lake	RBT, GRY	mile 29.7
2-Mile Lake	RBT, GRY	mile 31.2
1-Mile Lake	GRY	mile 31.9
Copper River	RSM, KSM	mile 1.1 McCarthy Rd.
Strelna Lake	RBT, SSM	mile 10.6 McCarthy Rd.
Van Lake	RBT, SSM, DVT	mile 11.1 McCarthy Rd.
Chokosna Lake	GRY, SSM	mile 23.5 McCarthy Rd.
Long Lake	LKT, SSM, GRY, DVT, BBT	mile 44.7 McCarthy Rd.

SEWARD HIGHWAY

Rabbit Creek	DVT	mile 9.2
Bird Creek	DVT, PSM, SSM	mile 25.8
Twentymile River	SSM	mile 46
Portage Creek	RSM, DVT, SSM	mile 48
Placer River	SSM	mile 48.6
Ingram Creek	DVT, PSM	mile 51.8
Granite Creek	DVT	mile 60.2-64
Resurrection Creek	DVT	mile 70.3; 20 mi. W on Hope Hwy.
Summit Lakes	DVT, RBT	mile 79.8 and 81.5
Jerome Lake	RBT, DVT	mile 88.4
Trail River	DVT, RBT, LKT	mile 102.8
Kenai Lake	RBT, DVT, LKT, WF	mile 104.1
Ptarmigan Creek	RBT, DVT	mile 105.1
Grouse Lake	DVT	mile 119.6
Salmon Creek	DVT	mile 121.1

STERLING HIGHWAY

Quartz Creek	RBT, DVT	mile 40.9
Kenai Lake	RBT, DVT, LKT, WF	mile 45
Kenai River	RBT, SSM, RSM, DVT	mile 47.8-58
Russian River	RBT, DVT, RSM, SSM	mile 55; ferry needed to access
Hidden Lake	RSM, RBT, LKT, DVT, KOK	mile 58; 3.5 mi on Skilak Lake Rd.
Ohmer Lakes	RBT, DVT	mile 58; 7 mi on Skilak Lake Rd.
Skilak Lake	RBT, LKT, DVT, RSM	mile 58; 8.5 mi on Skilak Lake Rd.
Jean Lake	RBT, DVT	mile 60.6
Kelly and Peterson Lakes	RBT	mile 68.3; on 1-mile spur to S

Body of Water	Species	Location
Watson Lake	RBT	mile 71.3; on 1-mile spur to N
East Fork Moose River	RBT	mile 71.3
Moose River	RBT, DVT, RSM	mile 82
Scout Lake	SSM	mile 85
Johnson Lake	RBT	mile 110; 0.5 mi. on Tustamena L. Rd.
Tustamena Lake	LKT, DVT, WF, SSM	Tustamena Lake Rd.; boat access only
Kasilof River access	RBT, DVT, SSM, KSM, STL	mile 111; use Cohoe Loop Rd. to
Ninilchik River	DVT, STL, KSM, SSM	mile 136
Deep Creek	DVT, STL, KSM, SSM	mile 136.7
Anchor River	DVT, STL, KSM, SSM	mile 157.1

STEESE HIGHWAY

Body of Water	Species	Location
Chena River	GRY	mile 28-50 Chena Hot Springs Rd.
Chatanika River	GRY, PKE, WF	mile 39-69
Faith Creek	GRY, PKE	mile 69
Birch Creek(North Fork)	GrY, PKE	mile 94
Birch Creek(lower)	GRY, PKE	mile 147.1

ELLIOTT HIGHWAY

Body of Water	Species	Location
Olnes Pond	GRY, RBT	mile 10.6; 1 mi. spur road to W
Chatanika River	KSM, DSM, GRY, WF, INC, PKE, BBT	mile 11
Washington Creek	GRY	mile 18.3
Globe Creek	GRY	mile 37
Tatalina River	GRY, WF	mile 44.8
Tolovana River (and W Fk.)	GRY, WF	mile 57.1 and 74.7
Minto Flats wetlands	PKE, INC, WF, BBT	mile 110; 10 mi. spur to Minto
Hutlinana Creek	GRY	mile 129.3
Baker Creek	GRY, PKE, BBT, WF	mile 137.4
Hot Springs Slough	PKE, WF, INC	mile 152

DALTON HIGHWAY

Body of Water	Species	Location
Hess Creek	GRY, WF	mile 23.8
Yukon River	BBT, DSM, KSM, GRY, PKE	mile 56
No Name Creek	BBT, GRY, WF	mile 79.1
Kanuti River	BBT, GRY, WF	mile 105.8
Fish Creek	GRY, WF	mile 114
Bonanza Creek	BBT, GRY, WF	mile 124.7 and 125.7
Prospect Creek	GRY, KSM, PKE, WF	mile 135.1
Jim River	BBT, DSM, GRY, KSM	mile 140.1 and 144.2
Grayling Lake	GRY	mile 150.8
South Fork Koyukuk River	GRY, DSM, KSM, WF	mile 156
Slate Creek	DVT, GRY, WF	mile 175

Body of Water	Species	Location
Marion Creek	DVT, GRY, WF	mile 178.5
Minnie Creek	DVT, GRY, WF	mile 187.2
Middle Fork Koyukuk River	DVT, GRY, WF	mile 188.5 and 190-204
Bettles River	GRY	mile 205
Dietrich River	BBT, DVT, GRY, WF	mile 207-232
Galbraith Lake	BBT, GRY, LKT, WF	mile 276
Island Lake	CHR, GRY, LKT, WF	mile 276.5
Toolik Lake	GRY, LKT, WF	mile 284.4
Kuparuk River	GRY	mile 288.8
Toolik River	GRY, CHR, LKT, WF	mile 294
Sagavanirktok River	GRY, BBT, DVT, WF	mile 323-408

Appendix C
Directory of Information Sources
For more information on lands and events, please
contact the following agencies and organizations

National Parks, Forests, and Wildlife Refuges

YUKON
Canadian Chilkoot Trail information
(403) 668-2116

Ivvavik National Park
P.O. Box1840
Inuvik, NWT X0E 0T0
(403) 979-3248

Kluane National Park
Box 5495
Haines Junction, YT Y0B 1L0
(403) 634-2251

ALASKA
Arctic National Wildlife Refuge
101 12th Ave.
Fairbanks, AK 99701
(907) 456-0250

Chugach National Forest
3301 C St., Suite 300
Anchorage, AK 99503-3998
(907) 271-2500

Denali National Park
P.O. Box 9
Denali Park, AK 99755
(907) 683-2294; bus and campground reservations (800) 622-7275

Gates of the Arctic National Park
P.O. Box 74680
Fairbanks, AK 99707-4680
(907)456-0281

Kenai Fjords National Park
P.O. Box 1727
Seward, AK 99664-1727
(907) 224-3175

Kenai National Wildlife Refuge
Box 2139
Soldotna, AK 99669
(907) 262-7021

Klondike Gold Rush National
  Historical Park
P.O. Box 517
Skagway, AK 99840
(907) 983-2921

Tetlin National Wildlife Refuge
Box 779
Tok, AK 99780
(907) 883-5312

Wrangell-St. Elias National
  Park and Preserve
P.O. Box 29
Glennallen, AK 99588
(907) 822-5234

Yukon-Charley Nation Preserve
P.O. Box 167
Eagle, AK 99738

Canadian Forest Districts

BRITISH COLUMBIA
Cassiar Forest District
General Delivery
Dease Lake, BC V0C 1L0
(604) 771-4211

Kalum Forest District
Room 200, 5220 Keith Ave
Terrace, BC V8G 1L1
(604) 638-5100

(*Note:* The area code for the above
two BC numbers will change to
(250) on October 19, 1996.)

Ross River Forest District
General Delivery
Ross River, Yukon XOB 1SO
(403) 969-2243

Watson Lake Forest District
Box 289
Watson Lake, Yukon YOA 1CO
(403) 536-7335

U.S. Bureau of Land Management (BLM)

Northern District
1150 University Avenue
Fairbanks, AK 99709
(907)474-2300

Glennallen District
Box 147
Glennallen, AK 99588
(907) 822-3217

Tok Field Office
P.O. Box 309
Tok, AK 99780
(907) 883-5121

State, Provincial, and Territorial Parks

ALASKA

Alaska State Parks
3601 C St., Suite 1200
Anchorage, AK 99503-5921
(907) 269-8400

Chugach State Park
HC 52, Box 8999
Indian, AK 99540
(907) 345-5014

Denali State Park
HC 32, Box 6706
Wasilla, AK 99687
(907) 733-2675 (summer only)

Kachemak Bay State Park
P.O. Box 3248
Homer, AK 99603
(907) 235-7024

Independence Mine State
  Historical Park
HC 32, Box 6706
Wasilla, AK 99687
(907) 733-2675 (summer only)

Tourism Bureaus and Chambers of Commerce

BRITISH COLUMBIA

Tourism British Columbia
Parliment Buildings
Victoria, BC V8V 1X4
(800) 663-6000

Atlin Visitors Association
P.O. Box 365
Atlin, BC V0W 1A0
(604) 651-7522

North By Northwest Tourism
  Association
Box 1030 SC
Smithers, BC V0J 2N0
(604) 847-5227

Peace River Alaska Highway
  Tourism Association
P.O. Box 6850
Fort St. John, BC V1J 4J3
(604) 785-2544

Stewart-Hyder Chamber of Commerce
Box 306
Stewart, BC V0T 1W0
(604) 636-9224

YUKON/NORTHWEST TERRITORIES

Tourism Yukon
P.O. Box 2703
Whitehorse, YT Y1A 2C6
(403) 667-5340

Klondike Visitors Association
P.O. Box 389
Dawson City, YT Y0B 1G0
(403) 993-5575

Silver Trail Tourism Association
Box 268
Mayo, YT Y0B 1M0
(403) 996-2290

Western Arctic Tourism Association
P.O. Box 2600Z
Inuvik, NT X0E 0T0
(403) 979-7237

Whitehorse Chamber of Commerce
302 Steele Street #101
Whitehorse, YT Y1A 2C5
(403) 667-7545

ALASKA

Alaska Division of Tourism
P.O. Box 110801
Juneau, AK 99811-0801
(907) 465-2012

Anchorage Convention and
  Visitors Bureau
1600 A St., Suite 200
Anchorage, AK 99501-5162
(907) 276-4118

Delta Junction Chamber
  of Commerce
P.O. Box 987
Delta Junction, AK 99737
FAX (907) 895-4628

Eagle Historical Society
Eagle, AK 99738

Fairbanks Convention and
  Visitors Bureau
550 First Ave.
Fairbanks, AK 99701-4790
(800) 327-5774

Greater Copper Valley Chamber
  of Commerce
P.O. Box 469
Glennallen, AK 99588
(907) 822-5555

Greater Palmer Chamber
  of Commerce
P.O. Box 45
Palmer, AK 99645
(907) 745-2880

Haines Visitors Bureau
P.O. Box 518
Haines, AK 99827-0518

Homer Chamber of Commerce
P.O. Box 541
Homer, AK 99603
(907) 235-5300, (summer only)

Kennicott-McCarthy Chamber
  of Commerce
P.O. Box MXY
Glennallen, AK 99588

Seward Chamber of Commerce
P.O. Box 749
Seward, AK 99664
(907) 224-3046

Skagway Convention and
  Visitors Bureau
P.O. Box 415
Skagway, AK 99840-0415
(907) 983-2855

Tok Chamber of Commerce
P.O. Box 389
Tok, AK 99780
(907) 883-5775 (summer only)

Valdez Convention and
  Visitors Bureau
P.O. Box 1603VG
Valdez, AK 99686
(800) 770-5954/(907) 835-2984

Topographic Maps

United States Geological Survey
4230 University Dr., Rm. 101
Anchorage, AK 99508
(907) 786-7011

Exploration and Geological
  Services Division
200 Main St., #345
Whitehorse, YT Y1A 2B5

Index

Hudson Hope, Yukon Territory 30
Hudson, N.R. 248
Hudson's Bay Company 11, 13, 23, 29, 30, 33, 42, 61, 62, 112, 135
Hudson's Bay post 76
Hungry Hollow 168
Hungry Mountain 120
Hunker, Albert 115
Hunker Creek 114, 115, 119
Hunker Creek Road 119
Hunker Summit 119
Hurricane Gulch 179
Husky Southwest Mine 124
Hutlinana Creek 249
Hutlitakwa Creek 249
Hyder, Alaska 15, 17, 18
Hyland River 44, 68, 69

I

Icefall Peak 162, 167
Icefield Ranges 53, 55
Iceworm Gulch 181
Iditarod River 175, 176
Iditarod Trail 175, 176, 192
Igumen, Father Nikolai 192
Independence Mine State Historical Park 185, 188
Indian Creek 215, 216
Indian Head Mountain 33
Indian Valley Mine 216
Ingram Creek 219
Inside Passage 1, 71, 82, 86, 100
Inuit 136, 142, 192, 196, 257, 260
Inuvialuit Indians 135
Inuvik, Northwest Territories 114, 127, 135, 136
Isabel Pass 161
Iskut, British Columbia 9
Iskut Burn 8, 9
Iskut Lakes 9, 10
Iskut River 8
Island Lake 144
Itsi Range 77

J

Jack Dalton's Porcupine Trading Company 104
Jack River 174, 179, 180
Jack, W.G. 172
Jack Wade Creek 137, 151, 152
Jack Warren Road 163
Jacksina Creek 206
Jacquot, Eugene 55
Jacquot, Louis 55
Jade City, British Columbia 12
Jake's Corner, Yukon Territory 40, 48, 57, 79
Jarvis Glacier 104
Jason claim 78
Jean Lake 227
Jerry Lake 174
Jew Hill 118
Jim River 255
Joe Irwin Lake 12
Joe Lake 174

Johnson, Albert 133
Johnson Lake 66
Johnson Lake State Recreation Area 228
Johnson's Crossing 47, 72
Johnston, George 47
Julius Creek 182
Jumbo Dome 182
Juneau, Alaska 178

K

Kachemak Bay 224, 226, 229, 230, 231
Kachemak Bay State Park 229, 232
Kalum Forest District 3, 15
Kantishna, Alaska 180
Kanuti National Wildlife Refuge 254
Kanuti River 254
Karshner, John 249
Kashwitna Lake 178
Kashwitna River 178
Kasilof, Alaska 228
Kasilof River 228
Kaska Indians 2, 13, 35, 44, 45, 64, 65, 74
Kaskawulsh Glacier 54
Kathleen Lake 100
Keele, Joseph 77
Kelly Lake 228
Kenai, Alaska 223, 228, 232
Kenai Fjords National Park 214, 220
Kenai Flats 232
Kenai Lake 220, 226
Kenai Mountains 214, 217, 223, 224, 227, 228, 230
Kenai National Moose Range 227
Kenai National Wildlife Refuge 224, 227, 228
Kenai Peninsula 220, 223, 224, 227, 228
Kenai River 226, 227, 232
Kenai Spur Highway 232-233
Kenaitze Indians 226, 229, 232
Kennecott Copper Corporation 213
Kennecott Copper Mine 158, 160, 207, 208, 212
Kennicott, Alaska 212, 213
Kennicott Glacier 211
Kennicott River 207, 211, 212, 213
Kenny Lake 208
Keno 700 Mine 126
Keno City, Yukon Territory 113, 117, 120, 122, 123, 124, 125
Keno Hill 122, 123, 125, 126
K'esugi Ridge 179
Ketchikan, Alaska 17
Ketza River 65
Ketza River Gold Mine 65
Keystone Canyon 156, 158
Kinaskan Lake 9
King, Alexander 223
King Solomons Dome 119
Kings Mountain 195
Kinnally, Pat 241
Kiska (Aleutian Island) 24
Kiskatinaw Provincial Park 29
Kitwancool, British Columbia 6
Kitwancool Lake 6
Kitwanga, British Columbia 3, 5, 6

About the Author

Erik Molvar.

Erik Molvar first came to Alaska in 1988 and has been returning to the Great Land ever since. An Alaskan resident, he has explored the length and breadth of the Far North, including all of the drives featured in this book. His master's degree studies at the University of Alaska have led to ground-breaking research on the ecology and behavior of moose in Denali National Park.

Erik is the author of *Alaska on Foot: Wilderness Techniques for the Far North*, and he has also written trail guides to Glacier National Park, Olympic National Park, the Bob Marshall Wilderness, and southern Arizona. It is the author's hope that his writings will create greater awareness and appreciation for the historical and natural features of the Far North so that these features may be preserved for the generations that follow.